WHITE GOLD

FOR MY WIFE, MOI

'APRES MOI LE DELUGE'
(attributed to Louis XV)

WHITE GOLD

THE INSIDE STORY OF THE UK'S
LARGEST EVER DRUGS HAUL

EUGENE COSTELLO
FOREWORD BY HOWARD MARKS

MAINSTREAM
PUBLISHING
EDINBURGH AND LONDON

First published in Great Britain in 2003 by
MAINSTREAM PUBLISHING COMPANY (EDINBURGH) LTD
7 Albany Street
Edinburgh EH1 3UG

ISBN 1 84018 733 6

Reprinted 2003

A catalogue record for this book is available from the British Library

Typeset in Avant Garde and Garamond
Printed and bound in Great Britain by
Mackays of Chatham plc

ACKNOWLEDGEMENTS

Firstly, and most importantly, to Chris Howarth, who served 11 years for his part in the following events, and Graham Dick, senior investigations officer with HM Customs and Excise, without whom this book could not have been written. Jeremy Holder, an *Evening Standard* sub editor, who painstakingly read every chapter, and made numerous suggestions for improvement. Norman Dowie, deputy chief clerk to the High Court of Justiciary in Edinburgh, for his unfailing courtesy and sterling work in helping me to access court records. Mark MacGregor of Customs and Excise for invaluable background information. Noel Hawkins, who, although reluctant to collaborate in great detail, agreed to meet me for an essential briefing and an enjoyable evening in a Waterloo pub. The renowned Howard Marks for his support, and for finding time to read my manuscript. David Hingston, who was Procurator Fiscal at the time of the events described in this book, for his helpful insights. Steve Hallworth at HM Customs and Excise press office for his prompt and courteous assistance on several occasions. Colin, a north London cocaine dealer, for his fascinating and revealing insights into his profession. Laurie Flynn, the legendary investigative reporter, for his support and encouragement. Margot Wilson and Bill Coles for their generous hospitality at Scotland Street, which ensured that I had a home from home when I had to be in Edinburgh for research and meetings. My mum and dad, Denis and Eileen, for their support throughout, and for lending me money when things got tight. Catherine Madden and Nick Bagot at the *Mail On Sunday* for giving me shifts to keep the wolf from the door. Gavin Giles and Jason Cross at NatWest for displaying a consummate understanding of a writer's precarious finances. Amir Gadwah, for ensuring that the manuscript actually arrived at the publishers when I cleared off on honeymoon. My editors, Ann Vinnicombe and Ailsa Bathgate for their thorough reading of the manuscript, and their many helpful suggestions. Everyone at Mainstream Publishing for their enthusiastic support, and particularly the publisher, Bill Campbell, who gave me such an unforgettable night at The Groucho Club that I can't remember any of it. And finally, to my wife, Moi, for her fortitude and forbearance, and tolerating the fact that there were three of us in this marriage – 'you, me and that bloody book'.

London,
October 2003

CONTENTS

FOREWORD

Writing forewords is on the verge of becoming my full-time straight job, but I am delighted to have been asked to do so for Eugene Costello's *White Gold.* Drug books tend to fall into one of two categories: (one) a story told from the point of view of consumers, dealers or smugglers who have got away with it and are prepared to lift the veil, shine some light on the reality of that world and narrate the stories behind the hysterical headlines; or (two) a story slavishly written by some naive journalist, blessed and sanctioned by some government agency – a sanitised account of events to vaunt the credentials of the particular agency and increase its budget. *White Gold* falls into neither of these categories. The writer asks interesting and awkward questions and answers them with tenacity and thoroughness while giving a compelling account of the UK's largest ever single drugs haul.

Drugs will continue to be produced and people will continue to want to consume them. For some of the poorest farmers in the world, drugs are their only means of survival. Social problems related to drugs almost invariably arise from their prohibition. This and other points are well articulated in the book. Reading about the lives of simple fishermen caught up in this extraordinary plot to import a record amount of cocaine serves to reinforce the folly of our existing laws. But *White Gold* is also a good read that will keep you hooked until the last page. Enjoy it. I did.

Howard Marks

CRAZY CHRIS

PROLOGUE

July 2002

Puffing and red-faced, I prayed that the plateau at the top of the mountain (all right, steep hill) was surely close by. Behind me, the view across the Kilbrannan Sound to Kintyre had to be one of the most beautiful on the west coast of Scotland – not that I was in any frame of mind to savour it. Spending most nights down the pub, along with my scarcely used gym membership, meant that all I could focus on was the searing pain in my lower abdomen while doing my utmost to gulp deep breaths of fresh air. Christ, I thought, this is meant to be a holiday, not a boot camp.

I was on the Isle of Arran, ostensibly to write a travel feature about activity holidays on that charming gem of an island but mainly to play golf with a couple of mates. I had arranged to come and visit a paragliding school for the article; unfortunately, the 'school' had no campus as such, and conducted lessons from the summits of various hills and mountains around the island. It was to one of these outdoor classrooms that I was trying to make my way.

When I finally reached the summit, I stopped to catch my breath and introduced myself to the instructor, a petite woman named Zabdi. We chatted for a little while about the sort of paragliding holidays she offers before finally she agreed to do what is known as a tandem jump with one of my mates, a large and well-built lad named Bob, who was dying to paraglide for the first time. As I had been paragliding on previous occasions, I was more than happy to let him jump in the driving seat while I attempted to regain my composure. Jumping in tandem means harnessing oneself to a qualified instructor before running off the side of the mountain together, the novice effectively sitting in the lap of the instructor. I wondered how such a small person would be able to carry someone twice her size; I didn't have to wait long to find out.

As they ran strapped together down the sloping hillside until it fell away in a sheer drop, Zabdi's view was obscured by Bob's mass in front of her. We heard a loud crack as her shin whacked into a large rock protruding from the ground, which she had not seen until too late as Bob jumped over it. The two fell out into space – the elegant soaring we had been expecting replaced by an awkward and rapid descent to ground, followed by a crash-landing. During their brief flight, if it can be called that, the air turned blue through the stream of colourful language we could hear through Zabdi's two-way radio. She was no longer enjoying herself.

Naturally, although concerned at her discomfort, I couldn't help but see the funny side. I began to joke about it with a man who was standing next to me, a cheerful guy with a Yorkshire accent, mid-forties with a shock of blond hair. We received word through the two-way radio that Zabdi had had enough fun for one day and would be taking herself off to the nearest pub at Blackwaterfoot; we could join her there.

I was left at the top with my new-found friend to gather up the accoutrements and make our way back down. His name was Chris, he told me, and he was on Arran to do a week's paragliding course that would mean he was entitled to jump solo back home in Ullapool. He went on to explain that he was determined to live life to the full while he could and that was why he was learning to paraglide.

As we gathered up the last of the equipment and began to make our way back down the hillside, he gave me a sideways look. 'You're a journalist, aren't you? I might have a story for you . . . You see, the thing is, I just got out of prison a few months ago.' In the same way you don't ask someone at a dinner party how much he or she earns, it is deemed equally impertinent in certain circles to ask what someone has done to earn a spell inside. I fudged the issue by saying, 'Really? How long were you in for?'

He gave me a grin and said, 'Well, I got 25 years but they let me out after 11 . . .' I must have stared at him in a sufficiently open-mouthed manner for him to take pity on me and put me out of my misery.

'Do you remember a case a few years back when a bunch of fishermen got caught landing half-a-tonne of cocaine near Ullapool?' he asked with a bashful smile. I said that I did and his grin widened. 'Well, I was one of the guys that got done for it . . .'

Over the next few weeks, we spoke several times over the phone and a couple of months later, I flew up to Inverness and took a hire car up to Ullapool – it really is that remote – to interview him for a piece I did for *FHM* magazine.

Based partly on what he told me, together with High Court records and extensive cooperation from several highly placed sources within Customs and Excise, the following is, at last, the inside story of Operation Klondyke, which resulted in the UK's biggest ever drugs haul.

CHAPTER ONE

1972

'Dad, I really want to be a diver,' said 15-year-old Chris Howarth over breakfast. Across the table, his father grunted, without lifting his head from the paper.

'You're too young,' he said, in a tone that would normally mean that the conversation had ended. Dave Howarth was a taciturn man who was the undisputed head of his household, brooking no dissent or challenge to his unspoken authority. But with the exuberance of youth, his son decided to chance his arm.

'Please, Dad, it's what I was put on this earth to do. I've been diving with you for fun since I was eight, and I know I can make a go of it – and there's good money to be made. All I need to do is a professional diver's course. I've checked out some diving magazines and there's a course at Stoney Cove.'

Stoney Cove is a disused quarry in Leicestershire, now flooded, popular with the UK diving community. Howarth had been for many weekend dives there with his father, a keen member of the British Sub Aqua Club (BSAC). It was also used by a firm called Underwater Securities, which trained North Sea divers, and was around an hour away from the Howarths' terraced council house in Doncaster, an industrial town in the heart of the once-prolific South Yorkshire coalfields.

'Go on, Dad, it won't cost that much. What do you say?' beseeched Howarth.

A few days later, Howarth returned home to find his father on the phone, and sat down on the stairs out of view to eavesdrop.

'Yes, he's done a fair bit of diving with me, just weekends and that . . . Yes, he's got his BSAC Third Class . . . £300!! . . . Oh . . . I see . . . OK, well, if that's how much it costs . . . OK, I'll bring the lad down Sunday, then . . . Right you are, see you then.'

As he put the phone down, he caught sight of his son through the banisters. At 5 ft 10 in. tall, good-looking and well built with a shock of blond hair and piercing blue eyes, the lad's appearance belied his age. Dave Howarth sighed. Unlike his well-behaved brother, who would go on to have a good career as a policeman, Chris had a wild streak that couldn't be tamed; once he had set his heart on something, there was no saying no.

'Right, lad, that's that, then. We're away down to Stoney Cove on Sunday to meet the instructors and work out which course will best suit you. It's costing me a bloody packet, so make sure you don't screw it up.'

Young Howarth could barely contain his excitement, and he didn't know how he was going to wait until the following Sunday. But the day arrived, and father and son set off down to Leicestershire in the family car, Dave's pride and joy – a brand-new, bright-red Ford Cortina Mk III. As they sped down the M1 towards Leicester, Howarth wound the window down to feel the wind rushing through his hair, making his eyes stream. In the background, the syncopated sound of avant-garde jazz musician Stan Kenton blared out – a saxophonist, Dave Howarth worked as a session musician with some of the biggest names in the business, such as the Three Degrees and the Four Tops, but, in his own car, his tastes were more eclectic.

In next to no time, they were at Stoney Cove, discussing the range of courses on offer. With one eye firmly on the booming North Sea market, about which he had read in diving magazines, Howarth plumped for one specialising in underwater cutting, oxy-acetylene welding and explosives. The cost would be £300 plus board (which consisted of an on-site caravan), and he was booked in for September 1972. Manhood seemed to be beckoning.

The four-week course went by without a hitch, and Howarth achieved such a good pass rate that even the instructors were impressed, especially with him being so young. It was time to look for gainful employment. With so much work from the North Sea oilrigs, new diving companies were springing up left, right and centre. A friend of Howarth's father, an ex-Navy Yorkshireman called Clarence Sayers, had started one such outfit in Hull.

'Right, son,' said Howarth's mother one morning in December 1972. 'It's time you got yourself a job.' In her hand was a piece of paper upon which she had written down all the train times from Doncaster to Hull. Howarth took the hint and rang Northern Divers (Engineering) Ltd.

'Hello, Mr Sayers?'

'Speaking.'

Howarth told him about himself, and how he was looking for work as a diver.

'Just a minute, you're Dave Howarth's son, aren't you?'

'Yes, that's right.'

'Righto, come in any day you like, and we'll see what we can find for you.'

Howarth came off the phone grinning from ear to ear. He was going to be a hotshot North Sea diver, with more money than he'd know what to do with. That Saturday, he set off with a kiss and a fiver from his mum, armed with his course certificates and his cockiness. On his way, he told anyone who'd listen that he was a professional diver, earning big money on the rigs; no one believed him for a second, but it made him feel like a player.

The train pulled into Hull station at midday. Compared to Doncaster, Hull seemed like an ocean of humanity, the platforms crowded with people meeting relatives, saying goodbyes, carrying Christmas shopping . . . Howarth's eyes were round with astonishment. 'So this is life in a big city,' he mused, wondering how the hell he would find his way to the docks. He spotted a man who didn't appear to be in a rush to get anywhere, and asked for directions. An hour later, after a few wrong turns, he found himself at a yard down in the docks, where a sign on a small building announced that he had found Northern Divers. He stood there for half an hour, trying to get his nerve up to go in, daydreaming about the future . . . the money, the women, the fast car, the big house. His life was about to begin.

'OK, Mr Sayers will see you now,' said the receptionist with the short skirt and the long, shapely legs. This was his moment. Howarth stood up, straightened his shoulders and puffed his chest out, causing the receptionist to smile, at which Howarth blushed. He went through the door with a plaque that read 'C. Sayers, Director' and found himself in a large, airy office, which was dominated by an enormous teak desk covered in papers. On the other side sat Sayers, a big, gruff Yorkshireman who, nonetheless, seemed dwarfed by the desk.

'It's Chris, isn't it?'

'Yes, Mr Sayers, we spoke on the pho . . .'

'Yes, yes, lad. Well, what can I do for you?'

Trying not to sound too breathless or cocky, Howarth launched into his patter, explaining how he had done his various courses, how he was desperate to be a diver, how he had even used explosives on a wreck off the Yorkshire coast when he was 13 . . .

'Under supervision, I hope,' Sayers interrupted sternly.

Howarth assured him that it was, that he had been working in Scarborough with a man called Bob Summers. Sayers appeared to relax at this.

'Ah, yes, I know Bob. He's a good guy – and a bloody good diver an' all.'

The atmosphere changed from feeling like a tough interview to an altogether more relaxed conversation. Sayers asked after his father and, after a few minutes chatting, said with a kindly smile, 'Well, lad, I think we should be able to find you something.'

Howarth's heart skipped a beat. His fingers were white from crossing them so many times. Surely he was home and dry. Sayers jotted down a few notes, humming to himself. Then came the question Howarth had not counted upon.

'Right, lad, how old are you?'

'Sorry?' stammered Howarth.

'What's your age?'

'I'm 15,' he replied in a small voice that somehow seemed to fill the room and echo back at him.

'Did you say 15?' asked Sayers incredulously.

'Yes, sir,' Howarth replied, now looking at the floor, reddening. Sayers picked up the piece of paper upon which he had been writing, screwed it up and threw it in the wastepaper basket.

'Sorry, lad,' he said, 'I can't do anything for you until you're 18.'

Howarth pulled out his diving course ticket, imploring Sayers to look at it, to take a chance on him. Sayers looked at it closely, then asked who had insured him. Howarth told him it had been Underwater Securities. With a shake of his head, Sayers handed it back, saying that he was sorry to have wasted Howarth's time, as well as his own.

As he stepped back out into reception, Howarth felt his face burn, and his eyes stung with anguish and shame. He could not bring himself to look at the girl at the desk, or even acknowledge her cheerful goodbye. His dreams and his pride, so rampant just an hour before, had evaporated in an instant; he made his way back to the station with the tears flowing freely down his cheeks. Doncaster, only an hour away by train, felt like a world apart, a world he had thought he would be leaving behind for a new and glamorous life. He was still just a boy, after all.

Over a year later, Howarth arrived back home one afternoon from signing on for his fortnightly dole cheque to find his dad reading the paper. As he shut the front door, his mother slipped into the kitchen noiselessly, closing the door behind her. His dad looked up at him through heavy-lidded eyes, tossed the paper to one side and jumped up to turn off the television.

'Right,' he blazed, 'what the fuck are you going to do with your life?'

Howarth had never heard his father speak to him like that before.

'What do you mean?' he asked nervously.

'You know fucking well what I mean. I'm talking about work! I shelled out over three hundred bloody quid on a diving course for you, and that's over a year ago. We're not letting you treat this place like some sort of bloody dosshouse. Get off your fucking arse and get a job; we're not keeping you any longer.'

All the impotent rage of youth rushed like blood to Howarth's head; 'Oh, fuck you!' he screamed. He didn't even see the punch coming.

'Chris! Chris! Are you all right?' Howarth's mother was bending over him, with a look of concern, and a wet cloth in one hand, which she was using to dab his face. 'You know you shouldn't speak to your dad like that, especially when he's had a few pints in the afternoon.'

Howarth managed to haul himself to his feet and stood there, dazed, with blood pouring liberally from his broken nose. He had heard the front door slam while he was lying on the floor and knew that by now his father would be safely out of hearing distance; still, it made him feel better to shout in the direction he had gone: 'One of these days I'll fucking have you!' Brushing off his mother, he grabbed a pile of diving magazines and ran up to his room, slamming the door behind him. He lay on his bed, his nose swelling and throbbing, while the saltiness of his blood and tears ran down his cheeks and the back of his throat. Clutching a cloth to his nose, he wiped the tears from his eyes and tried to focus on his beloved magazines, which offered him a glimpse of another world, away from his parents, the dole and the disappointments of Doncaster.

'Divers Make Bumper Profits From Scallops!' The headline seemed to jump off the page. The article said that it was a boom time for scallop diving off the west coast of Scotland, and claimed that there was more work than there were divers. 'Well,' thought Howarth, 'why not? There's fuck all for me here; it's time to get off my arse and get on with my life.'

Howarth headed downstairs that evening to let his parents know what he had decided. He looked a sorry sight, standing there with two black eyes, a bloodstained rag and a bent, bloody nose. If he had expected any attempt on their part to dissuade him, he was sorely misguided. 'Good,' said his father. 'The sooner you go, the better.' With that, he reached into a pocket, pulled out a tenner and threw it in his son's direction; it fell short and fluttered to the floor. No one said anything. Pragmatism prevailed over pride; Howarth knew he would need all the money he could get his hands on to start his new life. He bent down to pick it up and, with all the dignity he could muster in his pitiful condition, turned on his heel and went back up to his bedroom to plan his itinerary. Several articles referred to a place named Oban on the west coast of Scotland. 'Why not?' thought Howarth. 'It's as good a place as any.'

The following morning, Howarth was out of his bed at six o'clock, ready to see where his life would lead. After counting his money, he had the princely sum of £22. Not a great deal for someone starting out; he would have to be frugal. Hostels would be out of the question on his budget, so he packed all his camping gear including a small Primus cooking stove. Three hours later, he was ready to go out and conquer all he surveyed. Even his father got up to wish him goodbye and good luck – although neither of his parents asked him where he was heading or how he would get there. Money concerns also ruled out trains or buses, so he stepped out that crisp spring morning and headed for the A1 to thumb a lift north. He was not to know – could not have known – that it was the road that one day would lead to a 25-year prison sentence.

CHAPTER TWO

The cars roared past Howarth as he stood by the slip road leading to the A1 north. Every van and lorry that flashed by seemed to bear a legend showing that it belonged to a Scottish company, and was heading home after some delivery down south. Howarth had already been thumbing in vain for several hours. 'I wish one of these fuckers would stop,' he thought, a refrain taken up and chanted by hitchhikers the world over, like some sort of particularly ineffective mantra. Eventually, in the late afternoon, St Jude – patron saint of hopeless causes and Queens Park Rangers – must have taken pity on him, as a battered old hatchback piled high with luggage and personal belongings swerved and pulled in 20 yards ahead of him, hazard lights flashing. Two girls – university students – shouted out to him, 'Newcastle any use to you?' Gratefully, Howarth climbed in and squeezed onto the back seat, shoving bags along until there was just enough room to wedge himself in behind the passenger seat. The two girls were pleasant company and the three hours it took to get to Newcastle went by quickly enough.

As they reached the outskirts of the city, it was already dark and they suggested that he spend the night at their flat before hitting the road again the next day. Howarth amiably agreed and they soon pulled up at a flat in an area of tree-lined streets with the dilapidated Victorian housing stock favoured by students in most university cities. They spent the evening watching television, drinking and smoking a few joints, until the girls announced they were going up to bed. With hindsight, Howarth realised that one of them had other plans for him that night, but as a callow and inexperienced 16-year-old, he was too naive to read the signs. He collapsed into an armchair and crashed out. At six o'clock the next morning, he awoke to find grey light creeping in through the thin curtains, and no sign of movement from the girls. After splashing water on his face and having a perfunctory wash, it was time to hit the road again. He still had a long way to go.

He made his way back to the A1 and stood patiently awaiting a lift, thumb stuck out. It was an agreeable enough spring morning, and the sun was rising over Newcastle. Before too long, a car came screaming at speed down the carriageway, swaying from side to side, before swerving towards him at the last moment, forcing him to jump back out of its path. As he did so, he could hear the car's occupants laughing and shouting abuse at him out of the window. An occupational hazard for hitchhikers. After many tedious hours waiting, and a few short lifts that took him part of the way, his last ride dropped him off on the outskirts of Edinburgh. It was approaching midnight. With no clear idea of where he should head, he followed the signs for the city centre. After trudging along empty roads until two o'clock in the morning, he found himself walking through the main shopping thoroughfare, Princes Street. Years later, he would glimpse the same view through the wire mesh of a police-wagon window on his way to the High Court. On this occasion, however, the police were far friendlier. A Panda car pulled up next to him.

'What are you doing out at this time of night?' the copper in the passenger seat asked him, not unkindly.

'I'm hitchhiking up north to look for work, and I've ended up in the city, which wasn't part of the plan, so now I'm looking for somewhere to crash,' Howarth replied honestly.

The copper took one look at him, taking in the rucksack and tent on his back, then thought for a moment.

'All right, jump in,' he said. 'We'll give you a lift to the other side of the Forth Bridge. There are plenty of fields where you can pitch your tent, but keep it out of sight – I don't want some irate farmer on the phone when I get back to the station. All right?'

'Fine by me,' agreed Howarth, reflecting that what he had heard was not necessarily true – not all coppers are bastards, after all. What he didn't know, however, was that Edinburgh came under the jurisdiction of Lothian and Borders Police; across the bridge was the fiefdom of the Fife Constabulary. They were simply moving a problem along so it was not their responsibility. Still, it's an ill wind and all that . . . They dropped him off on the far side of the Forth Bridge at a good spot beside a cornfield, which was also close to the M90, where he could hitchhike north towards Perth the next day. As he got out, they told him to use discretion putting up his tent, wished him luck and sped off back in the direction from which they had come, towards the city and their own patch. Howarth followed the tail-lights until they disappeared.

All around was silence, with nothing to break it but the occasional hoot of an owl; against the sky across the firth was the orange, neon glow of the city. He sat down and rolled himself a joint; as he smoked it, he looked at a map he had retrieved from his bag. A smudge of peanut butter obliterated some of the letters of Glasgow; nonetheless, it was clear that that was where he should be, not east near Edinburgh. With the aid of the dull glow of his torch, he made out the word Ullapool in the far north. The name rang a bell and, after racking his by now stoned brain, he remembered why; his dad had a diving mate who had his own boat there. With the insight that passes for a flash of genius to the very stoned, or very optimistic, he decided there and then that that would be his destination. Forget Oban; surely this guy would be able to offer him some work, or at least introduce him to someone who might. Pleased with his bit of inspiration, he set about pitching his tent; no easy task in the pitch black when you're completely out of it. Finally, he managed it, crawled into his sleeping bag and slept like one of the innocent.

The heavy rumble of traffic close by awakened him late the next morning, and an acrid smell of rotting flesh that made him gag and dry retch. 'What the fuck is that?' he muttered, climbing out of his sleeping bag. His groundsheet was covered in maggots, and he dismantled his tent to investigate. He soon discovered the cause. Beneath the groundsheet was a dead rat, whose stomach was still pulsing and heaving as though it were still alive. Maggots were crawling all over the body, and parts of the decomposing rat had come away and were stuck to his groundsheet. Fighting back the vomit, he cleaned his tent as best he could on the dewy grass, and packed up, wisely deciding to skip the breakfast he had eagerly been looking forward to the night before. At last, at around lunchtime, he was ready to get moving again; he headed down to the road and stood patiently with his thumb out for the next couple of hours.

Coming up the hill towards him at breakneck speed was a sleek, black sports car; as it went by, the driver spotted Howarth's outstretched thumb and slammed the brakes on. The wheels locked, causing the car to go into a long skid, at the end of which it came to a stop half on the grass verge 300 yards further along the road. Howarth ran along to it; the driver was Italian, as was the car, and in broken English, he told Howarth he could take him as far as Perth. Howarth went round to the offside – it was a left-hand drive – and climbed in. When he shut the door, in the confined cabin of the car he realised that, not to put too fine a point on it, he stank. The rat was getting its revenge. The driver grimaced and wound down his window. If he had been driving fast before, now he was going like greased pork – well over 100mph, Howarth noted, glancing at the dashboard – desperate, no doubt, to be rid of his putrid passenger. As they approached Perth, Howarth watched with horror as a maggot fell from his shoulder onto the back of the man's hand, which was resting on the gear stick. To his eternal relief, the man didn't glance down, simply shaking it off without looking. Perhaps he was afraid of what he might have seen, Howarth thought wryly. The sign shot by in a blur: 'Welcome to Perth.' The driver seemed as relieved as Howarth was.

After making good use of public washroom facilities to restore himself to something that might reasonably be adjudged to belong to the human race, Howarth found a roundabout with a sign pointing to 'Inverness and the North'. He took up position and waited. A shabbily dressed old woman walking her dog passed him twice; the third time, she stopped and said hello. She commented repeatedly on Howarth's appearance, saying that he had perfect teeth. 'Great,' thought Howarth,

'I'm trying to get a lift and this old biddy keeps going on about my teeth.' She told him that she was in Perth with a visiting fairground, where she had a stall doing Tarot cards and reading palms; she told him she would read his for nothing. 'No, thanks,' said Howarth, with a chuckle; 'I don't want to know what's in the future.' In years to come, he would regret that on more than one occasion.

After the old woman had gone on her way, Howarth didn't have to wait long before a smart estate car pulled up. An attractive, trendy woman in her early thirties with an auburn bob asked where he was headed; when he said Ullapool, she told him she was headed for Wick and could give him a ride as far as Inverness. This was in the days before the new A9 had been built, and as it was already evening, it would be a long, hard slog north. Her name was Maggie, she told him, and she worked for a record company in London. What sort of local talent Wick could have nurtured to induce a record company executive to undertake such a gruelling journey, she didn't say, and Howarth didn't enquire.

Driving through the dark, along narrow country roads, the monotony was only relieved by the occasional village or small town. Howarth found himself dropping off repeatedly. At around midnight, Maggie pulled into a lay-by and suggested they got some sleep; it would only be a short journey to Inverness in the morning. Howarth stretched out in the back while she reclined the driver's seat and slept there. Howarth slept soundly until seven o'clock the next morning when he awoke with a smile on his face to find that Maggie had slipped her hand down into his sleeping bag and was slowly rubbing him into a state of alert. She had a look of intense concentration on her face and her free hand up her skirt. Inexperienced as he was, Howarth nevertheless tried to pull her over the seat into the back, but she told him just to lie back and enjoy it, saying it was the wrong time of the month for her to make love. As a lad of 16, Howarth did exactly what he was told by this attractive, older woman, and when she had finished the task in hand, it was time to move on again. In no time, they reached Inverness and the ever-bountiful Maggie told Howarth she had decided to take him all the way to Ullapool as they had 'become good friends'.

'Good friends, indeed,' thought Howarth with a wry smile, as they headed north out of the town. The road to Ullapool takes the driver through some of the most beautiful, and most desolate, scenery in Britain; climbing, it passes along bleak moorland, then drops through picturesque wooded canyons, such as the one at Corrieshalloch Gorge.

In less than two hours, Howarth caught glimpses of Loch Broom through the trees as they reached the outskirts of Ullapool, and, rounding a bend, he looked down on the small fishing village that was to become his home for the next 30 years, with the exception of one long, enforced leave of absence.

CHAPTER THREE

There has been continuous settlement of one form or another on the site of Ullapool since the days of the Picts and, later, the Vikings. But the modern port took shape in 1788, when it was designed as a model fishing village on behalf of the British Fisheries Society by Thomas Telford, famed for his Menai suspension bridge among others. By the mid-1970s, it had become the most important fishing port on the north-west coast of Scotland, renowned for the 'klondykers' – huge factory ships from the eastern bloc that would moor out in Loch Broom, buying up the majority of the local herring and mackerel catch to can on board and bring back to eastern Europe. As well as providing plenty of work for local fishermen, so many sailors of different nationalities congregating on this tiny place ensured a hard-drinking, hard-fighting culture that had earned Ullapool the sobriquet 'the Wild West'.

The original village seemed to have changed little in the intervening 200 years since Telford conceived it. Along the front was a tidy row of fishermen's cottages with a hotel at one end and a pub at the other. In front of these, the harbour was the scene of great activity – cranes were swinging girders into place, as foremen shouted up instructions to the operators. It transpired that the passenger ferry from the Isle of Lewis had come into harbour too fast, ploughing into the pier, all but destroying it; work was going on apace to restore it.

Maggie drove Howarth down to the front and dropped him off. She gave him her address down south and he promised to keep in touch, although of course he never did. As he sat on the pier watching boats coming in with their catch, the ferry pulled in, disgorging its passengers down the gangway. One dark-haired girl, struggling with a bulging holdall that was nearly her own size, asked him for directions to the Caledonian Hotel. With a bashful grin, Howarth explained that he was a 'blow-in' himself and didn't know the village, and the girl went on her way.

He decided it was time to find somewhere to stay. The local campsite charged a pound per night and, as he was down to his last £15, he decided to have a wander and see if he could find somewhere that he could pitch his tent free of charge; after a fruitless search, he concluded he would have to stay at the campsite after all. A little early in the season for tourists from mainland Europe, he practically had the place to himself. He had his tent up in no time and set off down to the front. It was time to find Darryl Campbell, his father's diving friend, who had inspired him to head for Ullapool in the first place.

After making enquiries at the local grocer's – a '70s, Spar-type outlet called Liptons – he made his way along to one of the cottages on the front. He rapped confidently on the door and, after what seemed like an eternity, it was opened by a man that Howarth instantly recognised as his father's friend. Short and stocky, with a dark beard, the most noticeable thing about him was the expensive diver's watch he was wearing. The man looked Howarth up and down. 'You're Dave Howarth's son,' he finally said, more as a statement than a question. Howarth amiably agreed that he was, and that he had turned up in Ullapool as he had heard that there was plenty of work for trained divers. The man stood with his arms folded across his chest, making no move to invite Howarth in. His wife was unwell, he explained unconvincingly, otherwise he'd offer him a cup of tea. As for work, there was precious little of it about. Howarth knew this to be untrue: he had seen boats arriving back that afternoon with huge catches of scallops; somebody had to be diving for them. The man bade him goodnight and practically shut the door in his face. 'Welcome to Ullapool,' thought Howarth bitterly, as he trudged back up to the campsite.

It was getting dark, and time to eat. He set up his Primus stove and cooked himself a simple but satisfying tea of sausages and beans. Replete, he sat back, contentedly surveying the twinkling lights of the harbour below him. It was time to get some ale down him.

He found himself in front of a large Victorian pub whose sign proclaimed that it was the Caledonian Hotel. A cacophony of noise spilled out from inside, which became deafening as he pushed open the double doors with frosted windowpanes. Inside was packed, the air thick with swearing and blue cigarette smoke. Oilskins and rubber boots lay everywhere, their owners spending the day's catch far more rapidly than they had earned it. At the bar, men stood with full pints and large whisky chasers in front of them, swaying as though still at sea. In front of him, two men stood screaming into each other's faces, skippers arguing over fishing rights. One grabbed the other's shirt, ripping it, and delivered three rapid punches to his opponent's face, causing blood to snake out in a graceful arc. The man staggered backwards, fell over a chair and landed in a heap against the wall, where he immediately fell asleep, the effect of the blows and the alcohol hitting him. Howarth could see why people called this town 'the Wild West'.

He forced his way through to the bar and shouted his order for a pint of bitter. 'Bitter is for the English, sonny,' sneered the barman. 'What you'll be wanting is heavy.' It certainly was, thought Howarth, sipping his pint and surveying the battlefield that passed for a pub in these parts. Then on the far side of the room, he saw a girl sitting alone at a table writing postcards; it was the one from the ferry who had asked him for directions earlier. He started to thread his way over towards her, squeezing past groups of men who made no effort to let him through; his polite requests to pass were met with retorts such as 'Fuck off, ye wee English prick' and 'Southern bastard!'

Eventually, he arrived at her table and asked if he could sit down; with a sigh, the girl said he could please himself. As he sat down, she glanced his way and, on recognising him, gave a smile. Her name was Mary McIver, and she was over from Point on the Isle of Lewis to work as a chambermaid in the hotel. She was sick of being chatted up by drunken fishermen, but it was good to come across a friendly face. The two of them chatted away and had a few drinks. She had heard of a party they could go to at ten o'clock, when the pub closed, so the two of them bought a few tins to carry out and set off to find it.

Although Ullapool was not a big place, they were unsuccessful in their quest, so Howarth suggested that they go back to his tent and have their own party. Slightly reluctantly, Mary agreed, and after a few beers, they ended up crawling into his sleeping bag. Howarth reflected that in all his years in Doncaster he had only been with two women; now here he was, with as many in two days. Things were looking up.

The following morning, he headed down to the pier to try to speak to some of the men on the boats; it was time to find some work. As he sat there, he saw an expensive-looking car pull up at the front. Out jumped Darryl, his father's friend, who disappeared over the wall to climb down to the jetty. Despite the blow to his pride when the man had shut the door in his face the previous evening, Howarth decided there could be no harm in trying again. As he climbed down the ladder, Darryl caught sight of him and, with a sideways look, half-heartedly asked whether he wanted to come along with them for the ride. Howarth didn't need to be asked twice. As he jumped on board the boat, a 40-footer called *The Stornoway Pilot*, two men came out of the wheelhouse and introduced themselves as John Hardcastle and Ken Walton, two divers up from the north of England to earn a few quid. Howarth took an immediate liking to Ken: although clearly an experienced seaman, he treated Howarth as an equal, looking him in the eye and smiling warmly as he gave him a firm handshake.

They cast off and headed out into Loch Broom, towards the Minch, the strait that separates the Isle of Lewis from the mainland. After around an hour, they dropped anchor. They had reached the fishing grounds. John got into his diving gear and climbed over the side with two bags for collecting scallops, one with a rope attached to it, the other under his weight belt. After he disappeared underwater, Ken explained that if he resurfaced after just a few minutes, it meant there was no great fishing there, and they would move on to other grounds. After a while, he reappeared, shouting excitedly that there was 'a big fishing' in only 60 feet of water, ideal conditions. Darryl quickly changed into his diving gear and slipped over the side. While the two men were down below, Ken and Howarth fell to chatting. Ken explained that he was just helping out for a bit of extra money while his own boat, a sturdy 38-footer called *The Emulate*, was being refitted; after that, he would be setting out on his own.

Howarth asked casually whether he'd be needing any divers and, when Ken said that he would in time, nonchalantly asked, 'What about me?', staring ahead of him lest he appear too desperate. Ken was reluctant to take on a rookie, but Howarth pointed out that he had his diver's ticket, and that everyone had to start somewhere. Ken looked out overboard, leaning on the railings, sucking his teeth. Finally, he said that he'd give him a go, but that he could only afford to pay him a living wage to cover beer and food; as for accommodation, he could sleep on the boat. It was all Howarth could do to stop himself punching the air with joy. He had a job! That evening, he telephoned his dad and persuaded him to fetch his diving gear up from Doncaster.

Over the next six months, Howarth and Ken worked well together.

Ken was from the old school – work hard, play hard – and taught Howarth everything he knew about diving for scallops, then spending the day's earnings in The Caley. Indeed, it was a shame the barman wouldn't let them pay for their beer in scallops, as they would have cut out the middleman, and the middleman's commission.

Howarth proved to be an adept student, and his prodigious talent for drinking, fighting and diving to unsafe depths shunned by others soon meant that he had acquired the nickname 'Crazy Chris'. When the season came to an end, he could count many friends among the fishermen of the area. Ullapool had taken him for one of its own.

CHAPTER FOUR

In the spring of 1976, Howarth landed what appeared to be a great job, up in Kylesku, a tiny remote community of around 40 people some 30 miles north of Ullapool. It is chiefly of note for the bridge that crosses between the inland Loch Glencoul and Loch a'Chairn Bhain, an estuary that sweeps out into the Minch. The bridge, just 300 yards long, was opened by the Queen in 1984, saving tourists more than a 100-mile detour; back in 1976, they made do with a ferry, *The Maid of Glencoul,* used as often for transporting cattle and livestock as for Dutch and German tourists with their Mercedes and BMWs.

On the southern side of the crossing, beside the slipway leading to the ferry stands a pleasant and spacious pub, the Kylesku Hotel, now run by an English couple who specialise in lunch and evening meals for the burgeoning tourist trade. Back then, it was not such a salubrious place, a drinkers' den for the fishermen who worked out of Kylesku, although it would become memorable to Howarth, for it was here that he met his first wife, a barmaid named Lenore.

The job that saw him heading up to Kylesku was one that sounded too good to be true. A skipper that he knew working out of Ullapool said that his father owned a boat in Kylesku, and was looking for a couple of men to crew it for him. Howarth got in touch with the man, who offered him what seemed like a good deal. Howarth would work the boat all week, in return for which the man would give him £10 spending money, food on the boat and a caravan in Ullapool to use at weekends. The rest of his money would be kept in a separate account and given to him at the end of the season.

It was a good time for Howarth, virtually his own boss, with only one other crewman to worry about – Duncan, who was as wild as Howarth. They would spend the entire day fishing from first light until eight or nine o'clock at night, then spend the evenings getting roaringly drunk in the Kylesku Hotel, where he got to see Lenore and enjoy some female company.

One evening after supper, Duncan suggested shooting a deer which he had seen milling about the area, a young, healthy beast well worth the bullet. He pulled an old .22 rifle from the boat's cupboard and set about cleaning it; when he had finished, he asked Howarth to go outside and see if the deer was still there. A young stag in good condition was indeed grazing on the brow of the hill, near some houses, around 300 yards from the boat. Duncan took the small rowing boat that they used to cross the estuary to get to the pub at night and set off in the opposite direction towards the sea so as to lull the stag into a false sense of security. He disappeared from sight, and Howarth stood watching the beast.

After some time, the peace was disturbed by a loud, sharp crack as a bullet hit the stag. It faltered, then found its feet again. Howarth looked around to see Duncan kneeling behind a large rock, taking aim again, then firing. Again, the beast took the bullet, but made no move to run away. Three more shots were fired, each time accompanied by a sickening thud as the animal was hit but refused to go down. By now half the village had come out to see what the commotion was about. Now out of bullets, Duncan pulled out a large carving knife that he had taken from the galley and ran towards the beast, which made no attempt to escape. With cries of horror from the villagers, he threw himself on the animal and started slashing at it in a frenzy. Howarth felt sick at the bloody spectacle; what was supposed to have been a clean kill with one bullet had turned into a frenzied attack.

It took Duncan a quarter of an hour to kill the deer, by which time most of the villagers had walked off in disgust. Howarth felt they had not made any new friends that evening and, right enough, when they walked into the pub later, the place fell silent apart from one woman who began to scream and curse them. It turned out that the deer was practically a pet and lived at the back of her house; it was so tame that it allowed her to feed it every day, and her kids played with it. After calling them every name under the sun, she stormed out in tears, inconsolable. Duncan followed her out and returned an hour later, looking even glummer. When Howarth asked him what was wrong, he answered that he had taken the woman a leg of venison as a peace offering, and could not understand why she and her kids had become hysterical.

At the end of the season, Howarth rang the boat's owner to tell him that there would be no more fishing that year, and that he would like to pick up his back pay, which he had calculated to be more than £3,000, a huge sum of money to him. After a long pause, the man said he could not afford it. Howarth couldn't believe what he was hearing. 'What! I've worked my fucking fingers to the bone for you from four in the morning till nine at night, and all for £10 a week spending money. How much *have* you got for me?' There was another long pause, before the man said hesitantly that he could let him have £70. Howarth exploded, but was told if he didn't like it, he knew what he could do. He slammed the phone down, and hitchhiked back to Ullapool. Over the next few days, whenever he tried to contact the owner, Howarth was told that he was unavailable.

By Saturday, he had got himself wound up into a highly agitated state. He saw the owner's son, the skipper of a local boat, working on his craft on the beach, and confronted him, demanding that something be done about the situation. The son pointed out that it had nothing to do with him, that Howarth's argument was with his father. Howarth blew his lid, and a violent fight erupted between the two men. After trading punches, Howarth then committed the grave error of picking up an iron bar that lay to one side and hurling it at the man's head. It missed by a few yards, and the fight petered out.

An hour or two later, as Howarth sat in The Caley nursing a pint and his grievances, two local coppers arrived and told him to get into the back of the car. Down at the police station in Ullapool, they told him he was being charged with attempted murder. 'What?' laughed Howarth. 'How can I be charged with attempted murder when I'm standing here with two black eyes and a bloody nose?' The sergeant replied that Howarth had recklessly thrown an iron bar at the man – and they had witnesses to back them up.

'But it missed him by a mile,' said Howarth, incredulously.

'Do you want to make a statement?' asked the sergeant.

Howarth mumbled that he did not.

'Well, shut your mouth, then – you're away down to Dingwall.'

Dingwall is an old-fashioned market town with a population of less than 5,000, the kind of place where the shops still close for a half-day on Thursdays and the whole of the first Monday in the month during the summer. The birthplace of Macbeth, it is some 45 miles south of Ullapool. It would be a lonely weekend for Howarth in the cells – Dingwall Sheriff's Court (the Scottish equivalent of a magistrate's court) wouldn't open until the Monday morning. When he was finally in the dock, the prosecution read out the charges and a summary of what Howarth allegedly had done. Concluding that what they had on him was 'a heap of shit', Howarth pleaded not guilty and, rather than incur the expense and hassle of a full trial, the sheriff bound him over to keep the peace for a year and put him on a bail bond of £50. There was only one snag: he had no cash, living as he did hand to mouth. Luckily for him, one of the coppers at the court that morning was based at Ullapool and knew 'Crazy Chris' well, in a professional capacity, of course. He kindly agreed to pay the bond and Howarth was on his way.

Back in his caravan in Ullapool, there was a knock on the door. It was the owner of the boat, whose double-dealing had got Howarth into trouble in the first place. He knew fine well that if Howarth went for him, he'd be back to court without his feet touching the ground, and was taking advantage of the situation to get Howarth out of the caravan as well. He said he would give him a cheque for £70 if Howarth would sign a statement agreeing to vacate the caravan and affirming that the money was in full and final settlement of any outstanding debt. Howarth had no choice but to sign, and by the evening he was once again homeless and unemployed.

In despair at how things were going for him, Howarth decided to skip bail and head for Morocco – he had never been there but travellers he had met had always spoken of it warmly, and he had heard that hash was plentiful and cheap there. As it happened, his parents and brother Stephen – the policeman – were heading for a family holiday to Brixham in Devon, so Howarth was able to cadge a lift that would take him as far as the south coast. From there, he would take a ferry to France or Spain and work his way down to Algeciras to catch a boat to Morocco. As his brother was far too straight for his liking, he took childish pleasure in rolling joints in the back of the car and blowing the smoke at him; he could do with chilling out, thought Howarth. Unfortunately, by the time they reached Bristol, the entire family was sick of him, and threw him and his luggage out on the hard shoulder of the motorway. 'Bastards!' shouted Howarth defiantly at the back of the car as it sped off, his fingers held aloft in a V-sign.

He managed to thumb his way down to Dover just in time to catch the night ferry to Calais and the next day set about trying to hitch down to Algeciras. At around 2,500 miles from Ullapool to Algeciras travelling by the most direct route, it might be supposed that Howarth had made some provision for his travels, but that, of course, would have been completely out of character. He made do with hitching, accepting any lift so long as it was going vaguely south. As well as the problem of being skint, he had the interesting added complication of not being able to speak a word of French. By night, he slept rough in hedgerows, bus stations and parks in small towns. After three weeks of living like this, he found himself in Perpignan, a French town not too far from the Spanish border. Here, he ended up living in a squat with some French heroin addicts. Without any money, they had to survive on a combination of begging and shoplifting. Much as he liked the junkies with whom he was living, after two months it was time to move on. He made it as far as the Spanish border, where a Customs officer stopped him, asking him how much money he was bringing into the country. Howarth emptied out his pockets; he had around 20 francs, less than £2. With a sneer, the man shook his head and pointed back to the French side of the border. 'You go back,' he said, and with two armed guards flanking him, Howarth was in no mood to argue.

He hitched to Marseille with a vague, half-formed plan of getting a boat to Morocco from there. Arriving in the city, it was clear that Marseille already had more than its fair share of vagrants, scroungers and vagabonds. After ten days in this city, Howarth felt utterly depressed. It was time to go home and face the music.

He managed to hitch back to the UK and headed for his parents' home in Doncaster; they were less than overjoyed to see him. Howarth made his way to the local police station and explained that he had jumped bail and been in Europe in defiance of a ban on unapproved overseas travel. South Yorkshire Police was completely indifferent to a breach of bail outside of its jurisdiction, but Howarth insisted that officers arrest him and notify Dingwall Sheriff's Court, which they eventually, though reluctantly, did. After a couple of days, two policemen from Dingwall arrived and took Howarth back to court, where he was fined £25 for jumping bail and put on probation. With nowhere else to go, he headed back to Ullapool. He was not the first to reflect that no matter how far you run, your problems will still be waiting for you when you get back.

CHAPTER FIVE

It was by now 1977. The year opened with Johnny Mathis at the top of the singles chart with 'When A Child Is Born', up and down the country street parties were being planned for the Queen's Silver Jubilee – and, back in Ullapool, Howarth was once again unemployed and homeless. Something had to change. He got back with Lenore, and they spent the season back in Kylesku. Howarth by now had gone into partnership with an Englishman named Harding; the arrangement was that they would share the work and any costs for diving gear, and in return split the profits.

It worked out reasonably well for the first year, although he was seeing less and less of Harding, who always seemed to be off on other jobs, turning up only to collect his share of the profits. In the spring of 1978, Howarth married Lenore and began to question whether he was really earning as much as he should. After another year of this, he had had enough. Even in partnership, it was the same old story – he seemed to be doing all of the work for very little return. He told Harding he was jacking it in, and that he could keep the inflatable boat in which they had invested. It was time to plan his next move.

But events soon overtook him. He brooded in the Kylesku Hotel one night, downing pint after pint until he was aggressively drunk and spoiling for a fight. Another fisherman made the mistake of engaging Lenore in conversation and conspicuously flirting with her. Howarth saw red. He flew at the man, dragging him across a table, before landing several heavy punches on his face. In front of a bar full of witnesses, and with his track record, he concluded that he didn't want to wait around for the police to nick him. The next morning, Lenore and Howarth packed up their few belongings and hit the road. It was time to say goodbye to Kylesku.

Some 185 miles south of Kylesku by road lies the fishing port of Mallaig, looking over the Sound of Sleat, a short strait that separates the mainland from the Isle of Skye. It is at the end of the long 'Road to the

Isles', the A830, which runs from Fort William to Mallaig along the shores of the hauntingly desolate Loch Eil. Howarth soon made friends and found work diving; in time, he bought his own boat, *The Stornoway Pilot*, on which he had first met Ken Walton several years earlier in Ullapool, with a loan from the fish buying company Walkers of Mallaig. He was back in business, and there was plenty of diving. Money was rolling in.

Unfortunately, he was spending it just as quickly as he could earn it. He had become a well-known face in the pubs around Mallaig, and the more Lenore nagged him about his drinking and their lack of money, the more he sought solace in the bottle. He had become good mates with two local characters, Cyril Simpson, from whom he bought diesel for his boat, and Jimsey Grant, a local fisherman. The three of them made a good fist of keeping the pubs of Mallaig in the black, and one night, during a typical drunken session, hatched a plan to do some poaching.

Cyril knew of a good spot for salmon down the A830 near Lochailort, a place called the Policeman's Pool. How it got its name, no one is quite sure, the roots being shrouded in nineteenth-century obscurity; whatever the reason, it would turn out to be particularly appropriate. The night was set for a Saturday in July 1978, and they employed the services of a local lad, who would act as driver and lookout.

After an evening in the pub getting well oiled, the three men were full of bravado and appetite for adventure. They went down to *The Stornoway Pilot* to pick up Howarth's diving gear and nets, loaded everything into the back of the van and set off for Lochailort at around two o'clock in the morning. They were in high spirits and passed around a bottle of whisky, from which all swigged liberally.

After an hour or so, they reached a roadside hotel, The Inn at Lochailort, and parked nearby. Removing their gear from the back, they set off down an overgrown track alongside a stream towards the pool where they planned to set up. It was a moonless night and Howarth could scarcely see ahead of him as he struggled down the path loaded down with his diving gear. After half an hour, he was short of breath; just ahead of him the path seemed especially overgrown, and he could barely make out what looked like a large amount of foliage across the path. As he stepped on it, he nearly jumped out of his skin; the bracken turned out to be a night angler, rudely awoken from his sleep by Howarth's size tens. The man jumped to his feet, demanding to know what was going on. Howarth flung his diving gear into the undergrowth as behind him Cyril Simpson did the same with the nets.

The angler shone a torch at them. As the arc of light caught the edges of the undergrowth, the man spotted the abandoned diving gear and nets, and his face creased with anger.

'Poachers, eh? Well, you've done it this time,' he hissed, drawing himself up. 'I am Detective Chief Superintendent John MacDougall of Strathclyde CID, and you men are under arrest.'

'Have you got a warrant, then?' demanded Howarth aggressively.

'I beg your pardon?' spluttered MacDougall indignantly.

Howarth repeated the question.

'No, of course I haven't, don't be so ridic . . .'

'Well, in that case, I'm Mickey fucking Mouse,' mocked Howarth as he sent his right fist crashing into the unfortunate policeman's eye, sending him flying. As he hit the ground, Howarth and his compatriots turned and fled back up the path, laughing hysterically. After a few minutes, they could see a flashing blue light up ahead of them on the main road, so agreed to split up and meet back at the van. Seeing flashes of torchlight on the path ahead of him, and hearing footsteps trampling the undergrowth as unseen officers of law enforcement headed his way, Howarth noiselessly slipped into the river, holding his breath as his body adjusted to the freezing temperature. He held his head above water by clinging to overhanging reeds and plants, pulling himself upstream as, above him, he could hear voices and the sound of men crashing along the path. After several minutes, when the noises had faded away, he hauled himself onto the path and ran back to the road near the pub, where he found the others already in the van. He jumped into the back and the van sped off, with its lights turned off.

They didn't get far; the Road to the Isles is the only route between Fort William and Mallaig and, within a few minutes, they were surrounded by police cars with lights flashing. As he was hauled from the van, he recognised a sergeant from Mallaig, who was apoplectic with rage. 'Do you know who youse fucking idiots have gone and battered?' he screamed at the men, the veins in his neck standing out red and angry. 'No,' replied Howarth flippantly, 'but if you describe him, I'll tell you if you're right.'

As ever, the police had the last laugh. Howarth had plenty of time to dry off in the cells at Fort William until the Sheriff's Court opened on Monday. He was convicted of assault and fined £60. Most of the locals treated the men as heroes and they dined out on the story for some time; Lenore, however, was not amused.

In fact, Howarth's drinking and brushes with the law were taking their toll on his marriage, and the cracks were beginning to show. Realising that he was coming perilously close to losing his wife, he resolved to leave Mallaig and head back north – not that he had been a model of restraint when he had lived there. Late that summer, he and Lenore loaded up the boat with their wedding presents and a few other possessions, and sailed off on their journey back north. Reaching Ullapool, it was clear that there were far too many boats operating there, too much competition to earn a decent living. They sailed on, back to their old grounds of Kylesku, where no other boats had been based since he last left. There would be enough pickings for him to make a reasonable living.

His first, most pressing concern though was where they would live. His drinking was now getting out of control, causing him to take days off work to nurse his splitting hangovers. 'I can't go on like this!' Lenore had screamed at him during one of their countless arguments. Another winter in the cramped, damp cabin aboard his boat would surely have finished off what remained of their marriage. He found an old crofter's hut, out at a remote spot called Nedd, three miles or so from the tiny village of Drumbeg with a population of around 50 people, a pub and a village shop.

Nedd forms part of the North Assynt Estate, which saw a test case in the early 1990s to challenge the ancient and detested 'lairdship' system of landowning in Scotland, which had changed little since feudal times. The estate was once owned by the Vestey family, who made their fortune in food distribution, owning the Dewhurst chain of butchers, among others. With the land changing hands many times over the last two centuries, often against the interests of those who lived there, a group of crofters formed an association to lobby for the right to buy their land and hold it in trust for the common good. They achieved their goal, and this right to self-determination against the interests of powerful lairds has seen notable successes since, including the high-profile cases where inhabitants bought the islands of Gigha and Eigg.

Back in the late 1970s, however, this was all yet to come. In return for the use of the croft, Howarth was required to spend one day a week working on the estate; the rest of the time, he was free to fish on *The Stornoway Pilot*. Drink, however, had really taken hold of him by now, and he spent most of his free time in a drunken stupor, watching brown envelopes arrive, accumulating in a pile to the tune of several thousand pounds' worth of debt. He blocked out his responsibilities, and, like many alcoholics, hoped for some sort of miracle to sort out his problems. And then one came.

One morning, he went down to the shore to examine the boat after an especially violent overnight storm. He surveyed the shoreline, but could not see his boat. Then he caught sight of it, tilting at an impossible angle, all but sunk. God – or at least the insurance company – had answered his prayers. With the boat classified a write-off, Howarth received a cheque from the insurers for £3,500. He paid off the majority of his bills; the rest, predictably, went on booze.

In a time of political turmoil, Margaret Thatcher had just come to power, promising that where there was despair, she would sow hope. Unemployment in Britain had reached the three-million mark by this point, and Howarth was once again one of those statistics. Then he landed a proper job, working on a salmon farm in Drumbeg. The pay was crap – £50 a week – but there was an end-of-season bonus of ten pence per pound of fish caught, which would add up to a tidy sum. He would enjoy the work, too: taking nets out to sea and setting them. At the end of his first day, he resolved to clean up his act, give up his boozing and become a more loving husband; he went home with a spring in his step, looking forward to his dinner. This would be a new start for him.

As he opened the front door, he knew immediately something was wrong; there was no fire in the front room, no smell of cooking wafting through the house. He called out for Lenore, but there was no reply. He went from room to room, looking in vain for her, but the house was empty. He concluded that she must be at a neighbour's and returned to the living room to start a fire. As he hunted for paper to light it, he caught sight of a note on the coffee table. It was brief, and to the point: 'Dear Chris. Can't take it anymore. We had some good times together, but now I'm leaving you. Sorry. Lenore.'

The words hit him hard, and he stood there with tears streaming down his cheeks, splashing onto the note. He sat in the dark room, reading the note over and over again by the moonlight that came through the small window. Eventually, he shook himself and stood up. He would find her, explain to her that he had changed, that everything would be different. As he slammed the door behind him, for what would turn out to be the last time, the cold night air hit him.

The moon, full and milky, cast eerie shadows of the outhouses as he walked up towards Drumbeg, three miles away. He felt utterly alone.

When he reached the small hotel, he could hear laughter and glasses chinking. He paused, then opened the door and entered. Conversation stopped and everyone looked towards him. 'Shit,' he thought, 'news travels fast in a small place like this.' His resolve to give up drinking now forgotten, he ordered a pint and asked the barman if he had seen his wife. The barman would not look him in the eye and lied that he had not. It seemed like an eternity before he could get any news about his beloved Lenore's whereabouts. He spent the best part of an hour trying to extract the information he so desperately needed from the villagers sitting at the bar.

Eventually, one man took pity on him. 'She has a job at a hotel in Lochinver,' he said, 'but she doesn't want you following her there.' Lochinver is 15 miles from Drumbeg and with no chance of getting there that night, Howarth spent his time and money in the company of the local barfly, getting drunk and telling him how much he loved Lenore. He spent that night on the wreck of his boat with a bottle of the best Scotch whisky the pub could sell him and a stack of memories, trying to blot out his unbearable pain and loss.

The following day, he set out on the road to Lochinver, his thumb out. As fortune had it, the first car along belonged to a friend who lived in the village. Concerned at Howarth's appearance, he insisted on taking him back to his home and cleaning him up, lending him some clothes. Then, still worried, his friend asked whether he could call a doctor. Receiving no reply, he went ahead and did so. When the doctor arrived, he gently asked Howarth some probing questions about his state of mind, whether he had entertained thoughts of self-harm and so on. He then said that he would like to admit Howarth to hospital for his own good, but Howarth refused point-blank. Left with little other option, and acting professionally, the doctor reached into his bag and took out a bottle of pills – Valium. He warned Howarth to take them only as necessary to calm him down.

Howarth arrived in Lochinver that afternoon and made his way to the hotel where his wife was working. He spent several hours drinking in the bar, hoping to see his wife and making new friends who were only too happy to accept drinks from him and listen to his tales of woe. Eventually, Lenore came out to the bar and took Howarth to a corner to speak to him. Gently but firmly, she told him that there was no way back, that their marriage was over and that he must put it behind him and rebuild his life.

Looking her in the eye, he said, 'Well, what I do now, I hold you responsible for.' He emptied out the entire contents of the bottle of Valium he had in his pocket, crammed them into his mouth and washed them down with a large glass of whisky. She held his gaze, shrugged and said, 'Please yourself', before walking away. That was the last time that Howarth would ever see her.

He made his way back to his new-found friends and carried on drinking. As he stood up to get a round, he suddenly felt woozy, saw bright lights exploding in front of him and felt himself falling.

When he came round, he found himself in what appeared to be a cot. A trail of wires was attached to his chest by means of pads, and an intravenous drip had been inserted into his left arm. A constant beeping from the electro-cardiogram on the trolley beside him indicated he was still alive, to his great disappointment. After a few minutes, a doctor in a white coat put his head around the door to check on him; his nervous manner and enormous black eye indicated that Howarth had not been admitted without a struggle. He took one look at the patient and quickly exited, closing the door behind him. Howarth looked around him. In the gleaming white ward, there were several occupants, all apparently very sick people. In the bed opposite was an old man, wired up to a machine that looked like it belonged to Mission Control, all buttons and flashing lights; he was grey and seemed to be having difficulty breathing. The smell of antiseptic was overpowering. Howarth could not stay there any longer.

He pulled the intravenous drip out of his arm and the wires from his chest, and began to rise from his bed. A nurse came running in with a look of alarm, and tried to persuade him to get back into his bed. When he refused, she disappeared and returned a moment later with the doctor. In a quiet voice, he told Howarth that he could leave if he signed a release form. Howarth staggered, still suffering from the effects of the alcohol and pills; he had a buzzing noise in his ear, which was clearly affecting his balance. The doctor explained that it was a side effect of his overdose and would take a few days to clear up. Howarth signed the form, got dressed and left.

He could not face going back to his croft so headed back to Ullapool, where his life in Scotland had begun several years earlier. A friend of his had begun a business hiring out canoes and rowing boats to tourists; Howarth persuaded him to give him a job in return for beer money. As for somewhere to live, he found an old fish bait store where he could sleep on a pallet with some borrowed blankets. He was at the end of the line, brought as low as he had ever been in his short life. At the age of

23, he had run out of moves and had lost any trace of pride or dignity. With enough money for sufficient alcohol to numb the pain, he was beyond caring; his wife had not only taken herself away, she had also taken any desire to live from him as well.

CHAPTER SIX

Over the next few weeks, Howarth's depression began to lift gradually and thoughts of suicide slowly receded. He started taking a little more pride in his appearance and began to think about looking for a more long-term solution to his housing problem. While in the depths of despair, he had been content to fall into his pit each night drunk; he now wanted to rebuild his life, and needed a secure base from which to start.

He put word around, and had a stroke of good fortune. A guy in the village had a business hiring caravans to tourists and had one that, although still sound, was not quite fancy enough to be rented out. He agreed to let Howarth live in it for a nominal rent.

And one evening that summer, something happened to help him begin to put the devastating collapse of his marriage behind him. One night, after a few beers, he joined the throng of people waiting for their late-night junk food at the hamburger van on the seafront. As he got to the counter, he saw a pretty young 16-year-old, dark-haired and vivacious with flashing eyes. She was working in the van and giving back as good as she got from her drunk customers as she handed over their post-pub packages of carbohydrates.

Howarth was immediately drawn to this fiery, no-nonsense girl and got chatting to her as the last of the pub evictees loped off to their homes. Her name was Fiona Forsyth and she was Ullapool born and bred. He started seeing more and more of her over that summer, and they soon became a regular sight around the village. Fiona began to spend more and more time at Howarth's caravan, to her parents' initial consternation, as they were worried about Crazy Chris's reputation, and within a few months, she had moved in. They put their name down for a council house; in the meantime, the caravan would suffice.

By now, Howarth had got his act together and acquired a boat, a 28-footer called *The Alison Jill.* He was diving for scallops once again, and making a reasonable living. Ever the maverick, he continued to go to dangerous depths and, at the beginning of the 1980s, suffered an extremely bad case of the bends which resulted in a spinal injury that doctors feared would see him in a wheelchair. He confounded them by recovering and continued to dive as before, even suffering another mishap, which meant a serious operation on his shoulder.

Finally, in January 1983 their council house came through and they were able to leave the caravan behind. Morefield Place is a terraced cul-de-sac; the last house is neat and well kept, a testimony to Fiona's house-proud ways, with a garden all around and a clear view across the harbour. In November of that year, Fiona gave birth to a girl, whom they named Gayle. Howarth was as settled as he had ever been.

He still had his wild streak, though, and an eye for the women that would always land him in trouble. When Gayle was still tiny, he went out for some beers one night and wound up in the bar of the Royal Hotel in Ullapool. He got chatting to a 20-year-old girl from Muir of Ord who was working there; her name was Val Allen, and Howarth hit it off with her immediately. He arranged to meet her again and, before long, they had embarked on a relationship, in what the tabloids years later would come to dub 'Crazy Chris's Love Triangle'.

Unsurprisingly, Fiona was less happy with the arrangement than Howarth was, and one afternoon in October 1985, after his affair had been going on for a couple of years, they had a blazing row. Howarth stormed out of the house and jumped on the old motorbike he kept as a run-around. He headed down to Muir of Ord, a village some 45 miles south of Ullapool, where Val was now living and working as a kilt-maker.

That evening, they headed out to a local pub in the village called The Moorings. Howarth was in a foul mood and began drinking heavily. As had happened with his wife several years before, when he saw a stranger talking to Val, the red mist descended once again. He grabbed the unfortunate man and clobbered him, sending him flying; for good measure, he picked up a soda bottle from the counter and hurled it at the row of bottles on optics behind the bar, causing glass to shatter and fly out everywhere. Within moments, he had calmed down enough to realise what he had done, and that the police would be there any moment. He didn't wait around to greet them.

Running outside, he jumped on his bike and kicked it into life; he took off like a greyhound out of the traps, heading for a back road. He took a country lane that bypasses Dingwall and heads through farmland by way of Marybank and Moy Bridge, reasoning that by the time he rejoined the main Ullapool road several miles north at Contin, the police would have given up pursuing him.

He was wrong. As he flew up the narrow country lane, he could see a flashing blue light in his rear-view mirror. Rounding a bend, he pulled sharply off the road by a bridge and took refuge under it; with satisfaction, he heard his pursuer shoot by above his head. He turned around and shot off down another lane, little more than a track, which would get him back to the main road. He tore off down it with the lights off and after a few minutes flew past a police car that was coming the other way.

'Shit,' he thought, 'I'm well and truly fucked here.' Luckily for him, the road was too narrow for the police car to do a three-point turn, so the car carried on in the wrong direction looking for somewhere to spin around. He had at most a minute or two to come up with something. Up ahead of him, a track led off from the road down towards a farm; he turned into it and hared down the track. It petered out after a few hundred yards, where a gate blocked the way. With visions of Steve McQueen in *The Great Escape*, he pulled back the throttle even harder, planning to hit the gate at speed and force his way through. Sadly for him, the gate was a good one, made of steel; when he hit it, he was catapulted over the handlebars at speed, sailed through the air and landed with a thud in a clump of bushes in the field beyond, badly winded.

He lay there frozen for a few moments, then slowly began to move his legs and arms to check nothing was broken. Everything appeared to be in working order, although there would be plenty of bruises to show for his night. Now, he could hear police cars close by; they had seen his bike and, what was worse, they had a dog with them. He lay completely still, wondering how he was going to get out of this mess. The fact that so many witnesses at the pub would be able to identify him did not lead him to consider giving himself up; whether it was the result of so many years of living hand-to-mouth or not, Howarth was not one to think ahead.

Suddenly, the bushes in front of him parted and he was sitting face to face with a growling police Alsatian. He kept perfectly still and the dog made no attempt to go for him, merely standing there as though keeping guard. After a minute or two, his handler called to him – 'Here, boy!' – and the dog was gone. Just yards from him, he could hear two policemen talking, speculating about how far Howarth could have got, and they set off with the dog, their voices soon dying away until there was silence.

Howarth lay there for a little while, then decided it was time to go. He got to his feet painfully, and contemplated his situation. It was the middle of the night, he was cold and wet and his bike was almost certainly knackered. Even he had to accept that things weren't looking too good. By the light of the moon, he could see that there was someone sitting in the driver's seat of the police car parked in the lane that led down to the field he was in. He sauntered over, as though without a care in the world, and rapped on the window.

The lad at the wheel didn't look as though he could be any older than 18. With a nervous look, he wound down the window. 'Y-yes?' he said.

'Err – I think it's me you lot are looking for,' said Howarth. 'I'm Chris Howarth, by the way,' he helpfully added by way of explanation.

Some time later, Howarth was in the back of a police van being taken to Tain on the east coast as Dingwall Sheriff's Court would not be open that Monday. He tried to strike up conversation with one of the coppers accompanying him.

'Here, that dog of yours is about as much use as a chocolate teapot, in't it?' he said. The copper glared at him.

'Nothing wrong with that dog, best dog in the Northern Constabulary,' the policeman replied.

'Well, it can't have much competition then – it just sat there, looking at me, didn't do a thing.'

'Aye,' the policeman replied, 'but if you'd have made a move, he would have had the arm off you.'

'Yeah, but I didn't move, did I?' Howarth pointed out cockily. 'Not much good as an attack dog if all you've got to do is sit there. Tell you what, though, he's a nice friendly dog, I'll take him off you if you like. The little one could do with a pet.'

The copper turned his back to Howarth in a manner that made it clear the conversation was over. The rest of the journey to Tain took place in silence.

At Tain Sheriff's Court, Howarth pleaded guilty to assault and breach of the peace; he was fined £500 and ordered to pay £100 compensation to the pub he had smashed up. Christ, these nights out were getting expensive, he reflected cheerfully, as he set off back to Ullapool.

Over the next few years, his tangled personal life didn't become any more straightforward. In June 1986, Val bore him a daughter, Amy, while in November of the following year Fiona had her second – naturally a girl, Lorna. Although living primarily at Morefield Place, he maintained his relationship with Val, spending time down in Muir of Ord whenever he could. He wasn't making life any easier on himself, as the arrangement naturally wasn't to Fiona's liking and rows would regularly flare up. The last decade had seen him in umpteen scrapes with the law, he had endured a broken marriage and suicide attempt and had fathered several children by different women. Still, that was Howarth through and through: still crazy after all these years.

OF CUSTOMS AND CANNABIS

CHAPTER SEVEN

In 1977, as Howarth was heading north to his new life in Ullapool, on the east coast of Scotland a fresh-faced 18-year-old Dundonian named Graham Dick was considering his career options. He was ready to leave Dundee, a handsome, once prosperous Victorian city, which sits overlooking a wide estuary where the River Tay empties itself into the North Sea. Its chief claim to fame is that it is the birthplace of marmalade – a Dundee woman, Janet Keillor, discovered the recipe in the late eighteenth century while trying to find a use for bitter Seville oranges. Her son opened a factory to produce this instantly popular confiture and the world was overnight made a more civilised place. It's also noted for the two-mile-long Tay Bridge. This was the scene of one of the world's most notorious rail disasters when, in December 1879, the central section of the 18-month-old bridge collapsed in a gale force 10, taking 6 carriages and 75 souls to their death in the icy black waters of the Tay. Perhaps, though, the greatest tragedy of the incident was that it inspired the world's worst poet, William McGonagall, to pen 59 lines of the most egregious drivel on the incident, 'Railway Bridge of the Silvery Tay'. Just how bad he was can be gleaned from these four lines of the first verse:

> Alas! I am very sorry to say
> That ninety lives have been taken away
> On the last Sabbath day of 1879,
> Which will be remember'd for a very long time.

Marmalade and McGonagall, alas, were not sufficiently strong lures to keep Dick in Dundee. He joined Her Majesty's Customs and Excise in 1977 and his first post was in Aberdeen, a granite-tough city further up the east coast and the nucleus of the Scottish North Sea oil industry. For the next five years, he cut his teeth in the VAT division, often visiting small family-run hotels to check that their returns were above board and that they weren't conducting too many of their transactions in undeclared cash.

It wasn't exactly the glamour and buzz he had been looking for. In 1979 he married Lorraine. By 1982, poring over people's VAT returns and surreptitiously watching barmen to see whether they rang drinks purchased into the till or not was leaving him cold. This wasn't why he had joined Customs and Excise: there had to be more exciting opportunities elsewhere.

In 1982 he applied for, and got, a job down south in the Investigations Division, based in London. This was more like it. He spent the next two years investigating gold smugglers. The scam was that unscrupulous dealers would buy bullion from the Channel Islands, for example, then import it onto the mainland by using false companies that had been set up purely for one or two movements before closing down again, thereby avoiding the VAT on the gold when they sold it on the London market. Compared to the work he had been engaged in back in Scotland, this was high-octane stuff – if not exactly *Miami Vice*, then at least Maidstone Vice.

In 1984 he was invited to join a new unit that was being started up – the cocaine target team. Up until then, cocaine investigators had worked according to a standard procedure whereby when they received a tip-off about a consignment coming into the country, typically they would stake out the airport or seaport and carry out surveillance, tracking the drugs in the hope of tracing them back up the chain to the organisers, or the 'principals' in Customs and Excise parlance. While this often yielded results, there were essentially two problems with this approach. The first was that the big guys, the money men, generally covered their tracks in such a way that they would leave little to connect them to the actual gear. What this meant was that it was generally the pawns – the landing and transportation crews, as Customs and Excise term them – who would be pulled while the real movers and shakers of the cocaine trade went untouched, living opulent lifestyles without getting their hands dirty. The second problem was that the risks associated with allowing huge consignments of drugs to move freely, albeit under surveillance, were so high that frequently the decision was made to take them out long before they reached their destination and those further up the chain.

The cocaine target team was set up to tackle the problem from the top down. The idea was to use a combination of informants, undercover officers and intelligence to identify who the heads of the organisations, or principals, were – to use the tabloid terminology, the drugs barons. Operations would then be established to watch these characters and their chains of command in order to destroy the supply network, rather than simply to disrupt it with the odd seizure of product. This has now become standard operating procedure within the investigations division of Customs and Excise.

In February 1989, Dick successfully applied for a position with Customs and Excise in Glasgow. He went straight into the drugs unit as a higher executive officer, working on a team of a dozen, answering to a senior investigations officer by the name of Andy Barr. One hectic afternoon in the summer of 1989, Barr called across to Dick, 'Graham, there's an incoming on line two, Customs guy from up the coast, Ullapool. Can you take it?' Dick picked up the phone. What the man had to say was very interesting. An informant had come to him with news of a large load of cannabis that had arrived in the Ullapool area – two tonnes of Moroccan hashish that had been brought up from Spain on a yacht called *The Eastray*, crewed by two men. They had landed the gear on a small uninhabited island halfway between Ullapool and Gairloch named Gruinard Island – better known to most people in the UK as Anthrax Island.

In 1942, fear of chemical and biological weapons being used by the Germans was rising – not so different to today, except the papers hadn't yet abbreviated them to WMD. British government intelligence suggested that the Germans were prepared to use anthrax against the civilian population in this country. A small island inhabited only by sheep was selected to test the deadly drug: the flock was wiped out instantly and indeed the island was so contaminated that it was deemed out-of-bounds for the next 50 years or so, finally having the quarantine lifted in 1990, the year after this drugs run.

The informant named several local people as being involved in the run. Libel laws prevent most of them being named but one will be familiar to readers – a scallops diver named Christopher Eric Howarth. The cannabis was taken off the island and back to Ullapool using a tug named *The Guardwell*, ironically a former Customs and Excise cutter that had since passed into private ownership. In an interesting coincidence, this boat was owned by one Harry MacRae, half-brother to Noel Hawkins, who would stand in the dock nearly two years later at the High Court in Edinburgh along with Howarth, accused of importing the UK's largest ever haul of cocaine. There is no suggestion that MacRae was aware that his boat was being used for anything to do with drugs; in a small fishing community, it is quite normal for friends and neighbours to lend boats to one another, assuming that it is for entirely legitimate purposes. The informant also stated that the hash was divided into two lots and taken away in vans, one to Edinburgh, driven by an Ian Rae, and one down to London, driven by a David 'Tam' Forrest.

Dick got cracking. In those days, Customs and Excise often called upon Coast Prevention Officers, or CPOs, who kept an eye on boats' movements along the coast, jotting down anything suspicious or out of the ordinary. One CPO had noted down a sighting of *The Eastray* in the Gairloch on 21 July, so Dick was able to date the landing of the gear to around then. As Dick says, 'These guys used to travel around areas, chatting to people, looking for new arrivals, basically keeping an eye on what was going on. We no longer have them, which is sad as hell, but we had them back then, and that's how *The Eastray* was sighted. The CPO will have made a log entry but it was only with hindsight that the significance became clear.'

Dick then cross-checked this information with the mainframe computer network shared by all law enforcement agencies, the National Criminal Intelligence Service (NCIS). Essentially a high-tech bulletin board for anyone working in law enforcement, it allows those in the field to upload information on suspects and those involved in 'higher level criminality' to a pooled resource. What he found was gold dust.

The name of the yacht used for the Gruinard Island run matched that of a yacht mentioned in a log from counterparts in Spanish customs. The intelligence stated that, according to an informant in Spain, a Scottish national we will call Jonathan Derek Chadwick* for the purposes of this book was planning to bring six tonnes of cannabis into Scotland using a vessel named *The Eastray* – the same name as the vessel given to Customs by their local informant in Scotland. Dick was looking at a fairly big player; this was no longer nickel-and-dime stuff.

---

* A contempt of court order was granted to the Crown in 1991 preventing publication of Chadwick's real name. Despite the fact that he has been named in several national newspapers, and there seems little real chance of him being prosecuted some 12 years later, the order is still in force. Customs and Excise and the Crown Office have made it clear to the author that they will fight any attempt to name Chadwick through the courts. The much-vaunted freedom of the press, it would seem, counts for very little when it comes to reporting on the workings of HM Customs and Excise, who have failed to bring this man to justice. For a publicly-funded body, they seem unwilling to have their use of taxpayers' money held to proper account, and officially refused to collaborate or assist in the writing of this book.

The chances were that this would not be a one-off: anyone with the wherewithal to orchestrate six tonnes from Spain into Scotland would not be doing it for the first time – nor, it could be assumed, would it be their last.

The NCIS log also gave the names of the two men who had sailed *The Eastray* up to Scotland. One was a German national named Ditus Neumann, the other an Irishman. It didn't take long for Dick to find out that these two men had checked into the Aultbea Hotel at Loch Ewe, near Gairloch, and a hop and a skip from Gruinard Island. This was high-quality information coming through from Spain: everything was checking out. It should be noted, however, that despite the evidence accumulated by Customs and Excise on the Gruinard run, none of the individuals named here were ever convicted in connection with that run.

Dick also discovered that the Irishman had broken his leg during the run, possibly when putting the gear ashore. Records showed that he had checked himself into Raigmore Hospital in Inverness. Unable to pull his weight, therefore, on the journey back down to Gibraltar and Spain, the men advertised locally for someone to come with them as crew, mainly to help out by cooking and cleaning. A local girl, unaware of the purpose of the trip, answered the ad and took up the offer. Dick spoke to her some time later and she confirmed that she had done the run down to the Med. Intelligence from Spain showed that *The Eastray* was in Morocco on 20 August – possibly to pay the Moroccan suppliers the balance of what was owed for the hash, having completed a successful run – and in Gibraltar on 22 August. The same source gave the names of two other men on the boat along with Ditus Neumann, neither of whom was the Irishman, so the inference is that he didn't make it back down south after breaking his leg.

A few days after being sighted in Gibraltar, *The Eastray* was seen berthed at the marina at Sotogrande, a seven iron from Jonathan Chadwick's home in Estepona, at the heart of the Costa del Sol. Dick was sure he was looking at a fairly major drugs smuggling network. It was time to do some homework.

CHAPTER EIGHT

When Dick found the NCIS log linking *The Eastray* to Jonathan Chadwick, he had a more immediate and pressing problem. Alongside the log from the Spanish detailing the informant's lowdown on Chadwick's activities was a note to say that the information had been passed to Madrid and then on to the northern headquarters of the Scottish Crime Squad (SCS) at Stonehaven, near Aberdeen, who were investigating. SCS was set up in 1969 to investigate major criminal activity affecting more than one police area, with branches in Glasgow and Edinburgh. In 1988, a year before the Gruinard Island run, a new office was established at Stonehaven to cover the north of Scotland and, by the look of the NCIS log, they were already getting their teeth into Jonathan Derek Chadwick.

In matters concerning major importation of drugs, Customs and Excise is normally the government agency that would have primacy; nonetheless, these matters always need to be handled with tact. Dick requested a meeting with his counterparts at SCS and on 12 September 1989 he met up with Commander Willie Anderson and a dozen other case officers at SCS offices in Glasgow. They had already done a fair amount of work on Chadwick – they knew that he had worked for several years as a freelance North Sea diver, latterly subcontracting to a company called Comex Houlder, who were in turn subcontracting to Shell. He had left this employment on 3 October 1988. They had an address for him at an apartment block in Estepona, Hacienda Beach, Carratera de Cadiz. They had also established that his parents used to run a family hotel in the Highland Victorian spa town of Strathpeffer, Mackay's Hotel.

When I tried to find out more about his background in Strathpeffer, I spoke to a Margaret Spark who ran the chemist's in the village for 30 years and, I was assured, knew everyone. 'The Chadwicks? Oh dearie me, I can't quite place them . . . Yes, that's right, of course. They ran a hotel here, Mackay's, but I believe they sold up and moved to Spain. I did hear that the father died but I'm afraid I can't tell you much more than that. They seemed pleasant enough.' And with classic Highland understatement and tact, she added: 'I did hear that one of the sons might have got in a wee spot of bother with the police . . .'

Jonathan Derek Chadwick was born on 25 June 1963, incredibly making him just 25 when he gave up diving to move into the more lucrative world of international drugs smuggling. He had a brother, James, four years older than him, who worked as a lorry driver, and a sister, who had emigrated to Australia. He seems to have been extremely close to his mother, Dorothy Jean Chadwick, but not a great deal is known about his father, also called James, who seems to have accepted instructions from his wife with meekness and equanimity. The Chadwick family appears to have been a matriarchal unit; there can be no doubt that Jonathan, her younger, good-looking son, was the apple of Dorothy's eye and could do no wrong. By 1989 he was living in Estepona and appears to have married a Moroccan woman, Moina Smaima Bent Laarbi, described as 5 ft 3 in. tall with black spiky hair – 'short and ugly' as one of the surveillance officers laconically noted.

In the summer of 1989, the Chadwicks sold up and left Strathpeffer. They got £211,000 for the freehold of Mackay's Hotel and, after settling their overdraft, closed their account and transferred their money to a bank in Gibraltar. The balance after closing their UK account was around £120,000, of which £100,000 went into a high-interest account, with £20,000 going into a current account. The Chadwicks finally moved to Spain on 26 September 1989, moving into the same apartment block at Hacienda Beach, Estepona, as Jonathan. Being the model son, he had secured apartment number 22 for them; he was living at number 69.

SCS had put together a list of known associates. These included Ian Rae, who would crop up again and again over the next 18 months, and, among others, a local diving acquaintance, though there is no suggestion that this man played any part in, or knew of, Chadwick's drug-related activities. Like most ports, however, there is a big drugs scene in Ullapool; recruiting people locally did not present a major problem for a man of Chadwick's charm and resourcefulness.

Chadwick was tall – over 6 ft – good-looking and urbane, the polar opposite of Howarth. The fact that they were both divers is about all these two men had in common. Dick talks of all the suspects in this case with something approaching affection, referring to them all by their first names as though they were old pals – after watching their every move for nigh on 18 months, it is as though he built up a relationship with them, despite the fact that the first time they spoke would have been after their arrests.

With one exception – he has little time for Chadwick. 'Jonathan came across as very vain, very arrogant – always preening himself and looking in mirrors,' says Dick. 'Anyone that came into contact with him – the girls at the car-hire desks, airline staff – that we spoke to afterwards couldn't stand him. He had a way of talking down to people that really got their backs up. Another character trait that emerged was that, for a major drugs smuggler, he was extremely tight-fisted.' One way this stinginess showed itself was in his choice of hire car.

Prior to diving for Comex Houlder, Chadwick had subcontracted to an oil industry services outfit named Wharton Williams Taylor. Alastair Willett, manager for diving projects for the company, recalled that Chadwick had worked for them between 1984 and February 1987. He started working as an air diver and progressed to the more lucrative saturation diving. The company had negotiated preferential car-hire rates with Hertz and all employees were given sticky discount labels to affix to their driving licence. Despite having left the company at least two years before the commencement of Operation Klondyke, whenever Chadwick flew into the country on his many trips, he would hire from Hertz without fail in order to get this discount. For a big-time drugs smuggler, he wasn't above saving a few quid whenever he could.

While Howarth was living hand-to-mouth diving for scallops in Ullapool, Chadwick had bigger things in his sights and diving was simply a means to an end. Even now, oilrig divers can command up to £500 per day – back then the work was even more lucrative due to a shortage of skilled divers. By 1985, he was doing well enough to have bought a flat in Great King Street in Edinburgh's fashionable New Town, the Georgian district made famous in the film *Shallow Grave*. The lad was doing all right for himself – according to New Town property specialists Rettie & Co., a similar property today would fetch up to £500,000. He also owned a red Porsche Carrera Turbo – again at today's prices, Porsche UK state that the price range for this model is £55,000 to £68,000.

One of the drivers on the Gruinard Island run was Ian Black Rae, a 35-year-old odd-job man and mechanic. After his eventual arrest at the culmination of Operation Klondyke, his wife Lucinda – or Lucy – was more than happy to talk. Both Dick and Howarth remember her as a stunningly attractive woman, slim, medium height with long blonde hair; both were mystified as to what she was doing with Rae in the first place.

It was clear that she had little time for Chadwick. She said, 'Jonathan is a long-standing friend of Ian's, though I don't particularly like him. He came to our wedding reception in 1986. Before I met Ian, he worked for a time on the oilrigs, as did Jonathan.' She went on to say, 'I remember Jonathan said to us a year or so after we were married in 1986 that he was going to invest in a drugs deal. He had money because he had been working as a saturation diver and had bought a flat in Great King Street, Edinburgh, and a Porsche motorcar. He had sold up and was moving to Spain. It was his last night in the flat. He said he was going to put his profits into a drugs deal. When we were with him in Spain in the summer, he was living in a rented apartment. He has since moved. He owns two boats, a motor cruiser and a yacht.'

She may be wrong about the date – there is a record of Chadwick leaving employment in Scotland in October 1988, so it is to be assumed that that is when he sold up and headed south. As Lucy Rae says, he knew Ian Rae from his days on the rigs. By the late 1980s, Lucy and Rae were living in a two-bedroom rented flat with their two children in a tiny hamlet called Glenisla in Angus, towards the east side of Scotland. They were struggling along on Family Credit and drove an old Citroen 2CV, and Rae was presumably very open to making cash, no questions asked. Rae had applied for, and received, a grant under the Enterprise Allowance Scheme to set up Glenisla Maintenance Services, a company providing labour in the areas of car servicing, gardening, building and so on. It had a workforce of one – Ian Rae.

An associate of Rae's whom he knew from his days in the Navy was a stocky Dundee man with a moustache, a 51-year-old lorry driver named David 'Tam' Forrest. Chadwick often stayed with the Raes when in Scotland and Forrest was also a frequent visitor to the house – presumably that is how they met. Forrest was known to Customs and Excise.

After moving to Spain in autumn 1988, it was only a few months before Chadwick was making regular trips back and forth to Scotland, staying with Ian Rae. He had identified Ullapool as the ideal place for bringing gear in and for recruiting a landing crew – he already had Forrest and Rae as the transport crew. Through his local diving aquaintance, who clearly would have had nothing to do with Chadwick's drugs run, he met another local man, a diver whom we will call Sandy Bennett. Bennett agreed to Chadwick's terms and the idea for the Gruinard Island run was hatched. Bennett recruited two more men locally to assist and arranged to borrow Harry MacRae's tug, *The Guardwell*, to land the gear. Again, there is no suggestion that MacRae was aware that his boat was being used for this purpose. And Bennett recruited another local man as a late draft on to the team, a man with a fairly minor, though important role, that of lookout and humper, helping to transfer the cannabis onto *The Guardwell.* That man was Crazy Chris Howarth.

Two months after the Gruinard Island run, Howarth was off to Amsterdam – one of the main hubs in the European drugs trade – with two Ullapool men. Says Dick, 'We're certain that this was the boys away to party with the money they'd made, there was nothing more to it than that. The fact that they chose Amsterdam is just coincidence, they were not big enough or smart enough to be negotiating business.'

Around about this time, Bennett fell out with Chadwick over money – it seems he felt that Chadwick had not given him as much as he had promised. He let Chadwick know in no uncertain terms what he thought of him and made it clear that he would not be doing any further business with him, under any circumstances.

This left Chadwick with a major headache. He still had four tonnes of hash down south that he had to get up to Scotland, but, through his stinginess and double-dealing, he had alienated his landing crew. Into the breach would step Howarth, who would be promoted by Chadwick from lookout to organiser of the landing crew – he could recruit others to land the gear with him. It was a decision that both would come to regret.

CHAPTER NINE

In September 1989, Howarth was down at the seafront in Ullapool one afternoon, a glorious late summer day, repairing lobster creels and contemplating the fact that the season would soon be over. Winter can be a bleak time for fishermen in the Highlands, with few prospects other than extreme weather and the dole. His unconventional arrangement with Val and his daughter Amy down in Muir of Ord meant that the rows between him and Fiona were regular enough to be a problem; tensions would rise with lack of money over the winter, and these were sure to get worse. The £6,000 he had been given for his part in the Gruinard Island run was disappearing fast, a large chunk of it having been swallowed up by debts, and it was doubtful whether he could get by until the next season.

He sighed, reflecting on the irony that he had once dreamed of being a diver; as with most things in life, the reality was far removed from the dream. The old proverb came into his thoughts: 'Be careful what you wish for – it may come true.' Howarth smiled ruefully: there was a lot of wisdom in the ancient saying. As he sat there on an upturned creel working away, he heard a car pull up on the pier a few yards away from him. He looked up to see a new saloon, the type not seen too often around Ullapool; a man got out and started to walk over towards Howarth. Around 6 ft tall, slim with black hair and tanned features, the man was wearing casual trousers and a designer leather jacket that looked as if it had cost a few quid, in contrast to the usual Ullapool uniform of jeans and sweater. He strolled over and struck up conversation.

'Lovely day, isn't it?' Howarth nodded agreement and, putting down the creel he was working on, began to roll himself a cigarette. Out to sea, the sun was setting in the west in a blaze of fire. In the evening light, the Summer Isles appeared to float as the sea merged with the shimmering sky; only the presence of a lone fishing boat, loaded up with its catch and heading back to an unknown port, offered any marker between the two.

'Getting your lobster pots sorted, then?' asked the stranger.

'Aye,' grunted Howarth monosyllabically, thinking sarcastically that this guy was as bright as a button.

'There's good money in lobsters,' said the man. 'What are you getting – about £6 a pound?'

'You must be joking,' said Howarth. 'Tell you what – if that's what you're paying, I'll come and work for you tomorrow.'

The man laughed, an easy laugh, showing his white teeth. Howarth couldn't quite place the accent – it sounded southern but had the faintest hint of a Highlands burr. He put out his hand.

'I'm Jonathan Chadwick,' he said. 'It's Chris, isn't it?'

Howarth turned to take a closer look at the stranger. Ullapool being a small place, he had heard who was the paymaster on the Gruinard Island run. Chadwick chatted away, explaining how he had grown up in Scotland, at Strathpeffer, near Dingwall, where his parents had run a hotel. He was now based in southern Spain, near Malaga, where he had a business exporting olive oil as a front – but he was making good money from his hash runs. 'Look, Chris, the reason I'm here is that I might have some work for you. Bennett and I have fallen out, and I need to put together a new crew. Would you be up for it?'

Howarth couldn't answer at first; he was so taken aback. Compared to the harsh life he had in Ullapool, this would be a dream come true. He pictured himself back at the helm of a yacht, sailing around the Med, getting a tan and berthing in marinas that were the playgrounds of the rich and famous. Perhaps after a few runs Fiona could come down with the two kids and start a new life away from stagnant Ullapool . . .

'Chris?' Chadwick cut into his reverie.

'Oh, aye,' spluttered Howarth, 'I'd definitely be up for that, I mean, I'm your man, and, like, when would you want me to start?'

Chadwick laughed at Howarth's eagerness, telling him to calm down. The job wouldn't be for a few weeks, sometime in November. That suited Howarth just fine, as it would mean that he could finish his season and Chadwick's job would simply be a bonus – a huge bonus – over the winter months. Chadwick told him that he would be paid £20,000 for doing the run on a yacht from Mallorca back up to Ullapool.

'Are you on the phone?' asked Chadwick, reaching into his leather jacket for a pen. Howarth gave him his home number, as well as Val's number in Muir of Ord, throwing in the number of The Caley for good measure. As Chadwick pulled away in his car, Howarth could scarcely contain his excitement long enough to put his creels away before racing home to tell Fiona the good news. He would be selective in what he told her; he could always say that he was simply delivering yachts.

He cut down to the end of the town where the houses stopped abruptly and jogged across some fields to enter his estate from the back. As he walked into the house, he was greeted by the smell of good home cooking and his two kids singing 'Daddy's home' in unison to some childhood tune. He rushed into the kitchen, where Fiona was busying herself over the stove.

As he raced through his story, Fiona had to keep telling him to slow down and take his time. When he had finally managed to convey his story, all she had to say was, 'That's good', clearly not sharing his excitement as she sat the children down at the table and began to serve up tea. Several years of living with Howarth had bred in Fiona an understandable suspicion of anything that sounded too good to be true – it generally was. She would believe it when she saw the money.

Just a couple of days later, the phone went. It was Chadwick. He wondered whether Howarth was free; he was planning to take a run up to a place called Clashnessie Bay some 40 miles north of Ullapool. He was toying with the idea of building a marina to cash in on the growing tourist economy in the Highlands and felt that there was money to be made from such a venture. He wanted to take Howarth along to look at the site and get his opinion. Howarth readily agreed. He knew the place well; it was just a couple of miles from Drumbeg, where he had lived with Lenore, and it would be good to get out of the house.

The drive north from Ullapool takes the visitor through some of the most hauntingly beautiful scenery in the Highlands, including Stac Pollaidh, the imposing mountain overlooking Loch Lurgainn, a favourite with hill walkers. It is dramatic, inhospitable territory, the odd crofter's hut the only sign of habitation. Clashnessie Bay is sheltered from the pounding of the Atlantic by a large headland known as Point of Stoer, with its lighthouse to warn sailors of the treacherous rocks all around. Opposite the bay is Oldany Island, inhabited only by seals, birds and red deer, who cross from the mainland at low tide. With beautiful sandy beaches on its leeward side, the approach from the sea is far more deadly, with waves crashing against the craggy rocks at the foot of sheer cliffs. A nature lover's paradise, but a sailor's nightmare.

Howarth and Chadwick got out of the car and looked out over the bay. Chadwick waved his arm expansively across the sweep of the bay as he spoke grandly of his plans. 'Imagine it, Chris – the Highlands' first and only marina. Think of all those Dutch and German tourists that come here; if we have a marina that means they can sail here instead of doing that enormous drive, we'd clean up.'

Howarth nodded his agreement. He was flattered that this sophisticated and smooth-mannered businessman was seeking him out for his advice – and Chadwick could be onto something. The sort of people who sailed yachts were big spenders; there could be good money to be made for someone like him who was good with boats and knew the tricky coastline like the back of his hand. He would not find out until over a year later the real purpose of this trip, and Chadwick's bullshit about a marina.

On the way back to Ullapool, they stopped for a beer at the Summer

Isles Hotel, run by the family of *Castaway* author Lucy Irvine, in the remote village of Achiltibuie. As he sat in the beer garden looking out to sea at the Summer Isles, Howarth felt a great sense of contentment and excitement at what was to come.

CHAPTER TEN

Six weeks later, early in November, the phone rang one morning. Howarth was in bed as he had been up late wintering all his fishing gear and sorting out his boat, *The Alison Jill*, beaching her for her annual four-month lie-up ahead of the cruel winter storms, which would soon be rolling in. He heard Fiona answer the phone downstairs, then shout up to him, 'Chris, it's some guy wanting to speak to you – it's long distance, so you'd better hurry up.'

Howarth glanced at the bedside clock. He'd forgotten all about Chadwick. Who would be ringing him at eight o'clock in the morning, he wondered, as he rubbed the sleep out of his eyes. He jumped out of bed and ran downstairs without stopping to put any clothes on. As he passed Fiona, she gave him a tweak between his legs, laughing as she told him to get dressed since her mother would be over in a few minutes.

Still half-asleep, he picked up the receiver.

'Hi, Chris speaking.'

'Hi, Chris, it's Jonathan Chadwick. I met you on the front at Ullapool a few weeks back . . .'

'Oh yeah, hi, Jonathan. How's it going?'

'Great, thanks.' Chadwick's well-spoken diction was curiously distant and the line had the slight time-delay that used to be a feature of overseas calls more than a decade ago. 'Look, the reason I'm ringing is, I've got a job on. It's a straightforward run from Palma in Mallorca back up to Ullapool, exactly the same as before. There'll be two of you – a German guy as skipper and you along as crew. Do you fancy it?'

'Oh, aye, brand new,' replied Howarth, 'brand new' being a colloquial phrase, meaning 'sound' or 'that's great'. 'When would you want me out there, like?'

'Well,' said Chadwick, 'I'm looking at the end of November – 26th, 27th, somewhere around then.'

'Fine,' replied Howarth. 'There's just one thing – I'm well skint. I couldn't afford to get to Mallaig – how the fuck am I going to get down to Mallorca?'

A chuckle came down the line.

'Don't worry, I figured that would be the case. I'm arranging for one of my guys to pick you up and drop you at Inverness station. He'll buy your ticket and give you enough cash to pay for the flight when you get to London. I'll be in touch nearer the time . . .'

Howarth put the phone down with a grin. Just then, the front door opened and in walked Fiona's mother, who covered her eyes when she saw Howarth standing there without a shred on. He made his apologies and raced back upstairs to put some clothes on.

By the time he came back down, the house was empty, Fiona and the kids having gone out shopping with her mother. There was nobody else for Howarth to share his good news with apart from Jim, his eight-year-old mongrel, so he grabbed the hound's front paws and danced a jig around the lounge, singing 'We're in the money'. Jim looked happy at the news – but then again, he'd have looked happy had Howarth told him that World War Three had broken out. He was only a dog, after all. Howarth dropped his paws and sank back into his favourite armchair, rolled himself a celebratory joint and switched on the television. It wasn't yet 9 a.m. but what the hell? After all, it wasn't everyday he landed a major hash run that would earn him tens of thousands of pounds, he reasoned.

On Monday, 27 November 1989, the phone rang again.

'Hello, is that Chris?' said a voice, one that Howarth did not recognise.

'Speaking.'

'Oh, hi, Chris. My name's Ian. Jonathan Chadwick has been in touch to say that the job is on this week. I'm to pick you up on Wednesday and take you to Inverness, where you'll get a train down to London to catch a flight to Palma on Thursday morning. Is that OK?'

'Aye, brand new,' said Howarth.

'Great. So I'll pick you up at one o'clock. Where can we meet? I don't know Ullapool that well . . .'

'Well, if you take the main road through the village, ignore the one going down to the front and you'll come to a great big pub in the village on the right. It's called The Caledonian Hotel.'

'Fine,' said Ian. 'I'll see you in the bar at one, then.'

On Wednesday, 29 November 1989, Howarth kissed goodbye to Fiona and the kids and set off with a stride to The Caley. He felt good about himself: Chadwick, this successful and wealthy businessman, had obviously liked the cut of Howarth's jib; he could see Howarth's potential. He looked around Ullapool, in all its small-town drabness and reflected that, if all went well with Chadwick, he wouldn't be sorry to leave all this behind for a life down in Spain, working the Med. He checked himself, telling himself not to get too carried away, that it was only one job. He got to The Caley in good time; with quarter of an hour to spare, he decided to drink to his own good fortune.

The bar was empty apart from a bored barman leaning on the counter as he did the crossword. Howarth sat there, watching the sunlight streaming through the windows creating shafts of light in which a million particles of dust were illuminated. Horrible to think of all that dust settling on his pint, grimaced Howarth as he took a deep draught. The door opened and a small bearded man, whose large head and long face seemed out of proportion to his tiny body, entered.

'Chris, is it?'

'Aye' said Howarth, thinking that, as he was the only person there, it didn't take a genius to work out that he was Chris. Without knowing why, he realised that he had taken an instant dislike to this man, that he distrusted him. They spent a few minutes in idle chat, then Ian said, 'Right, we'd better get going. The last train to London leaves Inverness at 2.40 – that'll get you into King's Cross just after midnight and you'll have to find somewhere to crash. You've to be at Gatwick by ten in the morning – Jonathan has reserved a seat for you but you'll have to pay for it when you check in, so you'll need to leave yourself plenty of time to get there.'

'Fine by me,' said Howarth, draining his pint and walking out with Ian. The car was parked a couple of streets away and they walked there in silence; Howarth couldn't think of anything to say to this man he had never met before.

When they reached the car, Howarth jumped into the passenger seat. In the back was a woman whom he introduced as his wife, Lucy. Howarth was struck by the woman's beauty. She was blonde, with a fresh, healthy complexion, and had such long legs that she had to sit sideways, with two young kids either side of her. It was all Howarth could do to stop himself from turning around to ogle her. For the life of him, he could not see what this gorgeous creature was doing with the runt in the driver's seat. As they headed down to Inverness through pine forests where sunlight would flash between the trees in their last autumn growth before winter, he would turn around to offer her the joints he was rolling in order to snatch another furtive glance at her high cheekbones and arresting features.

They soon arrived in Inverness, which was surprisingly busy for a weekday, so Ian had trouble finding somewhere to park while he went to the bank to draw cash for Howarth to use as spending money. It was almost three o'clock by the time he returned, looking flustered. Howarth had missed the train despite all their planning; he would have to take the overnight sleeper that left at half past six that evening and would get him into Euston at seven the next morning. Ian seemed worried by this, in case he would not have enough time to get to Gatwick but Howarth cut him short. 'Rubbish, I'll have three hours to do it, man, stop worrying,' he said with the authoritative air of one used to international business travel and to the manner born, rather than the Ullapool fisherman that he was. Reluctantly, Ian accepted that they had no other choice; he did, however, give Howarth the phone number for his home in Glenisla, near Blairgowrie, Perthshire, 'in case of any mishaps'. He handed over £300 to cover Howarth's expenses, and climbed back into his car, waving goodbye.

Howarth sauntered down to the station with a swagger in his step; with a wad of cash in his pocket, he felt like a proper weekend millionaire. He marched up to the ticket counter and, puffed with self-importance, imperiously ordered 'a sleeper to London' as though he did it every week. The ticket cost less than £50 and, keeping £150 back for his flight as instructed by Ian, he still had more than £100 burning a hole in his pocket and over three hours to start making some inroads into it. He checked his bag into left luggage and headed for his favourite pub in Inverness, the Eagle Bar on Baron Taylors Street.

The bar was doing brisk trade when he walked in. Although Inverness has since been granted city status, it is a small place compared to Glasgow or Edinburgh but huge in relation to Ullapool, and Howarth still felt like a country cousin there. He marvelled that a pub should be so busy in the hollow of a weekday afternoon. Howarth joined a group of men at the bar and bought their company by paying for their drinks – they were skint, naturally, or so they claimed. Still, buy a stranger a drink and there is an unwritten law that they are obliged in return to listen to your bullshit – and Howarth could bullshit with the best of them. Soon, in his cups and buzzing with adrenalin from his impending trip, he was regaling them with stories of his life on the ocean waves, appropriating anecdotes he had heard from a collection of seamen in his time.

Like the perennial angler's tale of the one that got away, Howarth recounted the numerous times that he had single-handedly taken a yacht through a storm force ten in the middle of the Atlantic. Ironically, if it was danger on the high seas he was looking for, he wouldn't have too long to wait.

After a couple of hours of this, it was time to leave. Several pints to the good, he lurched out into the cold evening. It was dark by now and the packed streets were emptying, with people rushing home from shopping or work, and he felt a sense of superiority over these drab people with dull, pedestrian lives. Leave them to their grey, work-a-day routines, he smugly thought – he was off to sail a yacht up from the Med. It didn't seem to occur to him that, if caught, he would be going down. He had been filled with a false sense of security from the Gruinard Island run and felt that it was no more risky than driving home from the pub when he'd had a few.

He picked up his bags from the left-luggage office and headed towards the train. He was greeted by a steward straight out of *Brief Encounter* with his shiny buttons and peaked cap. The steward consulted his clipboard; on it was a diagram of all the sleeping compartments, with each passenger's name pencilled into a box. He showed Howarth along to his berth, a tiny room with two bunk beds; Howarth chose the top one and stretched out. In no time at all, he was sleeping as the train rattled south. It was perhaps fortunate that he could sleep so soundly in a narrow, constricted bunk bed: he would have to get used to them in the coming years.

CHAPTER ELEVEN

Howarth slept soundly through the night, the rhythmic motion of the train proving soothing. He was awoken in the morning by a young lad, who, looking like a New York bellboy in his red uniform, had brought him a cup of tea. Howarth pressed his hand to his eyes to shield them from the sudden light from the corridor and asked him the time. The lad told him that it was half past eight and that they would be arriving at Euston approximately two hours late, just after nine o'clock on 30 November 1989.

'What!' yelled Howarth. 'You must be joking – I'm supposed to be at Gatwick at ten o'clock to catch a plane.' The lad apologised in a mechanical tone of voice, saying that there was nothing he could do about it, as he shut the door behind him. Just then, Howarth realised that he was not alone. The covers on the bunk beneath him were pushed back to reveal a big-framed old man with a bulbous nose and sad, drooping eyes. He asked Howarth what time it was; Howarth grumpily told him the time, then lay back on his bunk staring sullenly at the ceiling as he contemplated whether he could get across London and out to Gatwick in under an hour.

The old man got up and began to dress silently. As he did up his tie looking in the mirror, he made another attempt at conversation with the morose stranger with whom he was forced to share, mumbling something about the folly of relying on British Rail. Something about the man's mournful features and melodic Hebridean accent made Howarth feel ashamed of his churlish and sullen behaviour and he started to chat to the man. The old man told him that this was his first visit to London since the end of the Second World War and that he was down to attend his brother's funeral. Howarth tried to tell him that things had changed a lot since then, but the man reassured him that he would be all right. Something about the man's demeanour spoke to Howarth of a terrible sadness, something that went deeper than the death of his brother, something too deep to probe. They carried on making small talk until the train finally pulled into Euston at ten past nine, over two hours late. Howarth bade the man good luck, grabbed his bag and raced along the platform to start his mad dash to Gatwick.

On the station concourse, he was shocked to see so many homeless people begging, an unfamiliar sight in Ullapool. This, together with the old man with whom he had shared his compartment on the train, conspired to bring him down from his feelings of euphoria and excitement, and he found himself feeling depressed at the harshness of life. He raced along to a taxi rank and jumped into the one waiting at the head of the queue, saying 'Gatwick, please – as quick as you can' with all the confidence he could muster. As the taxi weaved in and out of the horrendous London traffic, the driver chatted away over his shoulder, but Howarth had difficulty understanding the strange southern dialect.

By the time they reached Gatwick, Howarth was seriously stressed; it was clear that he would miss the flight, which would be taking off in the next five minutes. His only option would be to explain to airline staff what had happened and see whether he could get onto the next flight. He made his way to the British Airways sales desk and explained his problem to an overbearing man in his neatly pressed staff suit, in sharp contrast to Howarth's jeans and khaki jacket. Standing a good six inches taller than Howarth and giving off an overpowering scent of aftershave, the man eyed him with something approaching distaste as he tapped away at a keyboard; sure enough, Howarth's details came up as having been reserved on the flight, which had just left. As Howarth began to go into detail as to why he was made late, the man cut him short, saying, 'I'm sorry, sir, there really is nothing I can do about it. It's a condition of a provisional booking that you turn up two hours before departure. There are no more flights to Palma today – all I can suggest is that you come back tomorrow.'

Just then, the phone began to ring in the office behind the desk. The clerk went to take the call; as he spoke, he looked up at Howarth and didn't take his eye off him as he listened intently to what was being said down the line. On returning, he told Howarth that he had just thought of a way around the problem; there would be a flight to Barcelona in around an hour that he could put Howarth on, and from Barcelona he would be able to take a connecting flight to Palma. As a sign of goodwill, he would simply charge Howarth the cost of a standard direct flight to Palma. Howarth thanked the man profusely and counted out his cash to pay for the ticket.

With a little time to kill before check-in, Howarth found a payphone and rang Ian to tell him what had happened, explaining that he would now be arriving in Palma at around four o'clock that afternoon, rather than lunchtime. Ian seemed very troubled by this and sounded worried that Howarth would miss his rendezvous. 'Christ, this bloke needs to chill out a bit,' thought Howarth as he told him not to panic, asking him to ring Chadwick and explain about the delay.

He toyed with the idea of getting a beer but decided it was a little early, even for him. He bought a magazine and had a coffee until it was time to board the plane. The flight was uneventful and, three hours later, they touched down on the tarmac at Barcelona. Howarth grabbed his bag from the overhead compartment – as he was travelling light, he had been allowed to take it as hand baggage – and set off to find his connecting flight. Unaccustomed to international travel, he wasn't sure which way he was supposed to be going, so set off down a long walkway where others seemed to be heading. Then something strange happened. Ahead of him, a uniformed guard stepped into his path, stopping him, and demanded to see his passport. Before he could get it out, however, the guard's superior came over, spoke to him in Spanish and turned to Howarth with a smile, saying 'This way, please'. The guard took him back the way he had come and along another passage to an area where passengers were waiting to board the Palma flight. Howarth thanked him for his trouble, thinking that Spanish officials certainly seemed to be more helpful than their British counterparts.

It is almost certain that Howarth attaches more significance to these incidents than they merit. With hindsight, he became convinced that the officials were being instructed by Customs and Excise not to hinder his progress in any way. If this is so, Customs and Excise have no record of the events. They simply noted him leaving for Palma and made sure that they would be waiting for him at the other end.

The plane landed in Palma around an hour later. Howarth made his way along interminable walkways, past baggage reclaim and Customs, and into the main arrivals lounge. As instructed, he made his way to the main meeting point and sat down to wait for Chadwick. Being late November, the airport was not especially busy, in contrast to the summer with its packed charter flights of English and German tourists. Howarth sat patiently, people-watching as he waited for Chadwick. After the best part of an hour, he began to panic. What if Chadwick didn't turn up? He had no phone number for him and was running critically low on the cash that Ian had given him; he certainly did not have enough for a return flight back to the UK.

Just then, a man approached who was wearing jeans and a T-shirt; with relief, he recognised Chadwick, although he looked quite different this time. His easy, relaxed manner had disappeared and he seemed strained and apprehensive, his eyes darting around as though looking for someone. After a perfunctory hello, he led Howarth to a car rental office within the airport and hired a car. It wasn't until they were in the car and driving into Palma city centre on the main carriageway that he appeared to relax, enquiring whether Howarth had had a reasonable trip and asking about things back in Ullapool. Howarth also relaxed and wound his window down, enjoying the cool salt air. They soon drove past the magnificent thirteenth-century cathedral with Moorish-influenced arches and towers, its walls bleached by the sun. Ahead of them, he looked out over the enormous horseshoe-shaped harbour with numerous marinas and jetties. He sighed and leant back in his seat. This was the life.

On the far side of the harbour, Chadwick pulled up at a rather plush hotel on the palm-lined promenade overlooking the sea. La Reina Constanza looked like a businessman's hotel; it was eight storeys high with smoked-glass windows and external lifts. The two men headed into reception and Chadwick booked two rooms, 704 and 705. Great, thought Howarth, there'll be fantastic views from the seventh floor.

His room was large and comfortable with an en-suite bathroom and, from the window, a fabulous view right out across the harbour. Out to sea, the sun was setting in a fiery blaze, dipping below the horizon. The sight of so many boats, riggings fluttering in the gentle breeze, gave him a burst of adrenalin; tomorrow he would be out on one of them, sailing out into the Med. With a start, he remembered that he had a small bag of grass in his coat pocket. 'Shit,' he thought, 'thank Christ they didn't search me at the airport.' He rolled himself a joint and sat looking out the window, taking in the view. When he had almost finished smoking it, there was a knock at the door. Howarth quickly threw what remained of the joint out of the window and flapped his arms desperately to try to disperse the smoke.

It was Chadwick. He came in, sniffed the air and tutted disapprovingly. 'Look, Chris,' he said, 'it's up to you what you do in your own time, but you have to remember that you're working for me now. I've taken you on to do a job and I expect you to be professional. You can smoke yourself stupid when you're back home, but not out here – and definitely not in front of the captain. Is that clear?' Howarth mumbled that he had got the message. He felt embarrassed at having to be spoken to like this and Chadwick seemed uncomfortable too. He changed the subject, asking Howarth whether he'd like to come down to the hotel bar for a beer – the captain would be there and it would be good for them to meet ahead of the trip. He left, telling Howarth that he'd see him there.

Howarth spent the next few minutes splashing cold water over his face in a vain attempt to straighten out, regretting having smoked the joint. He would have to do as he was, he concluded, looking at his red-rimmed eyes in the mirror. He took the lift down to the ground floor and headed into the hotel bar. The room was empty apart from Chadwick and another man, a tall, wiry and athletic guy in his 30s or so, around 6 ft 2 in. tall with blond, cropped hair and piercing blue eyes. The two were so engrossed in their conversation, leaning conspiratorially towards each other, that they didn't notice Howarth approaching. He coughed to signal his presence.

Chadwick jumped to his feet, saying, 'Ah, Chris, I didn't see you there. This is Ditus, who'll be skippering the yacht. Can I get you a beer?' Ditus refused a refill so Chadwick went to get Howarth one. While he was at the bar, Ditus made no effort to chat to Howarth and simply stared down at the table. When Chadwick returned with the beers, the men discussed what the plan would be. They were to head out to a point off the coast of Morocco to liaise with the suppliers, in the first instance delivering a large payment to them. Then they were to meet Chadwick back at Benalmádena and await instructions for the run back to Ullapool.

The conversation turned to yachts and boating, with Ditus making little effort to hide the fact that he was picking Howarth's brains to see how much he knew. Fortunately, Howarth knew enough to get through this grilling – and what he didn't know, he bullshitted. He clearly seemed to acquit himself to Ditus's satisfaction as the German skipper soon bored of the subject and talk turned to lighter matters. After a few more beers, Howarth was ready for his bed and left the two men talking into the small hours as he bade them goodnight. It would be his last night in a proper bed for some time, after all.

CHAPTER TWELVE

In September 1989, a Middlesbrough businessman, whom we will call Geoffrey Miller, took the heart-breaking decision to sell his pride and joy, a 57-foot yacht named *Shearwake*, berthed in a marina at Puerto Portals in Palma, Mallorca. He had owned the yacht for some years, having bought it from a colleague who had had it built especially to his requirements. It was a steel-hulled motorsailer, ketch-rigged. The trouble was, a big yacht like that takes some handling and, with the children grown up and starting to live their own lives, it would be too much for him and his wife to handle on their own. She'd been a good old girl, says Miller, and had seen them proud, with many memorable and happy family holidays chugging around the Med.

He put the yacht on the books of a yacht broker in Palma, a Dutchman who had a good reputation locally. The broker advised him that it should fetch £95,000. Satisfied that all was in order, he flew back to the Northeast as he had business to attend to, leaving his wife and the kids with *Shearwake* in Palma. While Mrs Miller was sitting on the yacht one day, a man came alongside, saying that he might be interested in buying *Shearwake* and asking whether he could take a look at it. Tall, with dark hair and a slight Scottish accent, he introduced himself as John Holt – however, we can be fairly certain that it was Jonathan Chadwick. He said he was representing a consortium, another member of whom he introduced under the pseudonym Steve Davis. Mrs Miller gave him a quick tour and he seemed impressed – *Shearwake* was in excellent order. He asked for a phone number for her husband and said that he would be in touch.

Over the next two months, Miller received plenty of calls from the shadowy Mr Holt. If Miller was out when he called, he always declined to leave a number. Whenever he did phone, it was invariably from a public phone, usually in a bar judging by the background noise. Miller's patience was being sorely tested; on one occasion, he thought they finally had a deal, flew out to Palma to do the paperwork only to find that Holt or Davis did not show up and he was obliged to return home empty-handed. On another occasion, he flew out, met up with Ditus Neumann, who claimed he was acting as Holt and Davis's representative and that they had asked him to give the yacht the once-over as he was an experienced skipper. Miller obliged, though there was something about Neumann he didn't like at all, particularly his cold, steely eyes that gave him a chill. In the wheelhouse on *Shearwake*, he noticed for the first time Neumann's forearms – they were criss-crossed with dozens of knife scars. Miller suddenly felt unsafe, alone on the yacht with this dangerous man. 'I don't frighten easily,' Miller now says, 'but alone in the wheelhouse with Neumann, I felt in fear for my safety. I was bloody glad when we stepped off the boat back into the sunshine with plenty of people around.' On that occasion, Holt was to have joined them but, typically, he failed to show up again.

Back in the UK, Miller's patience finally ran out the next time Holt called. He had a few choice adjectives for Holt, mainly of an Anglo-Saxon etymology, and told him to stop wasting his time and insisting that all future negotiations would be between the two of them, not Davis or Neumann. As he memorably puts it, 'I told him that I would only deal with Snow White *or* the Seven Dwarves, not Snow White *and* the Seven Dwarves as well.' Chastened, Holt apologised for messing him about and assured him that he was serious about buying the boat. Miller told him that he was sick of dealing with a man who appeared to have no telephone number or address, forcing Chadwick to give him a London address – 14 Draycott Place, London SW3 – and a number for a Vodafone mobile. He also agreed to courier up to Middlesbrough £5,000 as a deposit to show his intentions were serious.

Nonetheless, Miller remained deeply suspicious. All this cloak-and-dagger stuff had given him the heebie-jeebies; it was not the way to go about buying a £95,000 boat. He voiced his concerns to a friend of his, Bill MacDougall, a CID officer. MacDougall agreed to look into it for him. When he entered the London address that Holt had given him into NCIS, he saw immediately that it was the address of a drugs dealer who was a known associate of one Jonathan Derek Chadwick. The mobile number was also traced back to Chadwick himself. Dick had put a log into NCIS, requesting that anybody with any information that would assist in Operation Klondyke should get in touch with him. MacDougall contacted Dick to tell him what Miller had told him. Dick twigged immediately that John Holt was one of Chadwick's many aliases and arranged to fly down to Middlesbrough to meet Miller and MacDougall.

At the meeting, Dick explained that they were conducting a major operation into a suspected drugs smuggler based in Spain and that he believed that *Shearwake* was being purchased in order to transport large amounts of cannabis to Scotland. He indicated that, from the Customs and Excise perspective, it would be preferable if the sale of the yacht went ahead as they could keep the purchasers under surveillance in order to break the network. Clearly, it would be crucial that the purchaser had no idea that there was anything untoward; if Miller pulled out now, it was conceivable that the targets would realise that something was amiss, that they were under investigation.

Miller listened intently. He had reservations; he had no particular desire to be mixing with dangerous criminals. He was also concerned for his own safety and that of his family. Dick assured him that he would be under surveillance at all times and that if anything looked untoward, police and Customs would step in. Reluctantly, Miller agreed to be used as a pawn in the operation. He would continue to deal with the man calling himself John Holt and keep Customs informed about any developments.

Separately around this time, on 18 November, Ian Rae and David Forrest were intercepted at Gatwick Airport by Customs and Excise on their way back from Gibraltar, clearly having visited Chadwick. The Customs officers on duty had a sixth sense about these two characters and pulled them into a side room for a brief interview. As one officer spoke to them, another ran their names through NCIS. Their names were already in the system thanks to the informant who had tipped them off about the Gruinard Island run, so the guys at the airport realised these two were up to no good. As they were being interviewed, another officer went through their luggage. In Rae's luggage, they found letters that he was carrying from Chadwick, to be posted in this country. They took photocopies of the letters and some business cards that they found with them and then replaced them, Rae and Forrest none the wiser. They did not detain the men, or even do anything to give them the impression that they were being watched, and they let them go on their way. Forrest and Rae were now major targets in Operation Klondyke.

Back in Middlesbrough, Miller received a call from Holt, who said that he would like to go ahead with the purchase of *Shearwake*. Miller agreed to meet him in Palma towards the end of November to do the deal and flew down as promised. Given the history of his dealings with the mercurial Mr Holt, he was unsurprised that Holt failed to show. Finally, Miller received a call from Holt, apologising that he had let him down again but promising to come the next day with bankers' drafts to the tune of £90,000, the balance owing for *Shearwake*. Miller growled that he'd better look lively as he would be leaving the next day to fly back to the UK.

The following morning, Thursday, 30 November, Holt got in touch again to say that he would not now be able to make it but that he would be sending 'one of the dwarves', as Miller puts it, to meet Miller at Palma Airport to hand over two banker's drafts. Much to Miller's annoyance, the emissary turned out to be Ditus Neumann, the man he had grown to fear and detest. Miller took with him a friend, Ian Fairhurst, who was a yacht surveyor and resident on the island. He handed over the Lloyds Blue Book for the boat, the maritime equivalent of a car's logbook, to Fairhurst with instructions that he was only to give it to Neumann once Miller rang from the UK to say that the banker's drafts were kosher.

The banker's drafts had been drawn at a bank in Gibraltar the previous day by a man who was known to be involved with Chadwick and the drugs dealer who lived at the London address given by

Chadwick to Miller. A witness reported that the man had been dropped at the bank by a couple matching the description of Chadwick and his Morrocan wife Moina. They waited outside the bank for him – when he came out, he got into the car with them and the three drove off.

Neumann wasn't happy about it but had little choice but to accept the situation. Unbeknownst to him, the meeting was being watched. Detective Chief Inspector Cliff Craig of New Scotland Yard was on secondment to the British Embassy in Madrid. He agreed to fly down to Mallorca to carry out surveillance on behalf of Customs and Excise. Says Dick, 'Cliff was a tall, well-built guy with short, greying hair. He was a bloody good copper, and a hell of a nice guy, too.' It's not surprising that he has such warm words for Craig; he certainly came up with the goods for Dick. At 11.45 a.m. he saw Ditus Neumann pass through passport control, having arrived on Iberia Air flight 235 from Barcelona. He watched him meet Miller and Fairhurst in the main terminal building and the three men made their way to a cafeteria. They sat there for an hour talking and, from time to time, examining documents. At 12.50 p.m., he noted that the three men got up, shook hands and set off in different directions – Miller off to departures to fly back to the UK, Fairhurst out of the airport building and Neumann to a telephone kiosk.

After making a call – presumably to Chadwick to say that the deal was going through – Neumann sat down and read a magazine for an hour or so. Then at 2.15 p.m. he went to make another call – Craig was close enough to see that the first three digits he dialled were 952, the dialling code for Malaga and the Costa del Sol, where Chadwick lived. After a short conversation, Neumann bought some lunch, then left the airport, taking the taxi at the head of the rank. Along with a Spanish police officer, Craig jumped into an unmarked car and followed the taxi at a discreet distance. Neumann headed into town, past the Catedral de Palma de Mallorca and on round, past the marina with its myriad bobbing yachts. He entered the Hotel La Reina Constanza, checking into room 809.

Craig returned the following morning to check the hotel register. The previous evening, Howarth and Chadwick had also checked in, Chadwick surprisingly using his own name. For a man with so many aliases, it seemed careless. Craig next spotted Neumann, Howarth and Chadwick together at 12.45 p.m., having lunch at a bar in Puerto Portals, the main marina in Palma. An hour later, he saw all three of them on *Shearwake* apparently making the boat ready for departure.

Miller had clearly instructed Fairhurst to hand over the blue book, satisfied with the bankers' drafts. Craig would next see them – and *Shearwake* – at Benalmádena some nine days later. That afternoon, however, he went back to Palma Airport, where he established that Jonathan Chadwick was booked onto Aviaco Airlines flight 196 departing Palma at 8.40 p.m. for Barcelona, where he was booked onto a connecting flight, Iberia 363, to Malaga. If, as it turned out, *Shearwake* was off to rendezvous with the Moroccan hash suppliers, evidently Chadwick did not intend to get his hands dirty. That's what Howarth and Neumann were being paid for, after all.

CHAPTER THIRTEEN

Back at the Hotel La Reina Constanza on Friday, 1 December 1989, Howarth was awoken the next morning by an insistent rapping on the door. Feeling heavy-headed from the previous night's beers, he stumbled to the door in his boxer shorts and T-shirt and half-opened it to see Chadwick standing on the landing outside. 'Jesus, man, you took some waking,' said Chadwick. 'That's the third time I've been to the door in the last hour.'

'Sorry,' mumbled Howarth. 'I'm not used to this Spanish beer,' he added by way of explanation as he contemplated his throbbing head.

'It's no skin off my nose,' Chadwick pointed out. 'It's just that you've missed breakfast.'

The thought of food made Howarth feel queasy and sent him rushing for the toilet. Chadwick said he'd be back in half an hour and to be ready to roll; they had a lot to do getting the boat ready.

After checking out, they jumped into Chadwick's hire car and headed for a supermarket on the outskirts of town to get the 'stows' – food and provisions for the trip. Then they headed down to the marina and pulled up beside a yacht on which Ditus was already busy, getting it ready for the trip. They broke for lunch at a nearby bar, then carried on with their preparations. Chadwick told them that he had to get off to the airport as he was catching a flight back to Spain; he had some business to take care of. He wished them good luck and told them that he would see them in Benalmádena in around nine days before pulling away in the car.

Howarth looked at the bundles of cash. Judging by the weight of each one, there must have been around £500,000 on board. He joked with Ditus, saying it would be a shame if any were to go missing, labouring the joke until Ditus snapped. 'Look, we are being paid to deliver these packages and that is what we will do. Now, you will please give me a hand with this damn rigging.' Howarth was growing to dislike heartily the German skipper.

Howarth's first impression was that the boat was not the luxury charter yacht that he had been expecting. A 50-footer or so that was called *Shearwake*, it had an old-fashioned steel hull, not the modern fibreglass kind and, while it had three cabins below, they looked like they hadn't been refurbished for a decade or more. It looked out of place among all the plush cruisers with smoked-glass windows and comfortable leather pilot's seats that were moored alongside, with names indicting that they were registered from a variety of ports from Southampton to Santa Cruz. Still, it wasn't his place to worry about it; all he had to do was to help crew the thing.

By three o'clock that afternoon they were ready to set off. It was Friday, 1 December 1989, and there was a good west-south-west wind which would help them on their way. They passed the leading light marking Palma's harbour and headed out to sea, sailing in a south-south-west line towards the coast of Morocco. Howarth tried to strike up conversation with his German skipper. Around 45 (although it was hard to tell because the saltwater lines on his face had aged him prematurely), Ditus told him that he had been living on the Costa del Sol for ten years or so. Beyond that, he was not inclined to volunteer any information; taciturn and arrogant, he made it clear that he was here to work, not to enjoy himself or waste energy on frivolous conversation.

Howarth gave up and left him to pilot the boat as he took another look around down below. *Shearwake* was essentially a clumsy steel motor cruiser with sails, and two Perkins 60hp engines. Beneath the unusually large wheelhouse was a tiny galley with basic cooking facilities and, beyond, a narrow passageway leading to the cabins, two tiny ones at the bow end and a larger one at the stern. No prizes for guessing where he'd be getting his head down, thought Howarth bitterly, as he flung his bag onto a bunk in one of the smaller ones. He went back up to the galley and sat at the small table, looking back the way they had come. It was getting dark by now, and, in the distance, the twinkling lights of Palma were becoming little more than tiny fireflies against the black sky. Caught up in the romance and adventure of being back at sea, Howarth reflected that the view was like a long roll of black velvet that had been pricked repeatedly with a pin, and held up in front of a fire.

Ditus poked his head in and asked Howarth whether he could cook, in a tone of voice that made it more of an order than a query. Howarth said that he could, at which Ditus said with a sneer, in his curiously literal way of expressing himself, 'A British person who can cook? Now I have really heard something funny,' and before withdrawing back to the wheelhouse. Howarth's cheeks burned red with anger. Who did this fucking Kraut think he was? He was working for Chadwick, not this jumped-up prick. Right, he would show him. He went through the stows and got two good-sized pieces of steak and began to fry them up with a chopped-up onion. Meanwhile, he fried up some garlic in another pan and added in some mushrooms and a tin of tomatoes to make a sauce. Every couple of minutes, Ditus would stick his head through to watch Howarth's attempts with a sneering look on his face. Howarth thought, 'If we weren't on a boat, I'd wipe that fucking grin off your face,' but tried to ignore him. The combination of being so wound up and having every move watched meant that he wasn't concentrating on what he was doing, and he contrived to burn the sauce and leave the steaks on for too long. He cursed and dished out the burnt offerings onto two plates. Even he had to admit that it tasted terrible. Ditus, however, seemed to relish it all the more for being burnt; it gave him the immense satisfaction of telling Howarth that his fears about British cooking were justified. Howarth could feel his anger rising, ready to spill over, but, uncharacteristically, he chose to bite his lip: even he knew that fighting at sea was strictly taboo.

The first sign that Howarth's misgivings about the yacht were well founded came after two days out at sea when he awoke to find that the hum of the engines had gone, with only the sound of waves lapping against the hull. His initial thought was that Ditus had decided to put the sails up during the night for reasons best known to himself, but when he emerged on deck, the rigging still lay furled at the bottom of the two masts. The air was heavy with the smell of overheating engines and diesel, and Ditus was at the control panel, desperately pressing the engine starter to no avail. His brow was wet with sweat, his arms black with oil and, without even acknowledging Howarth, he rushed back to the engines and started tinkering with the port one, muttering to himself in German.

Howarth could tell from the way he was fumbling around that he didn't know what he was doing. Without looking at Howarth, he told him that the engines were overheating and, not wishing to display his ignorance, asked him casually whether he was any good with engines. Howarth replied that he knew a little and crouched down to take a closer look. Even as he approached, the heat off the engines was searing; it was no wonder they had shut down. He could tell instantly that the engine cooling had packed up. Boat engines take on seawater through valves called seacocks, which a water pump then takes on to cool the engines. It was pretty clear to Howarth what the problem must be. 'Well,' he pronounced to Ditus who was peering anxiously at him, 'either the water pump's packed up or the seacocks are blocked.' A look of irritation flashed across Ditus's face and he waved his arm impatiently at Howarth, signalling for him to get out of the way. 'No, no,' he disagreed, 'it has to be more than that.' All right, fuck you, shrugged Howarth; what else could it be? A while later, the engines started up again; the gauges on the control panel were still showing that the engines were overheating so Ditus thought for a moment, then said, 'Well, we will simply have to run at half-throttle. It means we will not make our rendezvous but the others will simply have to wait for us. There is nothing else that can be done about it.'

Over the next couple of days, the weather turned poor with heavy rain and storms that were against *Shearwake*, so putting up the sails was out of the question for the time being, forcing the two men to plod on with engines at half-throttle or less to avoid overheating. On their fifth day out at sea, they finally rendezvoused with the boat. It was a brightly coloured Arab-style fishing boat, with a long, sloping bow almost in the style of a *dhow*. Clearly a working boat with nets hanging over the side, there appeared to be three Arab fishermen on board, unless there were others below. They were a good distance out to sea as there was no sign of the Moroccan coastline.

Coming about was easier said than done in the heavy swell that caused the two vessels to crash against each other as they tried to manoeuvre into position; fortunately, both boats had sturdy fenders to limit any damage. Finally, they were alongside and ropes were thrown across to lash the boats together. In very poor English, the fishermen said that they had been waiting for them for two days;

Ditus shrugged indifferently, saying that it could not be helped. The two men fetched up the packages from below that they had been charged with delivering, and threw them across the choppy water into the hands of the eagerly awaiting fishermen. The two boats parted company, and Ditus turned the yacht around to start the journey westwards back to Benalmádena. Behind them in the east, what looked like a big storm with angry, black clouds and forked lightning was gathering; Howarth hoped that it wasn't heading their way. He was looking forward to getting back to land, where he could enjoy dry clothes, a decent meal and a few beers – and some company other than this miserable German bastard, out of whom he could hardly get a word.

CHAPTER FOURTEEN

It wasn't long after they had left the fishing boat behind that more alarms sounded to indicate that engine number two was developing similar problems, the needle jumping into the red to show severe overheating. They eased the throttle right back to just above tick-over speed and it began to cool. It would be a long journey back to Spain. Howarth once again tried to tell Ditus that the seacocks were causing the problem, but the German refused to listen, adamant that it was something else. In his frustration, Howarth slammed his book down and went to his cabin in a rage. He threw himself onto his bunk and fell into a restless, dream-tormented sleep.

A couple of hours later, the violent, rocking motion of the boat awoke him. The storm that had gathered from the east had hit them and huge black waves were pitching them into deep troughs of black water. Even though he was used to being at sea, Howarth felt nauseous and nervous. He headed up to the galley and sat clutching the table, praying for the storm to die down. With a howl of wind and spray that soaked him, the door burst open and Ditus fell through, losing his footing and ending up in a heap on the table. Howarth couldn't help but laugh but an icy glare from Ditus told him that the skipper didn't find it remotely funny. Ditus picked his glasses up from where they had fallen on the floor and pushed them back onto the bridge of his nose, his oily fingers leaving two dirty fingerprints on the lenses where his clear blue eyes should have been. Howarth tried to smother his laughter, but couldn't help but let out a whoop of amusement at the sight of his bedraggled skipper, who then stormed back out on deck, swearing to himself in German.

Howarth decided that he would make an effort to get on with Ditus for the last couple of days of their journey. He headed out onto deck to see whether he could help. They were really in the eye of the storm now; the sky was black and, apart from when lightning would light up the skies with a crack, visibility was negligible. Ditus shouted that, with the engines running at little over tick-over, they would be taken too far off course. He had decided to put up the sails and harness the power of the storm. 'You must be mad,' Howarth shouted back at him, 'it'll be suicide to try that in this weather.' Huge waves were crashing over the deck now and the idea of trying to put the sails up seemed folly. 'That is what I have decided,' Ditus pronounced. 'If it gets too much, we can always reef the sails.' This guy must be off his head, thought Howarth as the boat continued to pitch and tilt into the huge waves that were now crashing over the deck of the boat, which seemed to have shrunk in size, puny and fragile in contrast to the great forces nature was unleashing.

Still, Ditus was the skipper and Howarth had to do as he was told. He went below to change into his oilskins and stood at the door of the wheelhouse to wait for Ditus, pulling on a cigarette as if it would be his last. The German soon reappeared dressed for action and the two men headed out onto deck, the wind and spray hitting them with force as they moved outside. Howarth inched warily along the deck, clinging gingerly to the rail as he kept an eye on Ditus ahead of him. Halfway along the deck, an enormous wave hit the boat. The nose of the boat plunged forward, down into an enormous black valley of water where it seemed to stay, failing to rise on the crest as it had done with previous waves; this was far bigger than any they had hitherto experienced. A wall of water curled over the bow and began to roll along the deck towards them. Ditus shouted something, which was lost in the howling wind and the noise of the wave crashing over the boat. Howarth dropped to his knees and clung for dear life to the deck rail to prevent himself from being washed overboard. The wave hit him with such force that he was winded and loosened his grip. Sheer terror took hold of him as he realised he was no longer holding onto anything and briny seawater covered him completely. He flailed about in blind panic and after a few seconds that felt like an hour, he made contact with the rail again. The water drained away and Howarth found that he was wedged against the aft rail with his head stuck between the wires of the rail, looking straight down into the foaming water.

Dazed and winded, he crawled along the deck back to the wheelhouse, shouting out for Ditus. With his eyes full of saltwater, he could not see anything. After drying his face on a towel in the wheelhouse, he went back out on deck to look for him. He could see nothing at first but, as his eyes adjusted to the gloom, he could just make out the yellow oilskin marking the spot where his companion lay motionless on the port side. Another big wave would surely pull him overboard to be lost in this terrible sea. Howarth raced back to the wheelhouse and grabbed a safety harness, which he clipped to the rail, and began to make his way across to his unconscious skipper. As he got nearer, he could see that Ditus had a large gash on his head from which blood was pouring profusely. For all Howarth could tell, he was dead. This time around, Howarth made sure that he was ready for the next big breaker. And come it did, washing over the bow of the boat. He knelt down and gripped the rail firmly with both hands. Thankfully, it washed over him, and he was able to use the respite to examine Ditus. Although the gash was bad, it was not life-threatening and, after a few moments, Ditus began to come round. Howarth put the harness on him and somehow managed to haul him back to the wheelhouse and down into the galley, where he washed and dried the wound. Strictly speaking, it needed a couple of stitches but he had to make do with a plaster – Ditus would have a mean scar to show for this scrape with death. Howarth helped him to his cabin and got him into his bunk. Within seconds, he was out like a light, snoring away. Howarth looked in on him every hour and he remained in deep sleep, his body resting and recuperating after the blow.

Howarth took the wheel and sailed the boat through the night, keeping it on course through what must have been the worst weather in the Med for some years. With morning came respite from the buffeting. The clouds cleared to reveal blue skies, although the wind was still fresh. Ditus surfaced, sporting two black eyes and a bloodied plaster on his forehead. Putting the sails up was not mentioned again.

The following day, they reached the Costa del Sol. Ditus decided to put in at the first port they came to, Cartagena, in order to sort out the engines. The approach to the harbour seemed narrow with rocks either side. It was going to be hard to make the turn with the engines at tick-over and a strong wind against them. Ditus turned the wheel hard to starboard to make the turn, but nothing happened. The boat was now drifting towards the jagged reef. 'She won't come around,' he shouted, a look of panic on his face. Howarth reacted immediately. He jumped across to the control panel, pushing Ditus out of the way as he pushed the throttle down to give full revs. 'What are you doing?' cried Ditus. 'You will blow the engines for sure!'

'Shut the fuck up,' muttered Howarth tersely. 'We'll have a few seconds of full power before she overheats again. We don't have any choice.' After what seemed like an age, the head came around to starboard with a violent shudder and they began to move mercifully away from the reef and into harbour as the alarms came on. As though answering their prayers, a pilot boat came out from the marina and threw them a rope. The smell of diesel and overheating engines was overpowering and made Howarth feel sick. He sat there shaking as they came under tow. They had made it by the skin of their teeth.

Once moored, Ditus went to phone Chadwick to find out what they were to do. When he came back, he said that they were to get the boat looked at and then sail on to Benalmádena, where he would meet them. Ditus paid a local guy to find out what was causing the problems. He put on his diving gear and disappeared over the side. After half an hour or so, he emerged to say that the seacocks had been blocked with algae and moss, but that he had cleared them and they should have no more trouble with overheating, though the engines could do with an overhaul and the electrics needed looking at as well. 'Just as I said,' thought Howarth smugly, as they set off once again.

Late that afternoon, on 9 December 1989, they reached their destination, Benalmádena. The town itself was a somewhat unattractive resort, full of 1970s concrete and breezeblock holiday apartment complexes. By way of contrast, though, the marina was a swish affair, packed with expensive yachts and cruisers and with luxury waterside flats for the rich. They came into harbour and were directed to a berth by a small boat that came out to greet them. A relieved Howarth jumped onto the concrete jetty as they came alongside and tied the boat up. It felt good to be back on land. Once the boat was secure, Ditus and Howarth headed for a bar in the main marina complex, in among shops offering tax-free jewellery and leather goods. He felt that he had been waiting a long time for a pint. 'So what do we do now?' he asked Ditus, who didn't answer immediately, closing his eyes and enjoying a deep draught of beer, savouring the moment. After a moment, he shook his head as though to clear it, and said he would have to ring Chadwick to find out their next move. When he came back, he told Howarth that they were to stay put, that Chadwick would come down to meet them later that evening or the next morning. Fine by me, thought Howarth, as he ordered another beer and, putting on his shades, went to sit outside at a table in the sunshine. After a few more beers, he felt quite drunk – having had a few days off while at sea, it seemed to be having a more rapid effect than usual – so he decided to go and sleep it off on the boat. In his cabin, he remembered he had a little bit of hash left so he rolled himself a joint and, after smoking it, lay down on his bunk and fell into a deep sleep.

He was woken by the sound of people talking up on the deck above him. He recognised Chadwick's voice and he headed out onto deck. 'Hi, Jonathan,' he said as he emerged from the galley. 'Christ, what a shit heap you've got here.' Chadwick screwed up his face and began to defend his purchase. Howarth could tell he was annoyed. Clearly, he was irritated that Howarth and Ditus had shot his boat to pieces, although it wasn't their fault. Chadwick decided that there was nothing to be done that evening and that they'd have the boat looked at the following day. In the meantime, he would take Howarth and Ditus out for some food and a few beers that evening, music to Howarth's ears. To one side of the marina was a small building with toilets and showers. Howarth borrowed the key from the harbourmaster's office and went along to freshen up. When he came back, the three men headed up to the main drag to find somewhere to eat.

They walked up a side street full of bars with names like The George and The Horse and Hound, with boards outside advertising English football matches and promising English beer. 'Christ, it's like Blackpool,' thought Howarth as they walked past. Inside, the bars were full of women with peroxide hair and red-faced Englishmen laughing hilariously as they ordered another round. 'Why do they bother leaving home?' wondered Howarth, shaking his head at this little colony of Brits abroad. No wonder the English had such a bad reputation. They made their way up to the main thoroughfare and crossed the road towards a modern shopping centre, full of discos and bars. Outside, a mongrel dog was sniffing at something on the pavement before eating it; with revulsion, Howarth realised it was a lump of shit.

Although there was not much to choose between the bars, they settled on The Hungry Hippo, long since gone these days, tucked away in a quiet corner on the second floor of the centre. Howarth ordered steak and chips and a large glass of beer to wash it down. Food had never tasted so good. After several more beers, he was relaxed and laughing with Chadwick and Ditus as they recounted the adventures of the last few days; Christ, he was even beginning to warm to Ditus. They staggered back to the boat to sleep and Howarth agreed to stay on for a few days to help patch up the boat. 'That's it, though,' he warned Chadwick, holding up a forefinger in mock seriousness. 'No more sailing on this boat for me.'

The next few days passed quickly enough. They worked hard in the sun – although it was December, the weather was pleasant – fixing a new bracket to the mainsail that had looked decidedly vulnerable in the storm. Chadwick arranged for a man to come and repair the engines, fix new lights to the boat and take a look at the electrics. In the bay alongside them, a British film crew was shooting an episode of a new series for Granada Television, *El C.I.D*, starring Alfred Molina and John Bird as ex-CID detectives who had moved to the Costa del Sol for a new life. As Howarth stood watching them, Chadwick quietly told him to be careful not to get caught on film, that he needed to act more professionally. Howarth flushed at being accused of amateurism, particularly by this cocky younger man, but then simply shrugged and went back to watching the detectives. He would find out much later that other detectives were watching him.

After a few days of this, Chadwick told him that the hash run was off for the time being. He would cover Howarth's expenses and give him a bit extra. He gave no explanation why. Although Howarth had been rather dismissive about *Shearwake*, he felt the boat was more than capable of making the journey. There had to be another reason he didn't know about. One possibility was that Neumann had refused to carry on with Howarth on board, relations between them were so bad. Chadwick told him that he had a plane ticket for Howarth to go back home. He said it was a ticket that he had bought in his own name but would not be able to use. Howarth wasn't complaining; it would be good to get back home and see Fiona and the little ones, and he'd had enough of fucking about, waiting for a run that was clearly not going to happen.

He said cheerio to Ditus and the two men jumped into Chadwick's car and headed for Malaga Airport, some ten miles away along a busy dual carriageway. On their way, a thought crossed Howarth's mind and he asked Chadwick how he could use a ticket that had a different name to the one on his passport. Chadwick told him not to worry, that he would check him in using his passport. He would pass Howarth the boarding card and after that, Howarth wouldn't need to show his passport again. There shouldn't be any problems.

At the airport, Howarth asked about his payment for the job. Chadwick took out his wallet and peeled off £400 in sterling, handing it over without comment. Howarth had been hoping for a little more, given that the original plan would have netted him £20,000, but at least it was in time for Christmas. Chadwick told Howarth to give him his bag so that he could check it in and to meet him at the bottom of the stairs leading up to the departure lounge. Howarth did as he was told, then suddenly Jonathan rushed over, thrust a boarding pass and a ticket in the name of J. Chadwick at him and disappeared without saying goodbye. Howarth was confused, wondering whether Chadwick was pissed off with him for near-wrecking his boat. He had not yet got used to Chadwick's erratic anti-surveillance tactics.

He made his way along to the departure gate indicated on the board and, still puzzling over Chadwick's abrupt departure, absent-mindedly handed over his passport with the boarding pass. The woman flipped his passport open, then, looking up at Howarth, explained in broken English that he could not board as it was not his ticket. Howarth attempted to remonstrate with her, but she was adamant. Two airport policemen came over to see what the commotion was and led Howarth down to a small interview room. He tried to explain what had happened but the policemen simply laughed at him, apparently finding it amusing that someone could be so stupid as to attempt to board a plane with the wrong ticket. It seems that Chadwick's stinginess had expressed itself again, seriously jeopardising a multi-million-pound drugs operation for the sake of saving £100 or so.

Humiliated and fed up, Howarth headed out of the terminal building. Well, it was Chadwick's fault that he was in this mess, so Chadwick would have to sort it out. He got into the taxi at the head of the rank and asked to be taken back to the marina at Benalmádena. Twenty minutes later they were there. Not a moment too soon either, thought Howarth, as he saw Chadwick getting into his car, about to leave. He ran over and quickly explained what had happened, omitting the fact that he had volunteered his passport. Chadwick scowled and paid off the waiting taxi driver. He said that Howarth would have to wait until the following day when he would buy him a ticket in his own name. The following evening, Howarth was back home in Ullapool with Fiona and the kids. He told Fiona what a nightmare he'd had – skipping over the fact that it had been originally intended to be a hash run – and they agreed that he would be wary of accepting work from Chadwick again. It had been an awful lot of stress – and bugger all money to show for it.

CHAPTER FIFTEEN

The money Howarth had earned for his adventure in the Mediterranean did not last long. After buying decent Christmas presents for Fiona and the kids, what was left soon disappeared from his pocket, by some magical process to reappear miraculously in the tills of The Caley. Still, at least it had been one of the more enjoyable Christmases he could remember. He reflected on the job he had done for Chadwick. From heading down to Mallorca, expecting to earn £20,000, he had ended up practically being arrested at the airport and coming back home with £400. And then there was that twat, Ditus . . . it was nothing to do with Howarth whom Chadwick employed, but it certainly wasn't the straightforward hash run that he'd been led to believe was on offer.

From the Customs perspective, Graham Dick was pretty clear as to what had happened. He knew that Howarth was flying down in order to sail back to Scotland with Neumann, carrying a load of hash in a repeat of the procedure used for the Gruinard Island run. Howarth had been promoted from lookout to organiser of the landing crew and had assembled a landing team. What actually happened was more Groucho Marx than Howard Marks. Neumann and Howarth had carried out the rendezvous with the Moroccans as Howarth readily admits. They handed over large bundles of cash, which were either final payment for the Gruinard Island run or advance payment for the next one. They certainly did run into a terrible storm as Howarth describes, damaging the boat and making it incapable of undertaking the long journey back to the Highlands. Chadwick had a problem; he still had the hash down in the Med and he needed to get it back to Scotland. It's not clear why he sent Howarth home; it seems most likely that he had decided to defer the shipment for a time until he could plan what to do next, after the problems they had had with *Shearwake*.

Intelligence from Spain and Scotland suggests that the run had been put on hold until they were better prepared for it. Chadwick was too far in to pull out: he had a further four tonnes that he had paid for and that he needed to get to the market as soon as possible in order to recoup his investment. Then disaster struck. On 19 December 1989, around the time that Chadwick was working out how to get the gear up to Ullapool, after explosions on board and a fire, the Iranian tanker *Kharg-5* was abandoned, spilling 70,000 tonnes of crude oil, endangering the coast and oyster beds at Oualidia. More alarmingly than the loss of oysters, sad though that was from an ecological and gastronomical viewpoint, we can be reasonably sure that Chadwick was more concerned with how the hell he was going to move his hash. The oil spill had made that stretch of coastline unnavigable and, more worryingly, had attracted a flotilla of government vessels to the area to monitor the spillage. It was a grim day for Chadwick.

On 27 December Neumann sailed *Shearwake* to Sotogrande, where he stopped for a few days, before sailing the boat around Gibraltar and up to Vilamoura, an upmarket coastal resort in the Algarve, Portugal. *Shearwake* would remain berthed there for the following 11 months, under constant surveillance. Further reports from informants say that they were ready to do the run in March, but ran into an unforeseeable problem. It was the Muslim fasting month, Ramadan, which ran for 30 days from 27 March in 1990, and the Moroccan suppliers suddenly discovered some scruples, saying that they were not prepared to do business in the holy month. By April, Ullapool would be getting busy again as the season got underway and Howarth was committed to spending the summer diving down in Mull.

Back in Ullapool, towards the end of February, Howarth's thoughts had begun to turn towards the approaching season. He would need to start thinking about where he would fish that year. It was time to get the boat ready. He had a distant cousin in Newcastle, Tony McDonald, with whom he had made a tentative arrangement to spend the summer diving on the Isle of Mull. They had heard that there was good fishing to be had there and it would be good to get out of Ullapool. That wasn't likely to happen until May and so in the meantime he needed to try to earn some money. The *Alison Jill* had broken a plank and was beyond economic repair. For diving purposes, all he needed was a platform, rather than a flashy, expensive boat, so he tended to buy old heaps that were on their last legs and going for a song. The downside was that it had become an occupational hazard that these boats would die suddenly and without warning. He was half-heartedly doing up a 25-footer called *The Wolf* but for the meantime, he figured he'd be just as well off using an inflatable dinghy. He decided that he would try his luck along with most of the other Ullapool fishermen in Loch Broom for the time being.

On Tuesday, 27 February 1990, Howarth stopped off for a pint at The Ceilidh Place on his way home. He was to meet Chadwick there; the run was back on, apparently, though to say that Howarth was sceptical after the Benalmádena fiasco would be putting it mildly. Part-bar, part-restaurant, The Ceilidh Place also had a small hotel and a crafts centre attached. Now 32, Howarth was getting a little long in the tooth for the shenanigans and testosterone-laden atmosphere of The Caley every time he went for a drink. The Ceilidh Place was a relaxing and laid-back alternative, and Howarth was ready for a beer.

Earlier that day, Jonathan Chadwick had flown into London from Malaga and taken a flight on to Edinburgh airport. At 12.55, Lynn MacLeod at the Hertz hire desk, as she would later testify, hired out a Rover 216, registration G306 LYA to a J. Chadwick, clearly still abusing his discount card from the diving company for whom he had worked previously. Later that afternoon, at 5.35 p.m., Maggie McKeand and George Cockburn, investigating officers with Her Majesty's Customs and Excise, saw Chadwick pull into a parking spot opposite the Post Office in Ullapool. Five minutes later, he had entered The Ceilidh Place, and the two officers observed him in conversation with Howarth.

Over the next few months, Chadwick would spend a good deal of time in Ullapool and Scotland, although according to Customs and Excise surveillance notes, he was only seen with Howarth on three occasions. When in Ullapool, he often stayed at the Harbour Lights Hotel, using the name 'J. Holm' and giving the same address in London that he had given to Geoffrey Miller when buying *Shearwake*.

Whatever the reason for their meeting, and Howarth is vague on details 13 years later, for a conspiracy between two major players in a multi-million-pound drugs conspiracy, it was remarkably brief; the surveillance officers timed Howarth as leaving at 6.05 p.m., just 25 minutes after arriving, Chadwick leaving two minutes later. This was due to the fact that Chadwick had clocked McKeand and Cockburn, and was not happy. 'Fuck this,' he said to Howarth. 'They're Customs, no question about it. Let's get out of here.'

However, the two men did not go far. At 7.10 p.m., McKeand and

Cockburn spotted Chadwick's hire car in the car park of the Far Isles Hotel in Ullapool. There were no occupants. Howarth was seen by the two officers in the doorway of the hotel, making a call from the public telephone. A few minutes later, when the officers drove by again, they could see the car leaving with two occupants, presumably Howarth and Chadwick.

The following day, Howarth was observed heading down to The Ceilidh Place a little early – at 12.45 p.m., in fact, as noted by his watchers from Customs and Excise. He sat at the coffee bar and ordered a pint, and sat reading the paper. Fifteen minutes later, Chadwick entered. He greeted Howarth and bought a couple of pints, settling down on one of the bar stools. Considering that the two men were probably meeting to discuss and plan the most audacious drugs-smuggling operation in UK history, it seems exceptionally careless of Chadwick that they would have chosen to meet at a pub in which Howarth was well known in broad daylight, a pub he knew, or strongly suspected, to be under surveillance and to sit at the bar within earshot of the barman and in full view through the window of anyone outside (again, Maggie McKeand and George Cockburn, according to Customs and Excise surveillance records).

Howarth says that the purpose of this meeting was to discuss another hash run. He would put a team together. As ringleader of the landing crew, he would be paid £40,000, while his two main lieutenants would receive £20,000. Howarth had already lined up a friend and neighbour, a skilled skipper named Robbie Burns. The other man cannot be named for legal reasons; we shall call him Matthew Blake. Chadwick asked what Howarth was planning to do for work that season and Howarth told him truthfully that he was planning to go back to diving, much to Fiona's dismay after his bad accident in 1986, which had seen him airlifted to hospital and told that he might never walk again. He explained that he would start the season fishing locally but that he was hoping to spend the summer at the Isle of Mull with his cousin where there would be less competition. Chadwick was not happy with this as he could not be sure when he would need Howarth, but, as Howarth pointed out, he couldn't just sit around waiting for Chadwick to ring. They agreed that Howarth would keep Chadwick briefed about his movements and likely availability. They would look to do the run in the autumn.

Howarth suddenly realised that he had no contact details for Chadwick as he had left it to Chadwick to contact him previously. He pointed this out to Chadwick, who told him he'd give him his number in

Spain. Howarth picked up a leaflet promoting a local tourist attraction from a stand by the bar, as noted by McKeand and Cockburn, who were watching from their car opposite; they saw Chadwick write something upon the leaflet, which fits with Howarth's explanation that he was giving him his phone number. The two men finished their drinks, and stood up to leave. Chadwick said, 'Righto then, Chris – I'll be seeing you.' 'Aye – thanks for the beer, Jonathan, mind how you go,' replied Howarth, and the two men set off in opposite directions. It was 1.44 p.m. on Wednesday, 28 February 1990. Operation Klondyke was gathering pace.

CHAPTER SIXTEEN

After leaving The Ceilidh Place, Jonathan Chadwick climbed back into his rented Rover 216 and began to head south towards Inverness. McKeand and Cockburn followed him as far as the city. Here they handed over to a colleague, Tommy Martin, as dictated by best practice in anti-surveillance techniques, that is switching cars as often as possible to avoid the quarry detecting his pursuers.

Martin picked up the trail on the Kessock Bridge at 3 p.m., an impressive high-level, cable-stayed construction that spans the Moray Firth. The bridge carries the dual carriageway A9 over to Inverness and the road then takes motorists down through Aviemore and the beautiful mountain range, the Cairngorms.

For the tourist or day-tripper, it is one of the most scenic routes in the Highlands. Doubtless, however, Chadwick wasn't there to enjoy the scenery. Martin followed Chadwick as far as Dunkeld, where, at 5.07 p.m., he handed over to Graham Dick and Joe McGuigan, a Glaswegian with whom Dick often worked. McGuigan was Dick's joint case officer on Operation Klondyke and was around the same age as Dick. Seeing their quarry head out of Dunkeld onto the A923, Dick radioed ahead to Tony Jackson and Malcolm Sharp, who were waiting a dozen miles up the road at Blairgowrie, a stolid Perthshire red-sandstone town. They didn't have to wait long; 15 minutes later, right on cue, Chadwick appeared in the Rover. It was now 5.30 p.m. – Chadwick stopped in the main square and used the public phone box to make a call. He then turned north onto the A93 towards Braemar, practically back in the direction from which he had come. At Lair, he turned right onto the B951; at 6.24 p.m., Graham Dick and Joe McGuigan saw him pull into the car park of the Glenisla Hotel in Kirkton of Glenisla, on the border between Angus and Perthshire.

It had taken nearly five hours to reach Glenisla and Chadwick had come a strange route, staying on the A9 for far longer than he had needed to, rather than turning off south of Inverness and heading down through Pitlochry. One explanation is that he preferred to stay on the motorway for as long as possible, avoiding possible delays on the Pitlochry road. Another plausible explanation was that he had become aware of one of the tails, and only started to head towards his true destination once he believed that he had lost him at Dunkeld, when Dick and McGuigan took over. He was certainly jittery enough later that evening.

The Glenisla Hotel is a seventeenth-century coaching house that originally stood on the main Perth to Braemar coaching route. History holds that, at the end of the Napoleonic Wars, the government needed to raise revenue to pay for the cost of the war; a sharp increase in excise duty on spirits led to a corresponding rise in the number of illicit whisky stills in the glens. Excisemen grew wise to this and were despatched accordingly to smash the stills. As the main coaching house for the glen, these government agents would stop at the hotel to ready themselves for the following day's raids. However, the hotel was overlooked by the local manse, the Scottish equivalent of a vicarage.

When the minister saw the excisemen arrive, he would take to his horse and gallop through the glen, crying out, 'The Philistines be upon thee, Samson!', whereupon the locals would take to the hills with their stills, gratitude would lead them to attend church and everyone got along just fine, brought closer by this anarchic, two-fingered gesture of defiance to the Sassenach state. The records do not say whether the minister received a few bottles of the hard stuff for his efforts, although one can only surmise that it would certainly have been an added inducement to do the neighbourly thing.

Chadwick, however, had no collaborating cleric to warn him of the arrival of these latter-day excisemen. McGuigan pulled up in the hotel car park and Dick climbed out of the passenger seat. He walked across the car park to the main door of the hotel, through whose windows the flickering effect of a crackling open fire cast shadows on the walls and made a welcome beacon on a cold, dark night. There were enough people in the bar for them not to stand out. He beckoned to McGuigan to join him, paused for a moment, then the two men walked in.

Inside, there were a few knots of people in the snug bar, drinking or having their evening meal. Chadwick had pulled a stool up to the bar and was engrossed in conversation with the barman, the hotelier, a man named Michael Bartholomew. McGuigan and Dick took a table in a corner from where they could keep an eye on Chadwick, and bought a couple of pints. As they sat chatting, Dick kept glancing over towards Chadwick. On a couple of occasions, their eyes met as Chadwick was watching Dick and McGuigan in the long mirror that ran along the back of the bar. 'Who the hell is watching whom?' wondered Dick. He got up to go and use the public phone in the lobby and, as he started to dial, he heard the door to the bar open. He glanced over his shoulder to see that Chadwick had followed him out and was watching him. So as not to raise any further suspicion, he acted as though he had not seen him and phoned home, chatting nonchalantly to his wife about the imaginary hill walking that he and Joe would be doing. As he chatted away, he heard the bar door open again; Chadwick had gone back in.

When he returned and sat down, he said to McGuigan, 'Joe, he doesn't like it, he's just followed me out to the phone and given me the once-over.' McGuigan replied in the same low voice, 'After you'd gone out, I saw him nod in this direction and ask the barman who the hell we were, and the barman shrugged, as if to say, "Christ knows." Looks like he's rumbled us. What are we going to do?'

Dick had to think hard and quickly. The worst thing an investigator could do would be to let the suspect or target rumble them as it could compromise the entire operation. If Chadwick realised he was under surveillance, he would be very careful not to do anything incriminating, possibly even calling off the drop until he was convinced he was safe. 'Bollocks to it,' he said firmly. 'If we get up and walk out now, we might as well be wearing bloody jackets with "Customs and Excise" blazed all over the back, it'll be a dead giveaway. We're going to have to front it out. We're up here for a few days going hill walking, heading up to Aviemore. We both look the part, we've got waxed jackets and all the gear, let's just go for it. We'll order some food and just act completely natural.'

Dick made his way up to the bar and, without looking at Chadwick, stared straight ahead as he ordered two more pints and some food. He would find out much later from David Forrest, after he had nicked him, that Chadwick had made the gang watch a video of a BBC documentary called *The Duty Men* umpteen times. Much against his better judgement as an undercover investigator, Dick had been persuaded to appear on it. It seems that Chadwick felt he recognised Dick but couldn't quite place him, otherwise he would have been out of there like a Polaris missile.

After eating their meals, Dick got up to go to the toilet, Chadwick's gaze following him as he walked through the bar. McGuigan saw Chadwick say something to the barman in a low voice. The barman shrugged again, then came out from behind the bar to follow Dick into the toilet. As Dick stood pissing at the urinal, he had the unpleasant experience of having the barman come in and strike up conversation with him, something no man is ever entirely comfortable with, and certainly not when that man is supposed to be on an undercover investigation.

The barman nodded to him affably, then said, 'So, everything all right?' Through clenched teeth, Dick replied, 'Oh, aye, fine.' 'How was your meal?' enquired the man. 'Och, it was great,' said Dick, wondering how long this would go on. 'I've not seen you in here before, what brings you to the area?' The barman was cutting to the chase. 'Oh, we've come out from Glasgow to do a few days' hill walking; we're planning to head up towards Aviemore tonight and get some walking in tomorrow morning.' Aviemore is a resort in the Cairngorm mountains that has tried to establish itself as a ski resort to compete with those of mainland Europe. A lot of money has been pumped into developing a monorail, ski lifts and other facilities but it has never really taken off – Aspen, Colorado it ain't. 'Och, that's brave of you with all this snow, rather you than me,' replied the barman cheerfully before heading out again, not even bothering to pretend to use the toilet himself.

On returning to his table, Dick muttered to McGuigan, 'He's well suspicious, I think we'd better get the hell out of here.' The two men gathered up their things and headed out to the car park. As they climbed into the car, they saw Chadwick come out after them and give them another long look, before turning down the side of the hotel and pretending to have a conversation with someone through a side window. If it was unfortunate for Dick and McGuigan to have risked being rumbled, it's fair to say that Chadwick's anti-surveillance techniques were not exactly state-of-the-art.

In a statement to the police, the hotelier, Michael Bartholomew, said that Chadwick used his hotel reasonably frequently, whenever he was staying with Ian Rae, or 'Raz' as Bartholomew called him. Rae lived two miles down the glen at Brewlands Hall with Lucy and the kids (this incidentally made Rae's flat a nightmare to carry out surveillance on, as there was nowhere to stop on the road; all they could do was to drive past sufficiently infrequently so as not to raise suspicion). He said that Rae was a regular, coming in four or five times a week on his own and with the family at the weekends. The Glenisla Hotel seemed to form his entire social life. And Chadwick would visit regularly when staying with Rae, as he did frequently, coming up to the hotel for his evening meal and a few drinks. He only stayed the night twice – once when he was too drunk to get back to Rae's and Bartholomew put him into one of the bedrooms without charging for it, and once when he stayed with his wife Moina in October 1990.

Bartholomew remembers him as tall, 6 ft 2 in., slim with wide shoulders, athletic build. He says that he was flash, invariably arriving in the biggest car that the hire company had, and generally paying for his food and drinks with £50 notes. He says, 'On the occasions when Jonathan was in the hotel, he usually made a quick telephone call from the coin box and then invariably would receive a return call. On a number of these occasions, he asked if he could take the call in my study. On 20 October 1990, I remember my wife Kirsten telling me Jonathan wanted to send a fax and they couldn't work it. I offered to help send the fax. I held my hand out for the piece of paper but he wouldn't give it to me. I remember it [i.e. the fax] had a map and a road – the A-something – on it. Jonathan told me it was going to Spain.' This was presumably Chadwick setting up the big run.

Bartholomew recalled the evening Dick and McGuigan came by. He said: 'Jonathan was obsessed with people he didn't know or recognise. He often asked me if I knew who these people were, and if I knew whether they were the police. I would often speak to people I didn't know in the bar with a view to recommending the hotel and the bar food. I remember seeing Mr McGuigan in the bar, and I remember Jonathan being there at the same time, being very concerned that Mr McGuigan and his colleague were police. I remember speaking to Mr McGuigan's colleague in the toilets and then returning to Jonathan and telling him that they weren't police. Jonathan said, "They definitely are – I've seen one of them before." I remember the incident completely upsetting Jonathan and him leaving shortly afterwards. As a hotelier, I have an interest should the police be in the bar, from a customer-drinking-and-driving point of view.'

No one can doubt that, as a hotelier, Mr Bartholomew clearly put his customers' interests first, which is commendable. It's clear that Chadwick did recognise Dick from the BBC documentary, although it seems he couldn't quite place him. He was smart, Chadwick, that's obvious, and he was careful. But, as events would ultimately show, he wasn't quite as smart or as careful as he liked to think he was.

Two days after the incident in the hotel, Chadwick's hired Rover was seen parked outside Rae's flat covered in snow, implying that it hadn't moved. It was still parked there the following day when Tony Jackson did a drive-by – as well as Rae's battered old Peugeot, he noted the presence of another car, a cream and dark red Citroen 2CV, different to the 2CV owned by Lucy Rae. This car was registered to David Forrest of Aberlady Crescent, Dundee. The three men seemed to be spending more and more time together. Later that day, Chadwick was seen driving through Perth, taking the M90 towards Edinburgh. Records show that he returned the Rover to Hertz, caught the 3 p.m. shuttle to London and then an Iberia flight on to Malaga. He paid for a return ticket and was due to return to the UK on 21 March. He did not use this return booking, and did not try to fob it off on to anyone else as he had done with Howarth in Benalmádena.

Everything was fitting with their intelligence that Chadwick was the principal organiser, aided in his planning by Rae and Forrest, who took care of transporting the product to the market. As organiser of the landing crew, Howarth had a more straightforward role, meaning that Chadwick didn't need to spend as much time in Ullapool as he did at Glenisla, where Rae's flat appeared to be becoming the control room for the operation. The amount of time Chadwick spent with Forrest and Rae here could suggest that they had a far more important role than simply being couriers who knew very little, which is what they would ultimately be convicted of, leaving Howarth to be charged as the alleged ringleader. Few people who knew anything about the case could ever suspect Howarth of being clever enough or organised enough to have carried out that role.

CHAPTER SEVENTEEN

Back in Ullapool, Howarth carried on with his preparations on *The Wolf*, but it was clear that he wouldn't have the boat ready in time for the season. He'd have to stick with the inflatable for now. His diver's logbook records that he started fishing on Loch Broom on 14 March 1990. The harvests were small – Loch Broom had been overfished and there were too many small boats working out of Ullapool for there to be any bumper catches – but it was keeping his head above water. He heard from his cousin, Tony McDonald in Newcastle, who said he would be up for fishing on the Isle of Mull for the summer. Howarth was looking forward to it; it was always good to hang out in a new place and get away from Ullapool. A change was as good as a rest, he reflected, and there was a chance that the fishing would be better in new waters.

Some time towards the end of April, he got back from walking the dog one evening when Fiona greeted him with a smile. 'Jonathan Chadwick called while you were out – he said he might have some more work for you.' Fiona had obviously overcome her misgivings about Chadwick as she now had bigger concerns. Howarth had told her about his plan to spend the summer diving with McDonald and she wasn't at all happy. She had been there after Howarth's diving accident when the doctor had said that he should not go diving any more, that it could put too much pressure on his spine. To tell Howarth not to do something, though, was counter-productive and she was now looking on the work Chadwick had to offer as being the lesser of two evils. Howarth grunted and went to sit in front of the television. He had no intention of calling Chadwick back.

He didn't need to. Later that evening, the phone rang again. Fiona took the call, then came into the lounge. 'Quick, Chris. It's Jonathan and he's calling long distance. He wants to speak to you.' Howarth came to the phone and picked it up.

A series of beeps and whirrs came down the line. 'Chris, how you doing?' Fiona stood watching him, hoping in her heart that he would take whatever work Chadwick had for him and not risk his health by going back to diving.

Chadwick said, 'I've been trying to ring you for days now, there's never any reply. Where've you been?' Howarth felt like saying that he had been getting on with his life, that he had better things to do than sit around waiting for Chadwick's calls, but he bit his lip, saying simply that he had been fishing.

Chadwick continued. 'Look, the reason I'm ringing is it looks like we'll be going ahead with the run in the next few weeks.'

Howarth was apprehensive. He was reluctant to change his plans for Chadwick, who was unreliable and had let him down badly with the last run. On the other hand, he didn't want to alienate him – if the run did happen, the returns were big. He'd have to land a lot of scallops before he could even think about that sort of money. 'Well, Jonathan, the thing is, I wouldn't be able to do anything now until the winter, I'm afraid.' There was a long pause and after a few moments, Howarth thought that Chadwick must have hung up when he suddenly said, 'Why not?' as though he had a God-given right to know. Much to Fiona's evident dislike, Howarth snapped. 'Look, I can't just drop everything just because you ring up out of the blue saying you've got a run on. Last time, I got fuck all out of it, and that's not going to put food on my kids' plates. I've made arrangements to spend the summer diving and I can't let everyone down just because you want something doing.'

There was another long pause before Chadwick spoke again. 'Very well,' he said, a little tartly, 'we shall see if there is any work for you in the winter. Call me when you're not in such high demand.' With that, he put the phone down, leaving Howarth holding the receiver in his hand, waiting for the dressing-down from Fiona that was surely coming. 'Chris, you shouldn't have spoken to him like that. He might have had proper money on offer. You're going down to Mull with Tony and you'll do what you always do – earn a few quid, piss it up against the wall and come back here for the winter skint, moaning about how tough it is. I'm sick of it.' Howarth looked at her retreating back ruefully. There was no point arguing with her when she was like this. And she was right, after all. That's what made it so bloody galling.

McDonald came over to Ullapool in early May and they loaded up a caravan with all the requisite gear – oxygen bottles, the inflatable and their wetsuits. Saying their goodbyes to Fiona and the kids, they set off on the 150-mile drive. They headed south in McDonald's dark-blue Renault 18 estate, music blaring out while, as is required of the passenger, Howarth threw himself with alacrity into the role of being chief spliff-builder to the expedition. From Inverness, they headed south-west on the A82, taking them down along the banks of Loch Ness.

As they sped along the banks of the loch, with sunlight flitting between the trees, Howarth daydreamed in his stoned state about whether there really was such a thing as the Loch Ness Monster. He was drawn towards the unexplained and the supernatural, a tendency shared by many habitual smokers of cannabis, and he was inclined to believe in the beast. There had been too many alleged sightings for it all to be nonsense, he figured. He'd done a little reading about the legend and understood that the first recorded sighting of the beast was in AD 565 when, the story goes, a swimmer was in imminent danger of attack from a monster. Saint Columba, the Irish priest and prince who brought Christianity to Scotland, was watching and stood up and made the sign of the cross, bidding the monster to retreat, which it duly did. The next 1,400 years or so are largely quiet on the matter, but Nessie really came into her own in the twentieth century, with more sightings and explorations than you could shake a stick at. Howarth's own belief was that the monster was a plesiosaur whose ancestors had inhabited the loch when it was still open to the sea; with the shifting of the continents, the loch closed up, imprisoning its family of plesiosaurs until the present day. 'Wouldn't it be fantastic to see it?' he wondered, looking out across the sullen waters of the loch, hoping to see something break through the rippling water.

'Here, you twat,' said McDonald, cutting into his reverie cruelly. 'Are you going to smoke that all yourself, you selfish bastard?' Howarth laughed, forgetting about the hidden secrets in the depths of the loch. A while later, they were driving in the shadow of Ben Nevis, Britain's highest mountain and soon reached Fort William; from there, a short drive took them to Corran, where they took a ferry across an inlet to Ardgour, then another few miles to Lochaline, where they could catch the Mull ferry.

By now it was late afternoon and there were no passengers on the small ferry but themselves. It took them into Fishnish, a tiny ferry terminal – more accurately described as a slipway and some public toilets – towards the north side of the island. They had already decided to head for the Ross of Mull, the leg protruding from the south-west side of the island, opposite the holy island of Iona, the home of St Columba. The monastery that he founded on Iona is still a place of international pilgrimage. At this time of year, early May, the whin, or gorse, was out in full bloom, its flowers turning from yellow to orange, and the road to their destination, Bunessan, took them across the beautiful and dramatic interior of the island. A little over an hour later they arrived, the village being a small settlement on the side of a crescent-shaped bay. Out to the west lay Iona, and in the background the sky was a riot of colour, great swathes of orange and yellow cloud with a blood-red sun hanging in the sky. No wonder the ancients used to worship the sun, thought Howarth, the bringer of light and life. Still, that was enough poetry and philosophy for one day; the more pressing concern was, of course, getting a pint.

Although a tiny village, Bunessan had one thing to commend it to Howarth and McDonald – a large and welcoming pub, the Argyll Arms Hotel. They parked up outside the two-storey stone building and headed inside.

The older parts of the building date back to 1790. The story has it that the then Duke of Argyll, who gave his name to the hotel, had become so concerned about the level of illicit drinking and distilling among his tenants on Mull that he decided to provide a tavern at his own expense where locals could come to enjoy a dram without incurring the wrath and unwanted attention of the customs men. The attractive waterfront location of the subsequent hotel proved such a lure that the Duke began to use it as a hunting lodge to accommodate his stalking and fishing guests. With a history rooted in smuggling and fishing, it was bound to appeal to Howarth.

The present owners of the Argyll Arms Hotel are Duncan and Gillie MacLeod. Duncan's father was the late acclaimed accordionist and pioneer of Scottish country music, Bobby MacLeod. By coincidence, the owner back in 1990, an affable Highlander, was also a keen musician and squeezebox player. He greeted Howarth and McDonald cheerfully, asking them what they would have. As they stood at the bar supping their pints, they fell into conversation with the landlord, who was unencumbered with having to worry about any other customers; they were the only patrons. He explained that the place got busy in the evenings when they would often have live music, essentially himself and a few fellow musicians who would have the place rocking to Scottish folk music. He asked what brought the two men to Bunessan. When they explained that they were planning to spend the summer fishing, he couldn't have been more welcoming. He told them that they could keep their caravan in his field. Howarth asked how much rent he would want.

'Och, rent is for city folk,' said their genial host and now landlord in both senses of the word. 'Tell you what, though, you might help out with a little of your catch for the pot. What will you be fishing for, anyway?'

'We'll be diving for scallops, mainly,' said Howarth.

'Och, that's great. Give us a few scallops from time to time, do your drinking in here and we'll hear no more about rent.'

'Brand new,' said Howarth. 'Let me buy you a pint and we'll drink to that, then,' and the three men sealed the deal in the time-honoured manner. Later that evening, as the landlord had promised, the bar began to fill up with fishermen and locals, and later on the music started. Howarth and McDonald were in their element, buying drinks for their newfound friends and enjoying the 'craick', as a good piss-up and music is referred to in the Gaelic. It would be a good summer.

The following day, the two men headed out on the inflatable to do an exploratory dive and they were pleased with what they found. There were good crops of scallops to be harvested and virtually no competition. Back on shore, they got in touch with Caley Fisheries in Oban to arrange selling their catch. After agreeing a price, the company arranged to send down a stash of blue sealed fish boxes for the men to store the scallops they caught; once a week, they would send over a fish wagon to collect the produce and make payment for the previous week's consignment.

As predicted by Fiona, most of Howarth's earnings went into the till behind the bar of the Argyll Arms Hotel. Howarth and McDonald had become well known around Bunessan and they had grown fond of the locals. One day while out diving, they came across the wreck of a British munitions boat that had been torpedoed by the Germans in the Second World War. Howarth gave McDonald a querying look; through his mask, McDonald smiled, giving Howarth the thumbs-up. They swam through a hole in the rusting hulk and took a look around. Inside the hold, there were boxes of 'ack-ack' shells, anti-aircraft ammunition left over from the Second World War. They gathered up as many as they could, stuffing them into their diving pouches.

At the pub that evening, one of the locals whom they'd told about their find said that the best way to get the gunpowder out of the shells was to crack the casing in a vice. Borrowing a vice from their landlord, they split a pile of shells open and stored the gunpowder in a heap, a good distance from the pub. Fashioning a makeshift taper from twists of paper, Howarth lay down and held it at arm's length, trying to light the pile. Nothing happened. It seemed the powder was too wet to catch. Eventually, Howarth grew bored and drifted back to the pub for his nightly skinful. As he staggered out in the small hours, he remembered their project and decided to give it another go. Emboldened by beer, and less cautious after his early efforts proved fruitless, he didn't bother with the taper this time, leaning down over the pile and holding his lighter to it. There was an explosion of white light and a searing heat across his face. The powder had clearly dried out. When his sight returned, all he could make out was the sight of McDonald, helpless with laughter, clutching his sides as he pointed at Howarth.

'It's not fucking funny, man,' Howarth protested. 'I could have been blinded.'

'If you don't think it's funny,' retorted McDonald, 'wait till you get a look at yourself in the mirror.'

Howarth headed back to the caravan and found his shaving mirror. When he held it up, he couldn't help but laugh. He had to admit he looked comical. The explosion had completely burnt off his fringe and eyebrows, giving him the permanently surprised appearance of someone who has had one Botox injection too many. They might not be making much money down here in Mull, he thought, but they sure as hell were having some laughs.

On Monday, 3 September 1990, with the season ending, they called it a day. They packed up their gear, loaded up the caravan and said goodbye to their new friends. It was time to head back to Ullapool.

CHAPTER EIGHTEEN

While Howarth was down in Mull, Dick and his colleagues were getting a clear idea of what was going on from their intelligence. They had learnt that Howarth had put together a new landing crew, as he had promised Chadwick that he would. One of the crew was Howarth's friend and neighbour, Robbie Burns. Burns was described as one of the most highly regarded inshore fishermen on the north-west coast of Scotland and it was said that no one knew the coastline better than he did. He joined Howarth and McDonald down on Mull for a time that summer, skippering the boat while the two men dived for scallops. One Ullapool fisherman, who declined to be named, said: 'Robbie was a great skipper. Everyone in the village reckoned he was the best around, when he could keep off the booze. If you were off fishing and you saw Robbie's boat somewhere, you just moved on to other waters. There'd be no point fishing in the same waters: he'd have fished it dry. It was as though he had a sixth sense for where the good fishing would be.'

Drink played a big part in Burns's life. He was 34 by the summer of 1990 and lived with Karen Jacqueline Doffman, at this time aged 35 and the mother of his two sons. Doffman – who would be described in court by Howarth's barrister as 'that handsome, Amazonian woman' – had her difficulties as well.

She had split up with an earlier boyfriend in 1980 and despaired of being imprisoned in the suburbs living with her mother. Clearly being something of a free spirit, a 'hippy chick' as one neighbour described her, she decided to come and stay in the Hebrides, where she could be alone to grieve, commune with nature and to write poetry. In a statement to the police in January 1991, Doffman says: 'I had previously visited Glasgow and Edinburgh but never come this far up.'

She arrived in Ullapool with a half-formed plan to catch a ferry to Stornoway on the Isle of Lewis. Unfortunately, it was a Sunday and the ferry was not running. Lewis is the most north-easterly of the Western Isles, formerly known as the Outer Hebrides. Lewis is a long, flat island – its name in Gaelic, Leodhas, means marshy and the island is mainly covered with a layer of peat. The chief religion of the island is that of the Free Church of Scotland, or the 'Wee Frees' as they are known. This denomination is renowned for its asceticism and disapproval of hedonistic pursuits and particularly for its strict observance of the Sabbath. Until recently, no shops or businesses were open on a Sunday, or even libraries or sports centres, while the population attended services in draughty halls without any Popish imagery or adornment – even television viewing on a Sunday is frowned upon. Services are often conducted in Gaelic and the psalms are sung without musical accompaniment, as even music played on a church organ is deemed a little too racy for these dour souls. The Free Church rule is that only work 'of necessity or mercy' may be carried out.

To the shock and horror of the islanders, on Sunday, 27 October 2002 a British Airways subsidiary partner, Loganair, began operating a Sunday flight for a 34-seat, twin-propeller plane. The inaugural touchdown was met in the grey misty rain, the BBC reported, by a group of around 60 protesters who 'handed out leaflets to passengers saying that travelling on the Sabbath is a sin which will damage their own soul and the life of the island'. Church leaders on this staunchly religious island urged local people to boycott the new service and preserve a traditional way of life that includes strict observance of the Sabbath.

Calum Maclean, local representative of the Lord's Day Observance Society, said at the time: 'These Sunday flights are a breach of God's law and will have an adverse effect on the whole community life of this island as we know it. This is only the start.' It's fair to say that if you were booking a stag weekend or hen party, the Isle of Lewis might not be at the top of your list of destinations.

Still, it was what Doffman felt she needed, so she was disappointed to have fallen foul of the Sunday rule. She decided to repair to a seafront hostelry in Ullapool named the Seaforth, owned by Harry MacRae, for a consolation pint, something she would have struggled to do had she found an alternative means of crossing to the Isle of Doom and Gloom. Once in out of the mist and rain, she found that the Seaforth was doing roaring business, the windows steamed up and a fine time being had by all. No black-coated Wee Free minister would be doing the rounds with a stick to encourage people to go to worship in this town.

Ullapool people being a friendly bunch, it wasn't long before one rowdy group had started chatting to her, asking what brought her up to Wester Ross, as the region is called, and gently pulling her leg about her southern accent. One of the group in particular made a good effort to chat her up, buying her drinks and enjoying the craick. His name was Robbie, a local skipper, and Doffman found him attractive and good fun. Later that evening, she ended up going back to the boat Robbie was working on, *The Seafarer*. She realised how hungry she was and was delighted when Robbie offered to cook her a pork supper.

The next day, she agreed to go out fishing with Robbie and his crew, and to work in the galley as the boat's cook. After around four days, they landed at Lochinver, some 30 miles or so north of Ullapool, the fishing port where Howarth had pursued his wife Lenore when she left him; it was her spurning of him here that had caused him to take his overdose. Doffman said goodbye to Burns and the crew here and headed back to Ullapool to continue with her original plan of getting the ferry to the Isle of Lewis.

She says that she spent two weeks in a tent, communing with nature and being a free spirit among the peat, heather and rain. It is not known how much poetry she managed to write. Her time on the island dragged slowly, though, and after a fortnight she found she was missing Robbie, despite only having spent a few days with him, and headed back to Ullapool.

Their courtship seems to have been remarkably brief. When she returned to Ullapool, she moved straight in with Burns. Their first home consisted of a caravan situated by the Latheron Buildings in Ullapool, a commercial centre with a few government and voluntary bodies' offices. Says Doffman: 'Crazy Chris and his girlfriend Fiona lived in a caravan next to ours. Ever since I have known Robbie, he has always been a close friend of Chris Howarth's.'

They remained friends and neighbours over the years. Doffman gave Burns a son, Aaron, in 1983, the same year as Fiona Forsyth had Gayle, Howarth's eldest daughter, and so the two women were friendly. After Howarth and Fiona finally got their council house on the Morefield estate, Burns and Doffman were granted one in 1986 two doors down the same terrace, Doffman having given birth to her and Burns's second, Plato. Like many couples, they had their share of problems. In her police statement, Doffman says: 'When Robbie is working and sober, he is a really nice guy, but he often just goes on the drink for months on end, and when he is on the drink, he is completely different and can be very bad-tempered.'

Indeed, by 1991 Burns's drinking and violent mood swings had become too much for Doffman, who said that things had been carrying on in this vein for at least 18 months. On more than one occasion, it became too much for her and she travelled down to Mill Hill, the London suburb where her mother was living and where she had grown up.

In her statement, Doffman paints a picture of a joyless relationship, full of disillusionment and pain. There is a sense of suffering behind her veiled references to Burns's vile temper and alcoholic rages. By 1991, they were no longer sharing a bed and had not done so for a long time, Burns sleeping on a sofa in the lounge downstairs. Doffman concludes her statement by saying: 'I have often told Robbie before that if he gets involved with anything dishonest, not to tell me because I can't tell lies. If Robbie has anything to do with this cocaine, I can promise you that I do not know anything about it.' There is a pause noted on the statement after which she makes her point clear. 'I would not tell lies for Robbie.'

CHAPTER NINETEEN

In Malaga, Jonathan Chadwick had been keeping busy while Howarth was having high jinks down in Mull. After leaving Rae's flat on 3 March 1990 and heading back to Malaga, he did not return to the country for three months, failing to use the return flight he had booked for 21 March. He suffered a family bereavement in May when his father James died after a battle with cancer. Sadly, James Chadwick had only lived for eight months after retiring to southern Spain. Chadwick flew back to the UK on 19 May to bring his father's body home for a funeral but didn't stay long, flying back to Spain on 27 May. It was in April that Howarth had told him that he would be unable to do any work for him as he was spending the summer diving with Tony McDonald on Mull.

This may have been true, although another reason for deferring the job was given to Customs and Excise by an informant. He maintained that Howarth and Burns were unable to organise a boat. Neither had one suitable for the job and, with summer arriving in Ullapool, it would be impossible to borrow one. It is unlikely that Howarth would have been able to borrow Harry MacRae's boat, *The Guardwell*, which had been used on the Gruinard Island run, as there was no great love lost between the two men – when I spoke to MacRae, he made it clear to me that he had no time for Howarth. Chadwick would have to wait a few months.

He wasn't one for standing around and waiting, though. Over the next few months, he was in and out of Scotland the whole time. Is this consistent with simply arranging a fairly straightforward shipment of cannabis? Or did he already have his eyes on the bigger prize – cocaine? We know from the readiness with which he gave up his previous career as a successful freelance diver, with an already extremely affluent lifestyle, to go into cannabis smuggling that he was always willing to change his plans to look for the bigger bucks. It seems that he was always open to making as much money as possible in as short a time as he could. Chadwick was no Howard Marks, who was driven, in part, by an ideological belief in what he was doing, bringing cannabis to the people and having a bloody good time to boot. By way of contrast, Chadwick was cool, calculating and not particularly 'clubbable'. He was in it for the money, not for fun.

Indeed, there is every reason to believe that, over a year before the big job, he was already planning it without necessarily letting his co-conspirators know what he was up to. The fewer people that knew, the less that could go wrong. It seems likely, given what we know of the man, that the idea of earning enough money off one shipment never to have to work again would be irresistible to Chadwick.

On 17 July 1990 Chadwick was back, flying into Gatwick on British Airways flight BA425 from Malaga, arriving at 10.15 p.m. He was observed making his way to the south terminal on the monorail shuttle – from here he headed for the Hertz desk, discount card doubtless in his hand. He hired a blue Ford Sierra, plate number G187 FPR, as noted by a J. Jarvie and M. Stephens of Customs and Excise, and swung out of the car park at 10.50 p.m. He had a long way to go.

It's not clear why he chose to make the long drive up to Scotland, rather than take the shuttle up to Edinburgh as he usually did. He had a rudimentary grasp of anti-surveillance techniques, and had gone to the trouble of watching as many documentaries and reading as many books about Customs as he could, as David Forrest would testify later. Perhaps he had read that it was important to make it difficult for would-be watchers by changing his routine as often as possible, switching airports and times. The only problem with this theory is that it doesn't account for why he nearly always stayed at Rae's flat in Glenisla or at the Harbour Lights Hotel when in Ullapool. Perhaps he just wasn't very good at avoiding detection.

He must have driven pretty much through the night as he was spotted at 11.55 a.m. the following morning outside Perth, heading north, a journey, according to the AA, that takes the best part of nine hours. This would indicate that he had only stopped for a maximum of four hours on his way. Whatever was impelling him northwards must have been important. He had been spotted by two of Dick's colleagues, Frankie Cooper and Malcolm Sharp. Cooper was in his early twenties at this time, described by Dick as 'a bit baby-faced, a good-looking guy, and a great sense of humour. He was very funny, great lad to be on a job with.' Sharp was older – in his forties, he was married, a reasonably quiet man, balding with a beer belly and glasses. In other words, like most of the male population of his age, making him an ideal candidate for surveillance work.

At 12.30 the two men clocked Chadwick at Dunkeld heading north and handed over to their colleague Tony Jackson, an Englishman in his early thirties of medium build with a beard who lived for motorbikes. Jackson sighted Chadwick just south of Inverness, heading north on the A9 at 1.30 that afternoon. He was next picked up by Frankie Cooper three hours later, heading south again at Braemore Junction, some ten miles south of Ullapool. Clearly it had been a flying visit to Ullapool of no more than an hour and a half. Tony Jackson picked up the trail again and followed him between Contin and Tomatin before racing on ahead to avoid detection.

It was obvious to Jackson that Chadwick was on his way to Rae's flat at Glenisla, so he shot down there and drove past Rae's flat where he saw Rae's car and David Forrest's 2CV at 7.35 p.m. It looked like the Three Musketeers were planning another reunion. He looped back around to swing by the Glenisla Hotel, where, five minutes later, he saw Chadwick pull up in his Sierra and take a bag from the boot. Again, it must have been a brief meeting: an hour later, Frankie Cooper reported that Chadwick's car had gone while, over at the council estate in Dundee where Forrest lived, George Cockburn noted that Forrest's 2CV was back outside his flat.

The following morning, Forrest was on the move again. Cockburn discreetly followed him back to Rae's place at Glenisla, where, at 8.15 a.m., he noted the presence of Chadwick's hire car and Forrest and Rae's 2CVs. Two hours later, Chadwick was off again, heading this time towards Perth with someone in the passenger seat. It was Ian Rae. Dianne MacColl, a travel agent working for the UK chain A. T. Mays at the George Street, Perth, branch recalls the day. In a statement to police later, she said: 'On July 19 1990, two men came into the agency and one of them asked for me by name. I recognised him [i.e. Chadwick] as a customer I had dealt with on a previous occasion. The other man gave his name as Rae and told me he wished to book a flight for himself, his wife and two children from Gatwick to Malaga, Spain. I did the necessary booking.

'As it was a late booking, I arranged for Mr Rae to collect the tickets at the departure desk at Gatwick. He paid me £578 in cash. With regards to the man who accompanied Mr Rae, he had previously come into A. T. Mays some weeks earlier enquiring about cheap flights [definitely Chadwick!]. I cannot recall whether he gave his name or indeed whether he made any booking on that occasion. I would describe him as in his late twenties, tall, dark hair, slim build, suntanned, clean-shaven, casually but expensively dressed, well spoken, with no pronounced accent.' Despite his best-laid plans, things were ganging agley for Chadwick, who was leaving a trail like a slug all over the country.

Things were moving. Over the next three days, Chadwick was based at Glenisla and, finally, on 23 July, he headed to Edinburgh Airport, dropped the Sierra off at the Hertz counter and flew down to Heathrow, where he was seen coming through the domestic arrivals area. Two Customs guys from down south observed him head for the Underground and followed him down onto the platform, where he got onto a train heading for central London.

We know that Chadwick had links with big-time dealers in London – he had used the address of one of them on a number of occasions, as that dealer will no doubt be delighted to learn – and the lion's share of the cannabis he had brought in on the Gruinard Island run had been transferred down to the London market. It is likely that he was off to have a meeting with his clients, the wholesalers to whom he would be shipping the next load.

The following day, 24 July, Chadwick was observed boarding Iberia Air flight 611 from Heathrow to Malaga. The lad had had a busy few days in the UK and would probably be grateful for a breather down in the Costa del Sol. The day after, Ian Rae flew down to Malaga with Lucy and the kids on a Dan Air flight, the Ryanair of its day. They took flight 4360, departing Gatwick at 6.40 a.m., arriving in Malaga at 10.10 a.m. Lucy Rae does not have great memories of this holiday. She told police: 'We went out to Malaga for a summer holiday in 1990. It had been a long-standing invitation by Jonathan to go. I didn't want to go the year before because of Ben's birth. We paid for the holiday, which was a disaster. We were supposed to stay with Jonathan's mother. His father had recently died and she was too upset [for us to stay with her]. Jonathan found us another apartment and we paid the rent. He was there every single day and it annoyed me as I don't really like him, but he is Ian's friend and Ian is very loyal to his friends.' Very loyal, indeed. After this disastrous and unforeseeably expensive fortnight's holiday, the Raes flew back to Gatwick on 8 August on Dan Air 4361, arriving at Gatwick at 12.40.

Nothing of any great significance took place during the rest of August. Chadwick next flew to the UK, where, at 4.25 p.m. on Friday, 14 September, he hired a silver Ford Granada, registration number G271 OTN from Diane Wilkie at the Hertz counter of Inverness Airport. He appears to have slipped into the country without attracting the attention of Customs and Excise; for once, he was not followed.

Whatever the business that brought him to Scotland – and it can be safely assumed that it was not to discuss importing olive oil – it was a flying visit. He returned the car on Monday, 17 September, at 1.30 p.m. and, later that day, flew back to London and on to Malaga.

Perhaps he was missing potato scones and black pudding for breakfast – Chadwick was back in Scotland just three days later. He flew into London on British Airways flight 473 on Thursday, 20 September, and took a connecting flight up to Edinburgh Airport, where, at 6.12 p.m., Lynn MacLeod at the Hertz counter hired him another Ford Granada; perhaps the name reminded him of the Costa del Sol, where he had made his life. This time, though, Customs and Excise were on his case. Investigating officers John Buchanan and George Cockburn followed him north on the A9 until 7 p.m., just north of Perth, where, to avoid being discovered by Chadwick, they turned off, leaving it to their colleague Tony Jackson to pick up the trail. He spotted Chadwick at 7.16 p.m. as Chadwick sped past the Dunkeld junction of the A9. He followed him north, noting that Chadwick was alone in the car, past Aviemore as far as Inverness. Then Chadwick headed out of town on the A835 towards Ullapool, where Jackson's colleagues, Billy Reader and Frankie Cooper, would be waiting to take over.

Reader and Cooper were not disappointed. At 9.55 p.m. they saw Howarth standing at the entrance to his housing estate on the main A835. After a few minutes they watched him walk in the direction of the town centre as far as the Mercury Hotel. A minute later, Chadwick pulled up in his Granada, plate number H329 BBB, picked up Howarth and headed for the petrol station, where he did a U-turn and headed back towards town. At 10.45 p.m. he pulled into the car park of the Royal Hotel, where he left his car overnight. The following day, Chadwick set off at 10.56 a.m., heading north out of Ullapool. At 4.12 p.m. on Friday, 21 September, Customs and Excise investigating officers Frankie Cooper and Billy Reader observed their target, Jonathan Chadwick, pull up in West Shore Street on the seafront at Ullapool in a Ford Granada with the registration H329 BBB. A man they identified as Christopher Eric Howarth got out of the passenger side, waved and walked off. At 4.38 p.m., they noted that the car was heading south on Mill Street, the A835, near the Royal Hotel. By now, Chadwick was alone and they watched as he continued south out of Ullapool on the main Inverness road.

Howarth confirms that Chadwick was talking seriously about

putting another hash run together, and this time it looked like it was really going to happen. Chadwick gave him some tentative dates – it would be in the next six weeks – and assured him that everything down in Spain was set up. Howarth could only think of the £40,000, more money than he could dream of. In an instant, he'd contrived to put aside all his nagging suspicions about Chadwick and was thinking only of being at the helm of a yacht under a clear blue Mediterranean sky, hundreds of miles south of Ullapool and its winter storms and cruelly short days.

'Fine, that's agreed then,' said Chadwick, suddenly brisk and business-like. He turned the key in the engine. 'I've got to get going – I'm flying back down to Malaga this weekend and I've got a couple of things to see to before I go. Can I give you a lift anywhere?'

'Where are you headed just now?' asked Howarth.

'Back to the Royal Hotel to check out,' came the reply.

'Well, in that case, you can drop me down at the front. If you can't slip off for a pint on a Friday afternoon when the missus isn't looking, when can you?' he asked rhetorically. Chadwick laughed. 'True enough,' he agreed equably as he pulled off and headed the Ford Granada back towards town.

CHAPTER TWENTY

By late October, the old pattern was beginning to re-emerge. Winter was now setting in – it comes early to the far north – and Howarth was skint. He had had no word from Chadwick and, truth to tell, had assumed that the talk of work had turned out to be more of the man's bullshit. His distrust of Chadwick had come back and he was resigning himself to another long, cold winter on the dole. Fiona was unhappy with him and he had been sleeping in the spare room for two nights. One evening, he sat watching television with a rising sense of impatience and despair at his situation. Fiona's disapproval was emanating from her and hanging in the air like a bad smell from his poor dog Jim, who was looking up at him expectantly with mournful brown eyes.

'Christ, I cannot face another winter in this shithole,' he finally snapped. Fiona frowned and, showing no sympathy, said, 'Well, I told you not to fall out with Jonathan,' in a tone of voice as if to say 'I told you so'. Howarth protested, saying that he hadn't fallen out with Jonathan, that Jonathan had promised to ring if he had any work. The fact that there had been no phone call from Spain simply showed that there was no work on. 'Christ,' he said angrily, 'it's not like I'm the only bloke in the world that can crew a yacht, they're ten-a-penny. He's probably found someone in Spain that can do it for him and then he won't have to waste money flying me down.' Fiona was impervious to his attempts to reason with her, sitting on the sofa staring straight ahead at the television as though he was not even there. The sound of the rain beating against the windows only served to depress him further. He was a man who only felt free when he was outdoors, on a boat, doing a spot of poaching or even roaming through the fields. Despite the cosy warmth of the house, he felt cooped up, like a prisoner. If he had any money, he could at least head down to The Caley for a few pints to blot out the impotent rage that blew through him at times like a savage north-east wind.

Eventually, he could bear it no longer. 'Fuck this for a laugh, I'm going to ring Jonathan and see if this run is on or not. He can only tell me to piss off, can't he?' He went out to use the payphone at the end of the road. Chadwick had instructed him never to use his own phone when ringing him. Reading from a scrap of paper, he dialled the number; a moment later, Chadwick answered. 'Hi, Jonathan, it's Chris here,' said Howarth a little nervously. He felt funny about ringing Chadwick unbidden. It went against the grain of his stubborn pride. 'How's it going?'

'Fine,' said Chadwick in a laconic, noncommittal manner. 'What can I do for you, Chris?'

Nervously, Howarth stammered, 'Well, the thing is, you said you might have some work on and, like, I don't want to hassle you or anything, but I'm just trying to work out what I'll be doing over the winter and that and, I mean, I was wondering what the score was, like, and, you know, whether there might be anything on and if you think you might have any bits or bobs that you might be wanting doing . . .' His voice trailed off and there was a long pause, probably only a few seconds but to Howarth it felt like ages. 'It's funny you should ring, actually, Chris. I was just about to ring you myself,' said Chadwick. 'The thing is, I might have a run on in a week or two.' Howarth's heart leapt and he tried not to grin too much. 'Oh, aye, what's that then?' he asked with all the nonchalance he could muster.

'Well, it'll be a good run, from the Costa del Sol up your way, the usual sort of thing. Nothing complicated, you know the score from the

The MV *CITO* in 1987, gleaming proudly, clearly maintained
to the highest order by her Danish owners.

The *DIMAR-B* after being impounded at Halifax, Nova Scotia, in October 1991,
looking rather sorry for herself after two years under Torres's ownership.

The Pension Armando in San Pedro de Alcantara, Costa del Sol, where Chisholm put Howarth and Hawkins up before they were to set sail for the coast of Venezuela.

Surveillance photo of Johannes Ditus Neumann taken at Palma, Mallorca, aboard *Shearwake*, prior to rendezvousing at sea with the Moroccan hash suppliers.

The track near Oldany Island at Drumbeg where the huge haul of cocaine was loaded into Forrest and Rae's hire van.

The remains of the *DIMAR-B*'s Zodiac inflatable on the beach at Clashnessie Bay after Howarth and Hawkins's near-suicidal landing in a storm force ten.

The ice-encrusted carving knife that saved Howarth and Hawkins's lives when they managed to cut the rope free from the propeller on the inflatable's outboard motor.

The subtle and inconspicuous van that Forrest and Rae were using to transport half a tonne of cocaine to London, seen here in the compound at Inverness police headquarters.

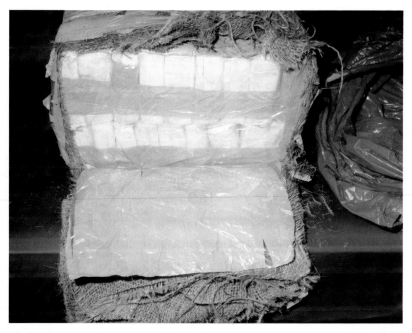

One of the hessian bales after being split open to reveal 32 one-kilogram packages of uncut Colombian cocaine.

The treacherous approach to Clashnessie Bay, looking out towards the Minch. Oldany Island is on the right, and the treacherous reefs that Howarth and Hawkins miraculously managed to negotiate can clearly be seen in the middle of the picture.

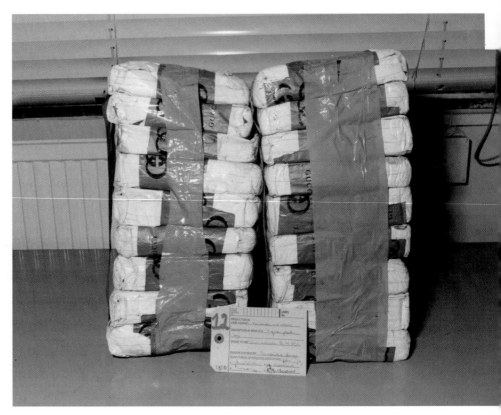

The contents of one bale after being seized by Customs,
with the stylish imitation Gucci masking tape.

Special delivery for the apparent attention of Virgilio Barco,
then President of Colombia.

Sr. Juez:

A usted, commo ministro, acólito, representante humano y material de ese soñado, utópico y platónico término que el género humano denomina, con la bella palabra, JUSTICIA va dirigida la presente carta.

Ante todo, le ruego, no ordene usted hacer la autopsia a mi cadáver pues desde mi humilde e intrascendente punto de vista, considero que no es menester, en este caso particular, malgastar tiempo, formalidad y dinero del erario público, que, a buen seguro, otras necesidades mas apremiantes lo requerirán; comparandolas estas con las patentes y evidentes causas de mi voluntaria muerte.

The elegantly handwritten five-page suicide note by Torres, addressed to 'Señor Judge'. This was after the first attempt in Halifax, Nova Scotia.

Chris Howarth at home in Ullapool, taken in 2003,
18 months after serving 11 years of a 25-year sentence.

last time. You organise the landing crew and the money will be the same as we discussed last time.' Howarth was elated. It looked like he was going to snatch victory from the jaws of defeat. Crazy Chris? More like Lucky Bastard Chris, he thought to himself with a grin as he listened to Chadwick down the line. He was giving Howarth further details on what would be required of him, and assuring him that this time Ditus would not be on the boat – music to Howarth's ears. In fact, he went on, he would let Howarth skipper the yacht and leave it to Howarth to recruit the second crew member. Howarth didn't foresee a problem with this; in fact, he had someone in mind for the job straight away.

'Righto,' Chadwick finally said, 'I'll leave it to you to ring me and let me know what you've managed to sort out, but don't leave it too long. I'm looking at getting you both down here a week or so into November.'

'All right, Jonathan – I'll be in touch shortly,' said Howarth, replacing the receiver.

When he returned home, Fiona greeted him expectantly with a half-smile on her face. 'Well,' said Howarth smugly with a smirk, 'I got a run.' There was great merriment in the Howarth household that night. He was once again the master in his home, the provider, and Fiona was over the moon. She would far rather see her man get involved with a wealthy businessman who could give him lucrative work, even if she remained naively unaware of the true nature of his business, work that would not see him end up in a wheelchair or worse, than carry on with his obsession with diving for scallops. They saw little money from it and she was worried for his health. Chadwick's runs had the added bonus of getting him out of Ullapool, where there were too many temptations and distractions. While Crazy Chris's exploits were legendary around the town, she no longer saw the funny side. She wanted what most wives and mothers want – a bit of money coming in and a safe and secure environment in which to bring up the bairns.

Even the kids were ecstatic. Gayle and Lorna, now eight and three, did not understand the ins and outs of what was going on, but they knew one thing – their mum and dad were laughing and kissing, and the foul mood that had sat like a heavy black cloud over the household had lifted and the sunshine of happy times was now pouring in. Howarth would not have to sleep in the spare room that night.

The only problem that developed was regarding the second crewman. Howarth had been planning to use Matthew Blake but, as the time grew nearer, Blake began to find a number of obstacles, meaning he would not be able to accompany Howarth down to Spain. The first of these was that he had lost his passport. 'No fucking problem,' said Howarth. 'You'll just have to get down to Glasgow and apply for a new one – but you want to look fucking lively, it'll be in the next couple of weeks.' A couple of days later, he called round to see Blake to check on his progress. It was bad news. Blake had now apparently lost his birth certificate. 'Well, you'll have to get a temporary passport then, using your driving licence, won't you?' said Howarth. 'Aye, Chris,' said Blake, not looking him in the eye. 'The only problem is, I'm not too sure where my driving licence is just now.' Howarth stormed off. Fucking unreliable twat, he thought, as he headed down to The Caley to consider his next move.

As the supposed ringleader of the landing crew, Howarth seemed to be encountering more than his fair share of human-resource issues. The following evening, he had a visitor – Noel Hawkins, a 20-year-old local man. He had known Hawkins since the latter was a young lad – Hawkins lived on the same estate at Kanachrine Place, the road leading into Howarth's cul-de-sac, Morefield Place from the main road, the A835 – and had practically watched him grow up. These days, he would often share a pint with him at The Caley, and Hawkins often popped around to Howarth's house for a joint. Hawkins was the youngest of four brothers and was born after the break-up of his mother's first marriage, leaving him with no knowledge of his natural father. At the age of three, he moved with his mother down to Canterbury when she remarried, while his half-brothers, Harry and John, stayed in Ullapool to work as fishermen. Although he lived down south for many years with his mother in Canterbury and, later, Cornwall, he would often return to Ullapool to see his brothers, and Howarth watched him grow into a strapping lad, broad-shouldered with dark hair. In 1987, Hawkins's stepfather died and he returned with his mother to Ullapool for good, picking up work on his brother's boat. The main work they had was ferrying sailors and, ironically, Customs men out to the klondykers, the factory ships moored out in Loch Broom.

A glance at Hawkins's list of previous convictions tells a similar story to Howarth, another true son of Ullapool. In August 1986, he was convicted of riding a motorbike in Strathpeffer without road tax and fined £20 on two counts. In January 1988 he was convicted of stealing 30 cases of beer off the back of a lorry and for breach of the peace, the latter the result of his drunken state when arrested. In May of the same year, he was convicted of malicious mischief – he slashed the tyres of a man with whom he had had a drunken argument – and fined £60, as well as being ordered to pay £100 compensation. And, intriguingly, he was convicted in January 1989 of an offence under the Explosives Act 1875. Although this at first seemed like a journalist's dream, the truth, as it often does, turned out to be far more mundane. He had thrown a firework into a fish-and-chip shop when he was pissed. In short, he was a normal, wholesome product of Ullapool with the full range of outside interests and pastimes shared by many his age. Howarth had always found him a pleasant and easy-going lad, and believed him to be a good seaman.

The evening that Hawkins popped round for a spliff, Howarth was getting stressed about whom he could take down to Spain with him. Hawkins was working at the time on his brother's ferryboat servicing the klondykers. He had worked for him a couple of years previously under the notorious Youth Training Scheme (YTS), first introduced by Thatcher's henchman Norman Tebbit, memorably described first by Dennis Healey as the 'Chingford skinhead' (Tebbit represented Chingford and Woodford Green as an MP, now served by 'the Quiet Man' of British politics, Iain Duncan Smith) and later by Michael Foot as 'a semi-housetrained polecat'. The year-old Thatcher government, having promised to soothe society's pain, introduced a workfare scheme, the YTS, whereby benefit recipients would effectively work for their dole, offering cheap labour to their capitalist chums while massaging the galloping unemployment figures downwards. Hawkins had objected to receiving a pittance for doing the same amount of work as waged employees, and he had said goodbye to working with his brother. By now, though, he was back with him as a short-term measure while he was waiting for a place at Lowestoft College to complete an Offshore Safety Certificate. The course had been paid for and was due to start on 14 January 1991, a couple of months later, so Hawkins could just about put up with the drudgery of Ullapool until then.

As they got stoned together, Howarth confided in him about the problems he was having with Blake. Hawkins knew that Howarth had been involved on the Gruinard Island run, and had made good money from it. It was common knowledge around the village and, to be fair, Howarth was not the world's best at keeping his mouth shut. In a small place, news seeped out fast, and Hawkins already had a good idea that Howarth was putting together another run. 'Well, what about me, Chris?' he asked. Howarth laughed. 'Don't be daft – you're still a kid.'

'Fuck off, man,' Hawkins retorted angrily. 'I know the coastline as well as anyone, and I can handle a boat better than half of the dozy cunts round here. What do you say, man?' Howarth reflected for a moment. He did need another man, that was true, but Hawkins was so young . . . on the other hand, Hawkins was right, he was a handy boatman, he knew the area and he would keep his mouth shut. Howarth paused a moment for dramatic effect, took a long pull on his spliff and, exhaling, said, 'OK. Why not?'

Hawkins's face lit up. The prospect of a few weeks' work in the sun and on the open sea obviously compared favourably with running errands out to the factory ships in Loch Broom during the winter. His grin disappeared suddenly as he seemed to remember something, then he frowned. 'The only thing is, I've got to be back by Christmas or me mum'll kill me.' Howarth chuckled again. 'Don't worry, it should only be for three weeks so we'll be back in plenty of time. And the money's good; £20,000 cash should do you nicely at your age. Just one thing; don't tell anyone just yet in case it doesn't come off. I wouldn't want you to lose your job because of it – you know what a twat your brother can be.'

'Aye, sound, Chris, sound man,' said Hawkins excitedly. He jumped up and tore out of Howarth's house with a new burst of energy. Howarth watched him go, smiling to himself and shaking his head. What it was to be that young and free, so full of vitality and with your whole life ahead of you. Howarth felt envious.

He finished his spliff and headed out to a phone box to ring Chadwick. The air would do him good. 'Hi, Jonathan, it's Chris here. Just to let you know I've got a man for the job, a good one an' all. There's just one thing; we'll be wanting return flights this time, just in case there are any little mishaps, know what I mean?' Chadwick chuckled down the line. 'Don't worry, Chris, I understand your concern after last year. It won't be a problem; these days a return costs the same as a single anyway.' Howarth felt relieved at this – better safe than sorry was not a motto he could remotely be said to have lived his life by, but under the circumstances it was good to have a get-out clause, should they need it. 'So when would you want us out there, like?' asked Howarth. 'Well, now, let's see . . . hmmm.' Howarth could hear the sound of rustling papers in the background. 'Well, it's the end of October now . . . I would need you out here by, say, 7 November. That OK with you?'

'Aye, no bother,' replied Howarth, buzzing with adrenalin at the prospect of taking the helm of a yacht under a cloudless sky. Life was sweet. It would be an adventure, he thought excitedly. He was not to be proved wrong.

CHAPTER TWENTY-ONE

After his last trip to the UK in late September, Chadwick returned to Spain for around three weeks. He then flew back into the UK with a woman travelling in the name of his mother, Dorothy, on 13 October, landing at Gatwick where he or his companion hired a Ford Scorpio, plate number G986 YTP in his mother's name and using her licence. Little is known of his movements for the next ten days; he had managed to slip into the country somehow without alerting Customs and Excise. We can speculate that, with a huge shipment being finalised, he was spending time in London arranging the distribution among wholesalers there who would arrange the flow into the market.

The first Customs and Excise knew about Chadwick being back was some days later when information came through from Hertz that he had hired a car on the 13th. Suddenly, it was all systems go once again. There was no sign of him at Rae's place in Glenisla, where he usually stayed, and he had not been picked up in Ullapool. Growing increasingly desperate, they tried addresses for known associates including David Forrest and a number of addresses in London. Finally, on 23 October, they got lucky. Frankie Cooper and George Cockburn saw his hired Scorpio at 10 a.m. outside his brother James's address, Garth Cottage in Caputh, between Dunkeld and Blairgowrie and just a few miles from Rae's place. It could be that, getting so close to the main event, he had grown twitchy and decided to change his routine by avoiding Rae's flat and the Glenisla Hotel. They were back on.

Graham Dick was cock-a-hoop. Chadwick was the main guy; without him, they had very little evidence to prove their case, and the fear that he had slipped through the net had been too awful to contemplate. With a firm sighting, they were back in control and the established surveillance procedures swung into place. Throughout the morning, officers would routinely drive past his brother's cottage, checking on the status of the car. It finally went on the move after lunchtime and Cooper and Cockburn were able to radio in the information that he was heading for the A9 once again.

They would find out later from Michael Bartholomew, the owner of the Glenisla Hotel, that Chadwick had in fact stayed there three nights previously. Bartholomew told police:

> From my records, I can say that he stayed the night of October 20, 1990. He was with his girlfriend Moina and I charged them £10 each for the room and they had food totalling £16.75, making a total bill of £36.75. Jonathan paid this in cash.' In case there was any doubt about who was with him, Bartholomew added, 'I would describe Moina as about mid-thirties, slim build, about 5 ft 5 in. or 5 ft 6 in. tall with black hair. I think she was from Morocco.

He was next spotted outside Dunkeld heading north at 3.25 p.m. – the officer reported that he had a passenger who we can assume was Moina. Maggie McKeand and Malcolm Sharp were waiting for them by the time they reached Ullapool just before 6 p.m. that evening, long since dark. They noted that he had a female passenger and that he headed for the north side of town, up towards the Morefield estate, where Howarth and Burns lived. They weren't gone long; McKeand and Sharp saw them arrive back into the town centre just before 7 p.m., where they pulled into the car park of the Harbour Lights Hotel.

McKeand and Cockburn dropped into the bar of the hotel and got a drink, sitting where they could keep an eye on the lobby of what was actually more of a motel. At 8 p.m., Chadwick came into the bar and ordered a drink, asking for it to be put on his room bill. Given that he had freaked the last time he had seen McKeand and Cockburn, clocking them as Customs, he stayed very calm. At 8.30 p.m., Moina joined him and the two made their way into the restaurant for dinner, supper or tea, depending on what part of the country you are from. It was a brief affair: at 9.10 p.m. the two left the restaurant and headed back to their room.

McKeand and Cockburn finished their drinks and left. They noted that the car was still in the car park at 10 p.m. and called it a day, handing over to Frankie Cooper, who was on the night shift. He observed that the car was still there each time he did his drive-by and handed over the following morning at 9 a.m. to Tony Jackson, heading off for some much-needed sleep. Jackson didn't have to wait long before something happened. He saw Moina and Chadwick come out of the hotel a few minutes later, climb into the car and head south out of Ullapool on the Garve Road, the main A835.

He followed a few minutes behind; eyeball contact was not necessary as the road only heads one way, down towards Dingwall and on towards Inverness. Trying to keep a target within eye contact was unnecessarily dangerous and could jeopardise an operation so it was only done when it was absolutely essential. He passed through Corrieshalloch Gorge, a local beauty spot and spotted Chadwick's car in the parking spot, keeping a good eye on the road.

This spectacular mile-long gorge, one of the finest examples in Britain of a box canyon, is 200-feet deep, according to the National Trust for Scotland. The river, which carved this channel through hard metamorphic rock, plunges 150 feet over the Falls of Measach at one end, as the National Trust website informs visitors. The wobbly suspension bridge a little way downstream from the falls was built by John Fowler (1817–98), joint designer of the Forth Railway Bridge, who bought the estate of Braemore in 1867. Further downstream, a viewing platform provides an excellent vantage point looking up towards the falls, the website also helpfully points out.

It is doubtful whether Chadwick was there for the views. Twenty minutes later, he was seen pulling out, his reconnaissance complete, and he headed south once more, being sighted at the Aultguish Inn on his way to join the A9. Three days later, he returned the hire car to Hertz at the Buckingham Palace Road branch, near Victoria Station in central London. One of the receptionists working on that day, Pamela MacClaren, recalled Chadwick. 'On 27 October at about 5 p.m., a man came into our office to return a car. He was tall, about 6 ft, short dark hair, clean-shaven, in his late-twenties and well spoken. I asked him where he had put the car and he replied that it was in the NCP car park, in the Hertz reserved bays.'

He asked MacClaren about getting to Victoria Station and she told him it was less than five minutes' walk. Displaying the sort of arrogance that alienated many of the people with whom he came into contact, Chadwick told MacClaren he had luggage and couldn't possibly walk; could she drive him? No doubt counting to ten under her breath, she agreed to do so, despite the fact that taking the car out of the car park into rush-hour traffic in central London and having to negotiate a savage one-way system was a major pain. Nothing was too much trouble for Chadwick, it appeared, to put people to.

MacClaren continues: 'Standing beside the car was a woman, dark-skinned, about 40 years old with black hair. She sat in the back of the car as I drove her and the man to the station where they unloaded the car and left' – it need scarcely be added, without offering a tip. MacClaren was able to confirm that the car had been hired in the name of Mrs Dorothy Chadwick and it can be assumed that this was another example of his rather ineffective anti-surveillance tactics.

COKE IT IS

CHAPTER TWENTY-TWO

Early November is a grim time in Ullapool when the season comes to an end and a general feeling of despondency settles over the town as fishermen winter their boats and put away their nets and gear. A sense of gloom is born of the realisation that work will be scarce until the spring and, throughout the terraced houses and cottages of the town, couples will argue over money, there will be no cakes and ale and the fortnightly highlight will be the dole cheque. Tourism has gone a little way to bring some work and money, but the winter months see little trade.

For Howarth and Hawkins, however, November 1990 had an altogether different feel. They would be sunning themselves down in the Med, mingling with the rich and famous in marinas and yachting complexes. And, after bringing the hash back to Ullapool, they would be loaded. Neither man yet had any inkling of the enormity of the operation in which they were becoming embroiled.

The two men packed their bags for the trip and dug out their passports. Howarth left his holdall sitting in the hall beside the front door, ready to leave at a moment's notice, like any experienced international business traveller. All they needed now was the word from Chadwick – they were ready for the off. Wednesday, 7 November 1990 came and went without a call from Spain, as did the following day. Howarth recalls that Hawkins was growing impatient and wanted to know what was going on, and was not satisfied with Howarth's protestations that it was not his fault. Howarth kept ringing the number that he had for Chadwick in Spain but there was no reply. By Friday, 9 November, things were looking shaky.

At 5 p.m. on that Friday, the two men were once again under close surveillance. Craig Paterson and Joe McGuigan of Customs and Excise observed Howarth enter the seafront chip shop where Hawkins was queuing for his supper, and asked him whether he was going to give him a lift. Hawkins replied that he would but that he wanted to speak to his girlfriend first; he would see Howarth in a few minutes. Howarth left the chip shop and headed to The Seaforth, a large pub on the front which is coincidentally now owned by Hawkins's half-brother, Harry MacRae. Hawkins was joined by his girlfriend a few minutes later and they headed over to The Seaforth. Ten minutes later, Hawkins left the bar and headed off toward the harbour. He wasn't gone for long; shortly before 6 p.m., he returned driving a red Mitsubishi pick-up, number H492 XST and stopped outside the pub. Howarth came out with another man, not identified by their secret admirers, and they climbed into the pick-up, Howarth in the passenger seat.

At this point, the surveillance was taken over by Maggie McKeand and Jim Conroy. At 6.03 p.m. they saw the pick-up in West Argyle Street, heading north out of town on the main A835. Keeping a discreet distance, they followed their targets for around three miles out of town to Ardmair Bay, a small crofting hamlet on the shores of Loch Kanaird, which is a local beauty spot offering panoramic views over the bay, across the Isle Martin and out to the Summer Isles. At 6.14 p.m. their followers noted that they stopped at a public phone box by the road and Howarth went in to make a call. Chadwick had given strict instructions to Howarth at one of their meetings that he was never to ring him from his own phone, always from public ones, using a different one each time. That was fine in principle, thought Howarth grumpily, but in a place the size of Ullapool, he had run out of payphones pretty quickly and was obliged to go further afield.

Not wanting to be spotted, the Customs officers drove back to Ullapool and waited in their car parked on the main road with the lights switched off. They didn't have to wait long. At 6.28 p.m., the pick-up drove past them on its way back into Ullapool. The two Customs officers headed back out to the phone box at Ardmair Bay, where, according to her notes, McKeand saw that the phone book was turned in at the page for Spain. This seems, on the face of it, a curious detail. Given his line of work, Jonathan Chadwick would be unlikely to list his number in the telephone directory. Besides, Howarth already had a note of his number and had spoken to him by phone several times previously, so presumably would have no need to look it up. Furthermore, without disparaging the many undoubted charms of Ardmair Bay, it is hardly the sort of cosmopolitan and happening part of the world where public phone boxes contain directories for overseas numbers. If McKeand meant that it was turned in at the page for overseas dialling codes, why not say so? Directories do not allocate a whole page to each country's dialling code (and Howarth would no doubt know the code for Spain by now in any case, having phoned Chadwick several times).

Anyway, no contact was made with Chadwick that evening. Hawkins had become pissed off with the delay and thought the whole thing had fallen through, taking his anger and impatience out on Howarth. The following evening, Saturday, 10 November, there had still been no word and when a mate named Alan called round to Howarth's house to see if he wanted to go to a Guy Fawkes (or Bonfire Night) party, he jumped at the chance of getting out. There was no point sitting by the phone willing it to ring, he told himself and Fiona; surely nothing would happen late on a Saturday night. Fiona just grunted, unimpressed with Howarth's latest scheme. He seemed to have the reverse of the Midas touch, in that everything he came into contact with turned to shit. 'Oh, sod you then,' said Howarth, banging the door behind him as he left. It would be the last time he would speak to her for some time.

'So what's the scoop with this party then?' asked Howarth as they made their way to Alan's van.

'Och, it'll be great,' replied Alan. 'It's a Burn Maggie Thatcher party – loads of booze, loads of dope, it'll be mental.'

'Sound,' said Howarth. 'Where is it, like?'

'Down Muir of Ord way – some croft out in the middle of nowhere,' said Alan, starting the engine. 'I'm picking up a few of the lads from the pub, then we'll get off.' While Alan popped into The Caley to pick up his fare-paying passengers – when everyone is skint, commodities like petrol need to be covered – Howarth jumped out and used the phone box to call Val Allen, the mother of his other child Amy, who was still living down in Muir of Ord.

'Hi Val, it's Chris. Listen – are you up for this Burn Maggie Thatcher party?'

'Yeah, course I am. Why don't you drop by my place first?'

'Sound,' said Howarth. 'See you in about an hour.' Back in the van, there was no room for any more passengers. Howarth squeezed into the back and they hit the road. Joints were being passed around like coconut macaroons at a vicar's tea party and pretty soon he was so stoned that he couldn't have told you where Spain was, let alone the fact that he was due to be flying down there. By some miracle they reached Val's place – it was less thanks to Alan's driving than the fact that they hadn't met anyone driving in a similar state coming in the opposite direction. He dropped Howarth off and headed on to the party; Howarth and Val would catch them up later.

Val was already in the party mood, having drunk a few glasses of wine. She greeted Howarth with a kiss and Howarth felt something stir for her. She was not unattractive, dark-haired and slightly plump – just Howarth's type. After downing some more wine and smoking a few joints they were nicely messed up by the time they came to leave. After taking a few wrong turnings down small farm roads, they eventually found the croft, an old stone cottage set back from the road with dozens of cars parked in the surrounding fields. They sat outside the croft for a few moments, trying to get their heads straight. Finally, they pulled themselves together and headed over to the cottage. As they walked in the door, the kitchen was full of people drinking and getting stoned; someone was standing over the cooker heating two knives over one of the gas hobs, then inhaling the fumes off some hash that was then burnt between the blades. It seemed everyone was intent on getting out of it.

Howarth immediately noticed a teapot standing steaming on the table – magic mushroom tea. Magic mushrooms – or *psilocybe* mushrooms, to give them their proper name – are popular particularly among dopeheads, especially those in rural areas or with easy access to the damp forests and moors where they can be found growing freely for a few months of the year, generally very late summer to early autumn. They contain compounds called psilocin and psilocybin which act as hallucinogens. The effects are not dissimilar to acid – LSD, or lysergic acid diethylamide – in that the user will experience often-powerful hallucinations at a higher dosage, shapes distorting, explosions of colour, and a profoundly advanced ability to find the most basic social situation inexplicably hilarious.

Purists argue that they are not hallucinogens, which create unreal visions, but psychedelics, which produce extremely enhanced and illusory versions of reality. Whatever. What's in a name when you're tripping your face off? What is worth pointing out, however, is that virtually every responsible guide to drug usage, under its 'dos and don'ts' of magic mushroom ingestion, will encourage the user to take magic mushrooms in a calm and peaceful environment, preferably where he or she can be at one with nature, but certainly not when the user has something important to do in the next 24 hours. Given that Howarth could be called upon to head for the airport at a moment's notice to fly to London, then Spain for a job of questionable legality and dubious morality, he was not following textbook guidelines. Perhaps he had never read the right books.

After making light work of the tea, colours grew more vivid and people began to look stranger and stranger; Howarth realised he was beginning to trip. He made his way into the living room with Val; it was carnage. There were bodies strewn about everywhere in the semi-darkness, all groping and snogging each other or rolling joints. Howarth shook his head. He was truly flying by now. They found a space in the sea of bodies and sat there, rolling joint after joint. Suddenly, it dawned on him that he was looking at Hawkins. He dismissed it as a mushroom-induced illusion but when he looked again, Hawkins was still there, looking anxious and agitated. 'Hang on a sec,' he told Val as he got up. 'I think Noel wants a word with me.' He stepped over bodies in his way with the exaggerated caution of Neil Armstrong taking his first steps on the moon. 'Shit, I'm off my face,' he thought as he made his way towards Hawkins at the door. Then it suddenly dawned on him why Hawkins might be there. 'Oh no, please not now,' he groaned. 'Not that fucking hash run.'

He followed Hawkins outside. 'Chris, they're here,' said Hawkins in a worried tone of voice. 'It's the Spanish job, these guys are here to take us to Edinburgh Airport. I've got your passport and your bag, you'd better get a move on.' He took another look at Howarth. 'Shit, you're tripping, aren't you?' Howarth couldn't deny it. 'Fuck, man, I'm tripping my nuts off. You'll have to try to cover for me, I don't want them to think I'm a headcase. How did they get here anyway?'

Hawkins laughed. 'I was in the same state myself at a party when Robbie [Burns] popped up looking for me. These two guys turned up at your house so Fiona went round to Robbie's to send him to look for you.' Val came out of the croft to see what was going on. Howarth told her. 'What!' she shrieked. 'You drag me off to some party in the middle of nowhere and now you tell me you're fucking off to Spain! You arsehole!' With that, she turned heel and disappeared back into the croft. Still tripping, Howarth couldn't help but laugh at the situation. They made their way over to the car and Howarth recognised the driver as Ian Rae, the man who had picked him up the last time he was heading down to Spain. In the passenger seat was a stocky man with a moustache, who was introduced as 'Tam', his real name being David Forrest, a driver from Dundee. Hawkins climbed into the back of the car, Howarth following him, and they set off south for Edinburgh.

Howarth slumped in the back, proclaiming that he'd had a bit to drink and was going to try to grab a bit of kip on the way. He let Hawkins strike up conversation with the two men. One odd thing happened; at one point, Rae turned round pointing an imaginary gun at the men, saying, 'Just remember what happens if you get caught and shoot your mouth off.' Given that Rae told the police everything he knew when he was finally caught, this was either an act of supreme irony by Rae or, more likely, a clichéd act of bravado by this small man with the disproportionately large head and mournful eyes. What is more revealing, however, is that it suggests a far more pivotal role in the whole enterprise than that of a simple and uninformed courier, which is what he would ultimately be convicted of.

CHAPTER TWENTY-THREE

Howarth had fallen into a drug-tormented sleep in the back of the car. Suddenly, Tam's hand was on his shoulder, gently shaking him. 'Wake up, Chris. We're here.' Howarth blinked, rubbed the sleep from his eyes and sat up. Outside, the snow was falling in swirling flakes, creating a soft white virginal blanket over the car park that had yet to be disturbed by any vehicle tracks. A couple of hundred yards away was the main terminal building. A large sign proclaimed 'Welcome to Edinburgh International Airport'. The clock on the dashboard showed that it was 3 a.m. Howarth stretched, letting out a heartfelt yawn. 'What about money?' he asked the backs of the heads of the two men in the front of the car. 'I'm just sorting it out,' replied Rae without looking up, counting out a wad of money by the glow of the dashboard. Satisfied, he turned around and handed over a pile of cash. 'There's £500 – that should cover your flights to London and Malaga, and there's a bit extra as well.' Howarth grunted, slipping the stash into the pocket of his combat trousers. It was time to go.

The two men watched the car speed off. 'Right,' said Howarth. 'It's fucking freezing and we've got four hours till the first shuttle to London. Let's go and get warm.' Inside the terminal, all the shops were closed, and the only people around were cleaners, gliding their machines in circular motions over the floor. The bright fluorescent lighting caused the men to wince; Howarth had not yet shaken off the previous night's excesses. They made their way over to a waiting area and stretched out on seats. Within moments he was asleep again. 'Chris, Chris – wake up, man.' For the second time in a few hours, he was reluctantly being dragged from his slumber. He opened his eyes to find a worried Hawkins looking at him expectantly. 'Have you got the tickets?' the younger man asked, with a sceptical expression. 'Er, no, not yet,' admitted Howarth sheepishly. 'Well, you'd better get your shit together 'cos the plane goes in 40 minutes,' said Hawkins with a slight edge. Some international drugs smugglers they made. From Howarth's account of the trip so far, it's doubtful that one would trust these two men's ability to pick up a £10 bag of weed from down the road and bring it back in one piece, let alone mastermind importing the UK's biggest ever drugs haul, as Customs and Excise would have it at the trial.

Tracey Gordon was working on the British Midland desk that morning, doing the early shift. She recalls the two men well – with red-rimmed, bloodshot eyes and dressed scruffily with holdalls, they were not the typical passengers that would catch the early morning shuttle to London – and remembers that the taller of the two men paid cash for the 7.10 a.m. flight. Howarth's recall of the events concurs. He felt atrocious and could see that his hands were shaking when he pulled out the bundle of cash to pay for the flight. He reddened but managed to get through the encounter. Returning to his seat, he groaned with his head in his hands, telling Hawkins that a pint would straighten him out. Hawkins did not reply. Oblivious, he carried on with his pointless one-sided conversation. 'You'd think they'd have a bar at a bloody international airport. I mean, it's supposed to be 1990, know what I mean? If we were in Spain now, we'd have no trouble. There must be somewhere here, maybe I should go and have a look . . .' Hawkins had grown tired of Howarth's twittering. 'Well, whatever you're planning to do, you'd better look lively – the plane's boarding in five minutes.' That seemed to signal the end of the conversation.

A couple of hours later, they were at Heathrow and wide-eyed at the sheer volume of people milling around the terminal on a Sunday morning. The airport had only come into being in 1946, in some fields beside a few cottages called Heath Row; at that time it was just a handful of tents serving only the most intrepid passengers. In less than 50 years it had grown into the world's busiest airport. Howarth and Hawkins were still suffering the effects of the previous night's drugs. As he walked around the brightly lit terminal, by now milling with people, snatches of the song 'People are Strange' by the Doors kept coming into Howarth's head. In his mind he could hear Jim Morrison singing about how 'faces seem ugly when you're alone'. 'They certainly do,' reflected

129

Howarth, feeling on edge at the sheer swell of humanity that felt as though it would engulf him. Day one of his adventure and he was already pining for the dramatic landscapes and open spaces of Wester Ross.

Christ, he needed to sit down. They found a cafeteria section and sat down for a coffee. Howarth had his back to a partition while opposite Hawkins sat with his back to the main crowd.

For the first time Howarth felt scared. Something was troubling him. A nondescript man in a tweed suit was sitting a few tables away, drinking a coffee and reading the paper. Howarth met his eyes over the paper and felt a jolt of understanding pass between them. He realised that this was the third time he had seen the man since boarding the plane at Edinburgh. Was he being followed? Surely not – they hadn't done anything wrong . . . yet. He looked away from the man and shook his head, wishing he could straighten out. He leant forward to tell Hawkins of his fears and when the two men looked over to where Tweedledum had been, there was no one there. All that was left was a still-steaming cup of coffee and a half-smoked cigarette still burning away in the ashtray, like a scene from a made-for-TV spy film. Hawkins laughed and said, 'Christ, Chris, man, I think you're getting the DTs. Pull yourself together for fuck's sake, we've only made it as far as London yet.' They drained off their coffees and stood up to go and find the ticket desk.

At the British Airways desk, the bookings clerk sold them two return flights to Malaga, as airline employee Andrew Porteous would later testify. Again, Howarth paid in cash. As they walked away out of earshot of the clerk, Hawkins muttered: 'Why the fuck do we need returns if we're coming back by boat?' Howarth started to tell him about the problems he'd had the previous winter trying to get back after his adventure to Benalmádena, but soon petered out and changed the subject. He didn't want to worry Hawkins unduly; after all, with return flights safely squirreled away in his pocket, what was the worst that could happen?

Hawkins seemed uneasy about the situation and kept pressing Howarth for more details about the job, but Howarth couldn't tell him much more than he had already done. Hawkins had an instinctive mistrust of Crazy Chris and his harebrained schemes; to this day, the two men have not spoken since being released from prison and Hawkins is emphatic that he will have nothing to do with Howarth.

This irritation with Howarth was already beginning to manifest itself back then, and Howarth could feel Hawkins's unease and incipient hostility. 'Come on, let's get a pint, for fuck's sake – my mouth feels like the bottom of a parrot's cage,' Howarth joked in an attempt to defuse the situation.

As they set off in search of a bar, Howarth suddenly caught sight of Tweedledum again. He had another newspaper in his hand and kept looking at his watch anxiously. He looked up and his eyes caught Howarth's; again, that electric surge as something seemed to pass between hunter and quarry. Howarth told Hawkins in a low voice that their watcher was back and Hawkins became twitchy as well. As they watched the man, he suddenly gave a beam of recognition and ran up to the arrivals area to hug a younger woman who was coming through the Customs channel. Both men relaxed and laughed. 'There you go,' said Hawkins. 'It's either his daughter or his bit on the side – that would explain why he was looking so guilty. Now let's get that fucking pint, my head's done in with all this shit.' As they walked away, Howarth glanced over; now both the man and the woman appeared to be looking at them. He said nothing to Hawkins, though; he probably was being paranoid after all those magic mushrooms. Shit, the state he and Hawkins were in, was it any fucking wonder normal people would be giving them funny looks?

In fact, as it turned out, it was paranoia. Graham Dick explains, 'We wouldn't have anyone following them that closely at the airport, there would be too high a risk of them realising. We knew they were flying down to London, we knew they were heading off to Malaga – we had that from the informant and we would be able to verify it from the airlines. The only problem was, we had people waiting for them in Malaga to keep an eye on them and somehow they slipped through the net when they got there.'

They found a bar and pulled up two stools, their enormous holdalls sitting to one side. The first beer was drunk in near silence but by the third, the two men were beginning to relax, ogling sun-tanned women showing lots of bare flesh, just back from their winter breaks in the Canaries or wherever. The two men carried on drinking, killing time until their flight was ready for boarding, their nervousness about being watched all but forgotten. Some time into the sixth pint, Howarth made some disparaging comment about English beer tasting like piss. 'That's rare, coming from you,' said Hawkins venomously. 'You're English yourself, in case you'd forgotten.' Howarth bit his tongue,

131

telling Hawkins he was in no mood for a political discussion and that that would be the end of it. Hawkins shrugged, telling him to please himself. The tension between the two men, suspended over their alcoholic armistice, had returned. It was time to board their flight.

CHAPTER TWENTY-FOUR

As the two men grabbed their bags and began to make their way to the boarding gate, Howarth remembered with a pang of guilt that it was his daughter Gayle's eighth birthday. He cursed, then spotted a payphone. Telling Hawkins he wouldn't be a moment, he dialled the number and spoke to Fiona for a few minutes before she put Gayle on. As he sent his birthday wishes down the line, Hawkins tapped on the kiosk pointing to his watch impatiently. Howarth assured his daughter he would be home before Christmas, then put the phone down.

The Tannoy was announcing the last call for the British Airways flight to Malaga, meaning Howarth and Hawkins had to make a run for it. Their heavy bags ensured that by the time they reached their gate, they were red-faced and out of breath. Howarth fumbled for the tickets and handed them over to the smartly groomed woman at the desk, who greeted each passenger with a smile as artificial and as efficient as the fluorescent strip lighting of the terminal. They bundled their way onto the aircraft and soon found their seats, shoving their holdalls into the overhead compartments where they lay strangely at odds with the neat holiday luggage of the winter sun seekers who made up the majority of the passengers.

The roar of the engines built up in readiness for the mad dash along the runway that would allow the plane to take off. As they left the terra firma of the UK, Howarth felt as though he had left his stomach behind. He loved flying and never ceased to wonder that such a huge mass of metal was capable of soaring like a bird and keeping itself airborne. In later years, this obsession with the principles of aerodynamics, wind patterns and thermals would lead to a love of paragliding; there would, however, be many years before he could experience the sensation of flying again, with or without engines.

Before long, members of the cabin crew were passing along the aisle, handing out meals and taking requests for drinks. This was in the days before the low-cost airline revolution when such things were always complimentary and Howarth was happy to take advantage of the free hospitality. Somewhere over the Channel, his previous night's abuse and the beers at the airport conspired to send him into a deep, contented sleep. When he awoke some time later, an announcement from the captain informed him that they were flying over the Pyrenees and would be turning south to fly down over central Spain and then to begin their descent to Malaga.

He looked out of the window and, sure enough, through a large gap in the white cloud beneath them, he could make out the snow-capped peaks of the Pyrenees. He continued to look, fascinated, as the terrain later gave way to the ochre and red of Spain, the soil apparently burnt by the sun even in what was for northern Europe the middle of winter. He shut his eyes again, daydreaming of visions of Spain snatched from the travel pages of magazines and television advertisements – cloudless skies, deep blue seas, bleached adobe buildings, lusty red wines, exotic seafood dishes . . . He was dreaming that he was on a boat, the waves gently lapping against the hull when he was awoken with a start by the scream of the engines as they were thrust into reverse. They were landing.

Howarth ran his hands through his hair and groaned as the captain wished them a pleasant stay in Spain. He hoped he didn't look as bad as he felt. In the aisle, Hawkins was stretching and pulling his jacket on. He looked pale with red-rimmed eyes. 'Christ,' thought Howarth, 'we must look a right state.' He caught Hawkins's eye and asked him whether he looked OK. A fit of giggling from Hawkins told him that he did not. 'Shit,' thought Howarth, 'we'll be meeting Jonathan in ten minutes and we look a right pair of muppets. He's not going to trust us with a skateboard, let alone a yacht.' He rubbed his eyes vigorously, getting the sleep out; this only served to make them water and leave them redder than ever. 'Well, there's fuck all I can do about it now,' Howarth reflected philosophically. 'If he doesn't like it, fuck him. We've got return tickets so we'll just get the next plane back.'

As they made their way down through Customs and passport control, his mind was racing, working out exactly what he would say if Chadwick gave him any gip. Working on the age-old strategy beloved of scoundrels, he concluded that the best form of defence would be to attack; he would lay into Chadwick, indignantly protesting that they had been snatched from a party without any notice whatsoever and driven straight to the airport. What the fuck did Chadwick expect them to look like?

When they passed into the main arrivals area, there was no sign of Chadwick. Hawkins let out a deep sigh, and looked at Howarth expectantly with his eyebrows raised. 'Shit,' thought Howarth, 'what do we do now?' He scanned the few people in the arrivals hall, most of whom looked like expatriate Brits who had made new lives on the Costa del Sol, greeting their newly arrived friends and relatives off the London flight. Towards the back of the hall stood a man in dark shades and a multi-coloured bush hat, who appeared to be beckoning to him. They walked over towards the man and, at the last second, he realised it was Chadwick. Without saying anything, Chadwick took him by his elbow and gently steered him out to the taxi rank with Hawkins following, and they climbed into the first vehicle. The taxi pulled out of the car park and onto the ring road; within a couple of minutes, they were speeding down the dual carriageway, the N-340 heading west following signs for Cadiz.

Once they were safely away from the airport, Chadwick visibly relaxed. He took off his shades and hat and said, 'So how you doing? Good flight?' in that familiar laid-back drawl. His easy-going attitude threw Howarth, knocking the wind out of his sails; the speech he was going to make to defend the state they were in went to waste. Chadwick lit a joint, then handed it to Howarth. 'Shit, Jonathan, it's not like you to smoke hash so openly,' exclaimed Howarth. Chadwick gave an easy laugh and waved his hand expansively as though to brush away any ill feeling. 'Oh, don't worry about that, Chris. I was a bit edgy the last time you were down. I was trying to put a business deal together and I was having a few problems with that boat that you were so fond of. Everything's cool this time.' Howarth took a few drags on the joint, then passed it to Hawkins. As he did so, the two men glanced out of the window to see a dog being hit by a car and flung into the path of another, sending it flying to the side of the road, its flank heaving as its life ebbed away. Neither driver stopped. 'Welcome to Spain,' murmured Howarth in a low voice to Hawkins, who was looking sick at the sight of what he had just seen.

After a couple of miles, Chadwick said that they would need to stop at a petrol station to get some fuel as he had run out on the way to the airport. He gave the driver some instructions in Spanish and a few minutes later they pulled up on a forecourt. Chadwick jumped out and returned moments later clutching a jerry can, the petrol fumes combining with the smell of hash to create a heady brew. Howarth closed his eyes; it was good to be back in Spain, which was warm even in November. The sight of the Med, blue and calm, was a tonic and he couldn't wait to be back on a yacht. Contentment and calm washed over him like the sun and he basked in it. Fuck Ullapool; this was the life. He must have dozed off in his reverie; he suddenly awoke as the taxi pulled up by a Jeep parked at the roadside. 'Here we go,' said Chadwick cheerfully, jumping out. 'Look lively, lads.' The two men pulled their bags from the boot as Chadwick paid off the driver, who then sped off. Chadwick made a big show of transferring the petrol from the jerry can into the tank and the three men hopped in, Howarth in the passenger seat and Hawkins in the back. As Chadwick turned the ignition key and the dashboard lights came on, Howarth glanced over and noticed that the needle on the fuel gauge was creeping up well above the halfway mark. 'Fuck me,' thought Howarth, 'either this Jeep has got a tank the size of a lawnmower or the fuckwit must have just stalled it earlier.' The third possibility, that Chadwick was employing a standard anti-surveillance technique (that is, switching cars to avoid being followed), was not one that suggested itself to him.

By now it was dusk and they were driving into the sprawl that is Marbella. Along this stretch of the coast one town spills into another (Torremolinos, Fuengirola, Marbella) with little to distinguish between them. The N-340 runs close to the coastline with evidence of the mass-tourism explosion encouraged in the 1960s by General Franco, and his ambitious young tourism minister Manuel Fraga Iribarne (who would later lead the Conservative opposition in the post-Franco democratic Spain), seen everywhere in cheap high-rise constructions in breeze block all along the road. The more hideous resorts of the Costa Brava and the Costa del Sol, such as Torremolinos and Lloret de Mar, stand testament to their enduring legacy. A few miles after Marbella, where the coastal towns become more upmarket, or 'money-raddled' as writer Laurie Lee memorably put it, they came to a town called San Pedro de Alcantara, where Chadwick turned right off the main road and turned up into the town, away from the sea. He drove up a wide street lined with palm trees; on the pavements, waiters with aprons stood outside cafés waiting for the first customers of the evening. The road bent round sharply to the right into a narrow street with tall houses on either side. Chadwick stopped outside one on a corner where the road bent back round to the left.

The Pensión Armando is a tall, four-storey townhouse with white and blue tiled steps up to the glass front door. Inside, there is no reception desk – simply enough room to turn, then another narrow flight of steps with the same typically Spanish tiling leading up to the next floor. The owner is evidently house-proud; you could eat your *bocadillos*, or breakfast rolls, in the morning off the steps, they gleam so spotlessly, and on every available ledge, window boxes are filled with bright geraniums and posies. It was here on the evening of Sunday, 11 November 1990 that Jonathan Chadwick pulled up with his newly arrived friends from the UK.

Howarth and Hawkins jumped out and Chadwick told them that their room was at the top of the last flight of stairs. There was no reception and no one to welcome them. If the room had been paid for, then it had been paid in advance by Chadwick as no money changed hands. Chadwick then pulled off, saying that he was going back to his flat in an apartment block at Estepona, a couple of miles further along the coast. He told the two men to get some rest as he would be back in a couple of hours to take them out on the town. The men waved as he pulled off and then started the climb up to their room.

When they reached the top landing, they pushed open the door to their room. It was basic, but clean and comfortable, two single beds and a window at the rear of the building, which looked out over the roofs of the town down towards the marina where yachts bobbed in the twilight. 'Wonder which one we'll be on?' said Howarth idly as he gazed down. Hawkins made no reply; he was already stretched out on the bed, fast asleep or pretending to be. Howarth realised how knackered he was and took a leaf out of his companion's book. 'Why do hotels abroad only give you one measly, under-sized pillow?' he asked rhetorically as he lay down, too tired to change even though he himself could identify the rancid odour of stale sweat and beer that came off him. It made little difference, however, and within seconds he was asleep like his companion. They couldn't be sure when they would sleep in a proper bed again.

CHAPTER TWENTY-FIVE

Howarth felt as though he had only just dozed off when he was awoken a couple of hours later by someone calling his name. At first, he thought he was still dreaming until he managed to focus to find Chadwick standing over him with Hawkins standing up by his bed, rubbing his eyes. Outside, it was dark and he could see the moon clearly in the cloudless Mediterranean sky. Chadwick laughed as Howarth squinted up at him. 'Come on, Chris, shift your fat arse. It's time to hit the town – you'll be sound after a few pints. I've got to pop out to make some calls, then I'll be back here for you in half an hour.' With that, he turned and walked out of the room. Howarth could hear him jogging down the stairs two at a time; a moment later, he heard a car start up outside.

Groggily, Howarth propped himself up on one elbow and looked over at Hawkins, who was changing his shirt, his back turned to Howarth. 'Well, Noel,' he said to his back, 'How do you feel about another night on the piss?'

'Why not?' Hawkins replied automatically. He did not look at Howarth.

Chadwick returned shortly, having changed into a pair of chinos and an open-necked shirt. The idea that one didn't need a jacket in the middle of November was most welcome to Howarth, who reflected that back in Ullapool, it would be pissing down and colder than a witch's teat. Chadwick was in a very relaxed mood. 'Come on, boys, let's hit the town. The beers are on me; you can put your money away – it's no good here.'

The three men headed downstairs and out into the night. San Pedro was beginning to get going for the evening and was a far more pleasant spot than Benalmádena – there were no pubs called the Jolly Skinhead here and little sign of British colonisation. This was café society, with restaurants all along the attractive, palm-tree-lined main drag. They headed for a bar near the front and took a table outside.

The beers were flowing fast and Howarth soon loosened up. After a few rounds, Chadwick nodded to the waiter, who brought the bill. Chadwick settled it without a murmur – uncharacteristically generously, thought Howarth. Standing up, he said, 'OK boys, let's go somewhere where we can have a spliff – I know a great place around the corner.' Howarth got to his feet, slightly unsteady through lack of sleep and too much abuse, and followed Chadwick with Hawkins behind him.

They headed up a narrow side street and came to a corner bar. Chadwick seemed to be something of a regular here – the barman nodded and the two of them had a brief chat before Chadwick led them to a table and ordered another round. 'Top man,' thought Howarth. He recalls that, at the time, this all seemed quite out of character for Chadwick. In a journal he kept while in prison, he says: 'This was so unlike Jonathan. He was full of it, with a happy, spend-as-much-as-you-like attitude – and in true Ullapool fashion, we did just that.'

As they drank on, getting more and more pissed, and aping the locals by rolling joint after joint, Howarth noticed that Chadwick kept looking at a pager he carried and going off to make phone calls. After one such phone call, he came back frowning, looking anxious. Hawkins at this stage had popped out to get some air and have a stroll around the town. Howarth laughed and said, 'What's up with you? Has the cat died or summat?'

Chadwick shot him a look and, sitting down, said: 'It's all off.'

'What do you mean, "it's all off"?' parried Howarth.

Chadwick looked down at his hands. 'I mean, everything. The boat run, all that – it's off.'

'Shit, man,' said Howarth, by now drunk, stoned and very angry. I can confirm that when Howarth is drunk and angry, the red mist descends and he becomes aggressive and potentially violent – I was close to being on the receiving end myself on one occasion. 'I hope this is some sort of fucking wind-up. What's the fucking problem now?'

He recalls that he could feel himself tensing up and was 'ready to go ballistic', as he puts it. Chadwick must have sensed it, too, as he became nervous at this point, stammering slightly as he spoke. 'Well, that particular job is off – but I do have another job for you.' Howarth, acting with uncharacteristic restraint, decided that he would listen first – 'and then twat the cunt', as he describes it.

Howarth was only too aware of the problems that he had encountered the previous year on a similar Spanish jaunt for Chadwick. 'Thank fuck we got return tickets,' he thought grimly. 'Go on,' Howarth said to Chadwick. 'I'm all ears.'

'Well,' said Chadwick nervously, 'it's like this. The boat you were going to take back to the UK isn't ready to go. We've got a few little problems, which means that the job's been put back, but I have got something else for you. I have some associates and we've put together another job. I can't tell you too much about it but what I can tell you is that it will mean joining a ship for a few weeks.'

Howarth looked at him and asked, 'How much?' Chadwick smiled, for he knew then that he had Howarth. 'Well, it's a lot more. As head of the landing crew, you'll get £150,000. Robbie and Noel will get £75,000 each.'

Howarth let out a long, low whistle. 'Fuck me, Jonathan, that is wild. What the fuck do we have to do for that sort of money?'

Chadwick shook his head. 'I can't go into the details just now. You'll find out in due course; we're on a strict need-to-know basis just now. The ship will take you back up to Scotland. Remember the spot near Drumbeg where I said I was thinking about building a marina?' Howarth nodded.

'That's where it'll be coming ashore. Can Robbie get a boat in and out of there?' Howarth thought about it. There wasn't much room for manoeuvre between the reefs and the cliffs of Oldany Island, but if anyone could do it, Robbie could. So that's why Chadwick had taken him on that goose-chase up there! He must have been planning this for over a year.

The two men talked, leaning in over the table so they couldn't be overheard. After a while, Hawkins came back. Howarth began to explain how the job they'd come for was off, but that there was something else on instead. As he talked, he glanced over at Hawkins, who was shaking his head. Howarth could practically read his mind: 'Not another Crazy Chris flop – I must have been mad to get involved.' His expression soon changed, though, when Howarth told him how much he'd be paid. 'Fuck me!' he gasped. 'What do we have to do?' Howarth explained that details were tight, but that they would be joining a ship in Gibraltar in three days' time.

Chadwick, who had been talking to an acquaintance, rejoined them, nodding to the waiter to bring another round of drinks. 'The ship sails from Gib on Wednesday, so you can do what you want till then. It's all paid for,' he said, meaning food, beer and hotel. Then as an afterthought, he tapped Howarth's glass of beer and added, 'Well, it is up to a point . . .'

Graham Dick does not doubt that the two men would have been aware of what they were getting into: 'Don't forget, at this time, we thought we were tracking a suspected importation of cannabis, possibly as much as four tonnes, which would have been big. In the event, when it turned out to be half-a-tonne, it was disappointing. That sort of amount is not unusual and would have been bread-and-butter stuff for us. Admittedly, boat jobs are always the hardest to do in surveillance and resource terms, but still we would hope back then to be doing a handful of those a year. The emphasis has shifted now as we are more likely to deploy resources into Class As, mainly cocaine and heroin. We will still seize cannabis and arrest those responsible but we just cannot investigate everything to this level of detail. These days we're far more likely to take it out in the port or at sea or we'll work with other countries to take it out before it even comes into the country.

'Now, £20,000 is a hell of a lot of money for a hash run. The street price for resin was around £120 per ounce, while the wholesale price for a kilo at that time would have been £1,500 to £2,000 so the Gruinard Island run would have been worth around, say, £3 million. However, buying that sort of amount would have probably cost £1.8 million or upwards wholesale, leaving a profit of only about £1 million.

'It sounds a lot but we don't know if Chadwick was a part-owner of the load, or simply supplying the transportation. As I say, the cannabis itself would have cost around £1.8 million from the Moroccan suppliers. If Chadwick was contracted for the transport, he would have agreed a set price. Out of this, he would have to pay the ship, the landing crew, Forrest and Rae – and still make a profit himself. If Burns and Hawkins were to get £70,000 each, Howarth would probably be getting more, and Rae and Forrest, who were much closer to Chadwick than the others, probably more again. You could be looking at around £400,000 just for their wages. Out of profits of £1 million? No way. The money just wouldn't be there if it was cannabis, so we're pretty sure that they must have known that they were getting into big-time stuff.'

Howarth has said that he had no idea that it would be cocaine. He was expecting that it would simply be a much larger consignment of cannabis. Hawkins seems to confirm this, saying, 'We weren't told that it would be coke – but for that sort of money, it had to be something pretty fucking big.'

The following morning, Howarth awoke late, when the sun was filling the room and causing him to squint. His head was pounding and his mouth felt like something had crawled into it and died. Christ, he groaned, could he manage to wake up just once in his life without feeling ravaged by a crushing hangover? Outside, car horns were tooting and San Pedro was going about its everyday business. The door opened and Hawkins strolled in, whistling cheerfully. He tossed a bag of something onto Howarth's bed, saying, 'I bought a couple of pies at a baker's down the road, don't know what they're like . . .'

Again, he didn't look at Howarth as he spoke to him. Relations between the two men continued to be strained. He went into the bathroom while Howarth opened the bag to be greeted by the smell of fresh baking. He was starving. He took a mouthful of a pie then, pleasantly surprised, crammed half of it in, realising how ravenous he was. 'Mmm, not bad,' he managed to call out, spitting crumbs all over the floor.

Hawkins came back into the room, zipping his flies up. Grabbing a pie, he pulled up a chair and sat down. He wolfed his pie down, then started tapping his foot impatiently.

'Well, what are we going to do now?' he asked. 'We've got two more days in this shithole before we get on that boat.'

Howarth was irritated at the aggressive tone and snapped back, 'How the fuck should I know? You're a big boy now, you can make your own decisions.' As soon as he said it, though, he regretted it. He had recruited Hawkins for this trip, after all, and there was no point in letting things deteriorate any further between them. He adopted a more conciliatory tone. 'Tell you what, why don't we go and check out the town? There must be things to see.'

As Howarth got up and pulled his clothes on, Hawkins spoke in a quiet voice. 'Look, Chris, I don't like it.'

'What don't you like?' asked Howarth.

'Jonathan. I really don't trust him,' said Hawkins.

Howarth tried to laugh it off. 'Oh, Jonathan's all right; he's just a bit tight.' Then, changing the subject, he said, 'Bollocks. I forgot to bring any sunglasses. I'll have to try and find a shop that sells them.'

Hawkins laughed for what felt like first time in ages, breaking the tension. 'You twat. Have you any idea of the price of sunglasses in Spain?'

The two men headed out into the sunshine; at midday, the streets were still bustling, although shortly afterwards, things began to wind down during the siesta. They looked at sunglasses in several shops before Howarth settled on a pair that set him back £30, a pair that would have cost a fraction of that in the UK. He cursed himself for not remembering to buy a pair at Heathrow.

There was no sign of Chadwick that evening. Left to their own devices, Howarth and Hawkins found a backstreet seafood restaurant where, he recalls, he had swordfish steak for the first time in his life. It was the best fish he had ever tasted. They later found their way back to the bar to which Chadwick had taken them the night before. It was Howarth's sort of place – loud music, plenty of beer and hash being smoked openly. They staggered back to their pension in the small hours and crashed out.

He has a hazy recollection of the following day, remembering only that, whatever they did, it involved drinking lots of beer. On Wednesday, 14 November 1990, it was time to get ready for six weeks at sea. Chadwick picked them up late morning and took them for a beer. Then they climbed into his car; he would take them to Gibraltar.

CHAPTER TWENTY-SIX

Howarth sat in the back of the car with the window wound down and his shades on. He smoked a joint and put his head back, enjoying the feel of the breeze in his hair and taking in the scenery. It's a 45-mile journey from San Pedro de Alcantara to Gibraltar along the coastal N-340 and he was chilling out, enjoying the scenery. In the front, Chadwick and Hawkins were blethering on, but he couldn't hear any of their conversation. He must have dozed off; he awoke with a start when Chadwick called out, 'Wake up, Chris. We're nearly there.'

He looked around him. They were driving along a seafront road. The Med sparkled brilliantly; across the water, though not visible, was Morocco. To the right of the road was a sprawling, ugly estate of high-rise flats. They were driving through La Linea de la Concepción, Gibraltar's Spanish neighbour, a rather ugly, industrial town whose main purpose appears to be to provide cheap labour for Gibraltar and Algeciras.

Chadwick pulled up outside a café, the Café Mirador, which overlooks the beach at La Linea, a few hundred yards shy of the border with Gibraltar. They ordered coffees and sat outside. Chadwick rummaged through a shoulder bag he had with him and pulled out a wad of money, around £500 in Gibraltar pounds. 'Expenses,' said Chadwick, counting it out. 'Should cover you for duty-free fags and booze. Make sure you don't buy all your cartons in one shop – they're looking out for fag smugglers so don't draw attention to yourselves.' He also handed over a large brown envelope to Howarth, instructing him to give it to the captain of the ship that they would be joining. Chadwick had become very businesslike. He drew them a rough map of Gibraltar, indicating where they were to meet their contact at 7 p.m. that evening. The contact would be wearing a navy pullover with a yacht motif; he would take them to the boat. Chadwick then told the men he had to get back to his flat at Estepona, down the road from San Pedro, and that he would see them in a few weeks. He jumped into his car, did a U-turn and sped off back the way he had come.

Howarth and Hawkins looked at each other. They had several hours to kill before meeting their contact. Beyond them, it was impossible to say when the sea became the sky. On the horizon, a large tanker could be seen, a trail of smoke coming from the funnel. The golden sand of the beach seemed to stretch for miles. Howarth shook himself and pulled himself to his feet. 'Come on then,' he said to Hawkins. 'Let's hit Gibraltar.'

The border was only a five-minute walk away. To cross it, one walked through a large set of gates, with Spanish police on one side and British police on the other. Howarth found it quite strange to see a solitary policeman wearing the same uniform as back home. There was no queue and the two men walked straight through the checkpoint, where they were told to wait. To reach the town, it was necessary to walk across a huge runway that protruded out into the harbour, the runway where, two-and-a-half years previously, in March 1988, three IRA members were shot dead in what was alleged to be a shoot-to-kill incident. Howarth and Hawkins were being held back to allow a plane to take off. After watching the jet hurtle across the runway, they saw it lift its nose before it reached the water and climb into the air, bound for London. They were then allowed to continue.

Over them loomed the Rock itself, which for centuries has been an extremely important strategic military site. From the top it is possible to see Morocco's Atlas mountains just 14 miles away and it has commanding views over the Straits of Gibraltar, where the Mediterranean meets the Atlantic and through which a quarter of the world's entire sea traffic passes. For the ancients, one of the twin Pillars of Hercules was the Rock of Gibraltar, and the other Jebel Musa in the Spanish enclave in Morocco, Ceuta. In mythology, Hercules reached the limits of the Mediterranean and raised two great columns upon which he inscribed '*Ne Plus Ultra*' – nothing further beyond – as this was the supposed limit of the known world.

Gibraltar seems an anomaly, a part of an overseas country that remains quintessentially British with red phone boxes, pubs and fish-and-chip shops. It has had an uneasy relationship with the Spanish, who, not unreasonably, want their territory back.

Howarth and Hawkins crossed the runway and made their way into the town by means of a gateway leading into Casemates Square, a large, open space with cafés and shops, which is the colony's main focal point. From Casemates Square, they headed up Main Street with its myriad duty-free shops selling everything from cameras to cigarettes. With cash burning a hole in his pocket, Howarth did what he always did in such circumstances. He looked for the nearest bar. Halfway up the crowded thoroughfare was an alley turning up to the left with a pub called The Cannon Bar. They headed in and downed a couple of pints in quick succession.

Howarth would have happily spent the next few hours in there getting pissed up, but Hawkins wanted to see the sights. He had heard about the cable-car trip to the top of the Rock and of the tailless Barbary apes that lived halfway up the Rock. Imported by the British from Morocco in the eighteenth century, they are reputed to be the only wild primates in Europe – other than the ones that spent Friday nights fighting at The Caley in Ullapool, of course. Hawkins wanted to take the trip. Howarth argued with him, saying it would be their last chance to sup a few pints for some weeks. 'Look, Chris, all we ever do is drink beer,' Hawkins pointed out, not unreasonably. 'We can do that in Ullapool, for fuck's sake. When are we going to get the chance to go up the Rock again? We might never be in Gibraltar again.' The same enquiring mind that would lead Hawkins to do a degree while in prison was expressing itself now. With a groan, Howarth said grumpily, 'Suit yourself, man.' He picked up his bag and they carried on up Main Street, sweating in the sun as they climbed the hill.

After ten minutes, they came to a cemetery for those killed in the Battle of Trafalgar. Howarth had had enough. 'Fuck this, Noel,' he said, throwing down his bag and sitting on a bench. 'I'm not going any further.' Howarth did not like not getting his own way. Hawkins attempted to remonstrate with him, saying: 'Come on, Chris, man, we're almost there. I really want to go up and see those apes.'

'Fuck the apes – I'm going to go fucking ape myself in a minute. I'm going to roll a joint here, I'm going to smoke it and then I'm going to go back to the pub for a few pints. You can do what you like.' With that, Howarth got up and went into the cemetery and found a bench to have a spliff in peace. He was getting hacked off with Hawkins.

Hawkins for his part stood there trying to decide what to do. Eventually, he came over to Howarth and as a sort of peace offering, said: 'Maybe you're right, Chris. Let's go and get a few pints.' It was getting later in the afternoon now and the sun was beginning to dip. It would be dark within a couple of hours and they still had three hours until they would meet their contact. Howarth knew exactly how to kill the time.

With a renewed spring in his step now he was getting his own way, he marched down Trafalgar Road and back down Main Street, Hawkins doing his utmost to keep up with him. He stopped at a pub several hundred yards down on the right called the Angry Friar. He looked at Hawkins, and said: 'Right, this'll do. Let's get a beer, for Christ's sake, and stop acting like kids.' Hawkins nodded his assent and they walked in.

Inside, the pub was a typical English affair, and could just as easily have been in Gillingham as Gibraltar. The long mahogany bar was festooned with brightly coloured card starbursts advertising its food. 'Chicken drumstix, only £2.99', 'Scampi in a basket, £3.95' and so on. Howarth ignored them and ordered two pints of strong lager and brought them over to the table. After several pints, he and Hawkins were laughing away like old mates, the ongoing tension between them forgotten for the moment. Eventually, he looked at the clock and said, 'Right, we'd better shift. I want to get some fags before we meet this guy.'

They picked up their holdalls and set off back into Main Street. Remembering Chadwick's advice about not buying all their cigarettes in one shop, they ducked into the first few duty-free shops they came to until they had bought about ten cartons each. That should keep them going for a few weeks. Night was closing in now and Main Street was beginning to lose its shoppers, and gaining those out looking for the nightlife that Howarth and Hawkins would not see. They headed back down the hill into Casemates Square, went through an arch in the great wall that surrounded it and soon found the bar where Chadwick had instructed them to meet their contact.

A sign on the door said, 'Closed until further notice.' 'Great,' thought Howarth. Well, they would just have to sit on the grass verge outside and wait for the guy to show. Just then, a man appeared around the corner and started to walk towards them. Howarth jumped to his feet and stretched out his hand in greeting, but the man simply gave him a funny look and walked past them. Hawkins began to laugh at this, saying, 'You twat, he probably thought you were begging.' Howarth felt his anger rising again at this, but bit his lip and said nothing. They didn't have to wait long.

A man appeared as if from nowhere and said, 'Chris, Noel, how you doing?' in a Spanish accent. He was short and plump, balding with a thick grey beard. Sure enough, he was wearing a navy pullover with a yacht motif. 'Come, please. My car is this way.' They followed him to the back of a building and through a door. They found themselves in a supermarket and walked straight through, trying to keep up with the man who was trotting at a brisk pace. Walking through the front door, they found themselves in the middle of Main Street, more or less opposite the Angry Friar. Howarth cursed. The way they had walked had taken them the best part of 30 minutes and now they were back there in less than five.

They reached a small hatchback and the man climbed into the driver's seat, opening the passenger door for Howarth and Hawkins to get in. It was a tight squeeze with their luggage on their laps but it would not be a long journey. He sped off down through the town towards the docks and slowed down as he drove past the main gates, peering intently at the guards who were on shift, before turning around and driving back around the way he had come. They did this for two circuits in silence; finally on the third run, he seemed to recognise a guard, gave him a wave and turned into the docks.

They pulled up and got out of the car. 'Right,' the man said. 'There is your ship out there,' waving an arm towards the dark outline of a 300-foot cargo ship out in the harbour. 'And here comes your taxi,' he added. They could make out an inflatable dinghy, and could hear the putt-putt of the outboard motor as it headed towards them. Someone had been expecting them. Suddenly, there was a scraping sound and the engine cut out before being restarted. They had misjudged their speed and hit the breakwater too fast, bouncing off it. Hawkins gave a snigger and said, 'I hope to Christ they don't berth the big one like that.' Hawkins was very good at handling small boats – Howarth had seen him in operation back in Ullapool – and there was no way he would have been so amateurish.

A head appeared over the wall, but in the darkness all they could make out was the man's eyes and teeth. Spotting Howarth and Hawkins, he called out, 'Hi, hi, hi' and waved them over. They would learn that that was about the sum of his English. They said goodbye to their contact and headed over to the inflatable. Arms reached up for their bags and the two men jumped down into the boat. There were four others in the inflatable, all chattering excitedly in Spanish. They patted Hawkins and Howarth on their backs by way of greeting, started up the motor and began to head back out to the big cargo ship in the harbour. It was beginning to rain. Even in the dark, he could tell that Hawkins was frowning, a worried expression on his face. In a quiet voice, he said to Howarth: 'I hope to fuck you know what you're getting us into.' Howarth said nothing. He wasn't convinced that he did.

CHAPTER TWENTY-SEVEN

Howarth felt scared now, nervous about what lay ahead. They were too heavily committed to turn back; he prayed to Christ that everything would be all right. He looked back at the receding docks and the orange glow of Gibraltar becoming smaller in the distance. One of the crew passed him a bottle, which he took out of politeness. He took a swig, then spluttered as the rough, fiery liquid hit the back of his throat. His eyes watering, he passed it to Hawkins, saying, 'I thinks it's brandy, but your guess is as good as mine.' Turning around, he could see the huge, dark hull of the ship looming; on the side was the ship's name, carelessly painted on, the *DIMAR-B* and, beneath it, the name of its home port, Balboa, in Galicia, north-west Spain. So this would be their home for the next six weeks, he mused as they came alongside.

One of the crew snatched at a rope ladder with wooden rungs that hung down from the deck 15 feet above their heads. He motioned for the two men to climb up and Howarth followed Hawkins. It wasn't an easy climb; the rungs were wet and greasy with oil or diesel. Finally, he reached the top. He was dazzled by the powerful lights that illuminated the deck; blinking, he pulled himself over the rail and swung down onto the deck. At the bow end, the forward end of the ship, was a climb up to the forepeak, which is where the ship was tied to a heavy mooring buoy. To the rear of the forepeak was a short, stubby mast with broken rungs and chipped, flaking paintwork.

Howarth silently told himself that he would never climb that mast. Moving aft, huge hatches ran the length of the deck, a good four feet high. There were smaller inspection hatches from time to time, all of which were open. Howarth climbed up and looked into one. Inside, it was dark and Howarth could not see the bottom. It was a big hold. He looked along the length of the deck towards the stern where he could see what had to be the galley and above it, the wheelhouse.

All around was a hive of activity. Engines and generators hummed and the crew shouted instructions to one another in a strange-sounding Spanish dialect. Another ship was alongside, pumping fresh water aboard the *DIMAR-B*. Howarth was joined by one of the men who had been on the inflatable. He took Howarth by the elbow and steered him towards the galley and wheelhouse. It was a relief to step in out of the driving rain. Howarth realised he was drenched through and through. Inside, they stepped into the galley. A fat, sweating cook was labouring over his oven, preparing something in a huge pot. From the smell, Howarth wasn't sure if he was cooking or simply boil-washing his underwear. His newfound friend thrust a mug of coffee into Howarth's hand, which he gratefully took. The man nodded towards the sugar bowl and Howarth heaped three spoonfuls into the mug. He needed this. He sat down at a table that was bolted to the floor, with a bench either side of it, big enough to seat eight people at a go.

He looked around him. The galley was a large room, around 20 feet long and 15 feet wide. There were several doors off it; in time, he would learn that these included toilets and showers, a TV room for the crew and one that led to the captain's quarters and the wheelhouse. There was also a passage to one side, filled with oilskins and wet weather gear. Halfway along the passage was a large hatch with steep rungs leading down into the interior of the ship. The fat cook had a counter and work surface at one end of the room where he worked away. Pots and pans hung above his head along with large legs of smoked ham, swaying back and forth in the gentle swell.

The cook opened a huge fridge to fetch something and Howarth could see that it was well stocked. Clearly, the ship had just taken delivery of supplies. Empty boxes lay all around him. The cook took a bottle from the fridge and, lifting the lid from his pot to allow a cloud of steam to escape, added a few drops to his concoction. With a spoon, he took a slurp and murmured in approval. 'By Christ,' thought Howarth, 'I hope it tastes better than it smells.' Just then, the noise increased as the door to the deck opened, and a crewman came in carrying Howarth's bags. He dropped them at Howarth's feet without saying a word and disappeared through the aft door. Howarth followed him into a small, carpeted passage with doors off to the left – the showers and toilets. On the wall were a couple of aerial photographs of the ship, taken in better days, when she stood proud and elegant against the blue seas. She had come down in the world since then.

At the end of the passageway was a door through which the man disappeared. Howarth followed him through the door, where there was a flight of carpeted stairs. To the left was another door through which he could hear Hawkins's voice so he pushed the door open and went in. The room was luxury compared to the rest of the ship, carpeted with plush seats and pictures on the wooden-cladded walls. Through one of the portholes, he could see the fresh-water ship pulling away, thankfully taking most of the noise with it.

A short, somewhat chubby man with a beard, no more than 25, jumped to his feet, saying, 'Hi, Chris, good to meet you. I am the captain. You can call me Franco,' he added, thrusting a paw out towards Howarth. 'Please sit down,' he insisted, waving an arm expansively towards the comfortable seats. Hawkins was already sprawled in one, enjoying a bottle of beer and as Howarth sat down, the genial captain was already handing him one. Howarth handed him the envelope Chadwick had given him and the captain opened it and pulled out a bunch of maps and sea-charts. Just then, the door opened again and three well-dressed men with heavy gold jewellery and watches came into the room, bringing with them a waft of expensive aftershave, which made Howarth's eyes sting.

The captain jumped up and bustled over to greet the men, introducing them to Howarth and Hawkins without telling Howarth and Hawkins in return who they were. They all shook hands, eyeing each other with deep suspicion. One of the men looked intently at Howarth with his black eyes and held his hand longer than was comfortable, saying, 'Remember, you must not touch the cargo.' Howarth laughed nervously; no one else smiled. They then turned to the captain and spoke rapidly in Spanish to him. Judging by the nods they made towards Howarth and Hawkins, it was clear that they were the topic of conversation. Eventually, they seemed satisfied and one pulled out an enormous bundle of banknotes, handing it to the captain, who pulled a hinged picture to one side to reveal a safe. He turned the dial three times in opposite directions and, as it opened, Howarth got a glimpse of lots more money and papers before it swung shut again.

The captain sat down, saying to the three men, 'We shall speak English now as our friends do not speak Spanish and we must not display ignorance.' Turning to Howarth, he said in a friendly manner, 'So, Chris, tell us a little about yourself and what life is like in Scotland.' Howarth couldn't think what to say and spent five minutes chattering aimlessly about Ullapool, diving and Fiona and the kids. It was clear from the way that the captain fiddled with his beard and looked at his watch that he wasn't really interested and was simply being polite. Eventually, their three visitors put Howarth out of his misery by interrupting to say they had to leave. The captain went out of the room with them and, when he came back, said in response to the question he could see framing on Howarth's lips: 'Those men are the owners,' – whether of the ship or the drugs, he didn't say. It was clear that he was now more relaxed. He offered them another beer each and joined them, chatting in a more relaxed manner. When he saw Howarth yawning, he said: 'But you must be tired. This is enough conversation for one night; we can talk again tomorrow.' He called one of the crew and told him to show the two men to their quarters, pleasantly bidding them goodnight, before opening a door to what was clearly his cabin, with a bunk, desk and comfortable seat.

Howarth and Hawkins followed the man back into the galley, where the fat cook was still slaving over his pot, grease and sweat pouring down his face. The tiled floor was as filthy as his bloodstained apron upon which he continually rubbed his hands. Howarth picked up his bag from the table where he had left it and they headed back the way they had come. When they reached the large hatch in the stern passageway, the man climbed down the ladder, beckoning for the two to follow him. The ladder seemed to go on and on but eventually they found themselves in a long gangway about seven feet wide running the length of the ship.

Looking along the length of it, there were doors off to either side. Immediately to their right, one door was open, revealing the ship's stores. Howarth was pleased to note that it was piled high with boxes of food, bottles of wine and yet more hams. If he could get over the revulsion he felt for the cook, he thought wryly, he'd live well on the ship. As they walked down the corridor, he saw that the white paint was yellowing and flaking, in places showing the rusty hull behind. They passed another corridor leading off to the right but continued on. The

TO OPEN: TEAR DOWN PERFORATIONS AND PEEL APART

WENTWORTH (01924 444501) Ref. 6609

ship seemed even bigger once on board than it did from the outside. Finally, they reached a door at the bow end, which would be their cabin. Opposite, another door opened onto the engine room with a 20-foot ladder leading down to it. Engine parts and tools littered the floor and in the middle was the huge black engine that powered the ship.

Their guide slipped noiselessly back the way he had come and they entered the cabin. He had seen worse. Two bunks lay on the right-hand side with the pillows at the same end as a porthole through which only the night could be seen. It was as tatty as the rest of the ship with peeling paintwork, cheap Formica and wood-edged furniture, and threadbare carpet. He turned on the tap in the small sink and a brown sludgy liquid came out. Hawkins said, 'I wouldn't drink that, if I were you. Apparently there's drinking water in the cupboard.' Howarth checked. Sure enough, there were several cases of bottled water, enough to keep them going.

Howarth sat down at the small table and lit a cigarette. He was dead tired, but still buzzing on adrenalin. It had been a big day. 'Well, what do you make of all of this, then?' he asked Hawkins, who had stretched out on the top bunk. There was no reply. Hawkins was already fast asleep. Howarth realised he was still drenched from the rain so stripped off and put on clean underwear and a T-shirt before climbing into the bottom bunk and lying on his sleeping bag. He turned out the light, but, despite his exhaustion, lay there unable to sleep for a while. He felt very apprehensive and very alone. Thank God Hawkins was with him, he thought. They may have their differences, he reflected, but this would all be just too weird to face on his own. Before he knew it, he was in a deep sleep, dreaming of Ullapool, and Fiona. He would not see them for some time.

CHAPTER TWENTY-EIGHT

The next morning, he was woken by the noise of the engine, which seemed unbearably loud. He would have to get used to it. The room was dark and gloomy, with precious little sunlight coming in through the porthole. The ship was rolling and outside there was no sign of land. Howarth shouted up to Hawkins, but there was no reply. He jumped out of his bunk to find Hawkins's bunk empty.

First things first. He lit a cigarette and sat on the edge of the bunk. He switched the light on, which only served to make the cabin look even more tatty. When he finished his smoke, he washed himself in the viscous brown water at the sink, taking care not to swallow any. Next he brushed his teeth, squeezing a little paste onto his toothbrush and dribbling some of the drinking water over it. It wasn't ideal, but it was better than nothing. Suddenly, the engine noise rose massively before dying away again. Somebody must have opened the door to the engine room. He stuck his head out the door and looked along the length of the corridor but there was no sign of anybody. He closed the door and went over to the porthole, opening it to gulp down a few lungfuls of fresh air.

Seagulls wheeled and circled overhead, doubtless following the ship in the hope that scraps would be thrown overboard. The sea was a deep blue with the occasional white cap in the distance, though other than that, it was a perfect sunny, silvery day. It was time to get up on deck. He wanted to meet the rest of the crew and have a look around the vessel that would be his home for the next few weeks.

The corridor lights were all on as he headed out. It felt strange to walk with the rolling gait of the ship. Howarth was used to smaller yachts, which were jerkier and more reactive than this ship, whose movement was slow and rolling as it pitched on the waves. He would soon get used to it. He clutched at the handrail, which ran along the corridor, interrupted only by the doors to the cabin where it was replaced by a sissy bar, a rail to clutch at for those who had not found their sea legs. Howarth was not ashamed to take advantage of it, even if it meant he was a sissy for now, he joked to himself.

As he neared the end of the corridor, the fat cook came out of the stores. He didn't see Howarth and turned back towards the steep steps up to the galley. With a shock, Howarth saw that he had a body slung over his shoulder. Then, with relief, he realised it was the headless body of a pig. Where the head had been, only a dripping stump remained, spilling blood and gristle down the man's already filthy back. He must have just decapitated it, Howarth concluded. As he went to climb the steps, he noticed Howarth and nodded in recognition. Howarth stepped forward to help, but the cook motioned him away. It was clear that he had managed it on his own hundreds of times.

Watching him climb up, Howarth grinned as he reflected that it was impossible to tell where the pig ended and the man began as his enormous buttocks spilled over the waistband of his trousers. It was no sight for the faint-hearted to watch the mountains of flesh, both pig and man, disappear through the suddenly small hatch at the top. As Howarth climbed up, the cook's face suddenly appeared again. He thrust a rag at Howarth and indicated that he should wipe the stairs. His first job on board, Howarth reflected cheerfully as he began to wipe the blood and gristle from the rungs.

By the time he had finished and climbed up to the galley, the cook was back at his worktop, lifting a heavy cleaver over his shoulder and bringing it down on what was left of the pig. Howarth offered him back his rag and, giving him a dirty look, the cook snatched it from him, flinging it under the counter where it lay among a pile of rotting cabbage leaves and potato peelings.

Howarth looked over to the table where two of the crew were playing cards. One was dressed in black jeans and T-shirt and had a gold tooth that sparkled when he smiled. He looked over to Howarth and smiled at him, indicating that Howarth should come and sit next to him. Howarth went and sat down and realised that the guy was older than he first appeared. Judging by the deep, heavy lines etched into his face and neck and his milky eyeballs that were showing early signs of cataracts, he must have been around 60. The other man was small and squat, a pot-holed face testament to the ravages of youthful acne. He had heavy, lazy eyelids and short curly, black hair.

Howarth watched as they played. He couldn't understand the game. It certainly wasn't poker or, at least, not a variation that he'd ever seen. The two men were taking it in turns to slam down cards, going faster and faster like a wild dance. Suddenly the one with the gold tooth let out a cry of glee and scooped up all the cards. He had clearly won. The other man scowled, got up and sloped off. 'Bad loser,' said Howarth's new friend to him, winking conspiratorially. After putting the cards back in the pack, he looked at Howarth once more, this time slowly, as though examining him. Finally, he said, 'You must be Chris.' Howarth was warming to this man. 'Yes, I am,' he replied. 'And you are . . . ?' 'Jorge,' the man completed the sentence for him, offering his hand. Howarth took it and shook it firmly. 'And the other one?' he asked. 'Oh, him,' said Jorge. 'We call him Chito.' And he laughed, as though at some private joke – the men involved in such a risky operation were unlikely to be using their real names. Howarth liked this guy, though. He said he'd see him later and headed out on deck.

The sun hit him straight away. 'Thank Christ I bought those shades,' he thought. He could see Chito leaning over the stern, looking down at the white wash from the churning propeller below. When Chito caught sight of Howarth, he smiled, then raised one finger to his lips while rolling his eyes upwards to the wheelhouse. 'El capitán,' he mouthed, 'he no see.' With that, he surreptitiously passed Howarth a half-smoked joint in his cupped hand. Howarth understood. As events would later prove, the captain might be a big-time drugs smuggler, but he didn't tolerate it on his ship. For him, it was clearly a simple matter of business.

Chito headed off, carrying two bins back to the galley that he had just emptied overboard. Howarth stayed smoking the joint, watching the gulls swoop for scraps in the wake of the boat. He finished the joint and flicked the roach down into the wash. He wondered what he should do. About his feet lay numerous lengths of rope so he set about coiling them into some semblance of order. A glance at his watch told him that it was not yet 11 a.m. It would be a slow few weeks.

He set off to walk the length of the ship and explore his new habitat. There was by now a welcome and cooling breeze. Halfway along, he stopped and leant on the rail, looking out to the sea that had played such a big role in his life. It never ceased to amaze him how beautiful it was. He carried on towards the bow when something flashing in the sea caught his eye. There it was again. After a minute or two, he twigged. Dolphins! Of course! He could have kicked himself for not realising straight away. He had seen them hundreds of times before, yet they continued to hold some fascination for him, these beautiful, sleek creatures with their mouths in a perpetual grin, full of playfulness and sport. He climbed up a ladder onto the bow deck and stood watching them leap out of the water, darting back and forth just ahead of the ship's bow in some sort of game of marine tag.

There must have been three or four dozen of them playing, not so much a school as a university of dolphins. Enrapt, Howarth watched them for half an hour or more. Eventually, he turned around and looked back down the length of the ship towards the wheelhouse at the stern end. He could see a figure on the bridge waving at him. It was Hawkins. He was shouting something, his hands cupped over his mouth, but the wind whipped the words away. Howarth shrugged to show he couldn't hear and indicated that he would come and join him. He walked back along the deck to the side of the galley where there was a set of steel rungs leading up to the wheelhouse. He climbed up to find the captain standing with Hawkins.

Howarth had to stop himself laughing at the sight of the captain. A short, chubby Hispanic man – more like a boy, Howarth thought – with a beard, he cut a ridiculous figure in long Bermuda shorts, flip-flops and an open-necked flowery Hawaiian shirt. On the deck were two or three life rafts and, in the middle, the enormous funnel from which smoke poured every few moments, sending out with it a little shower of soot. It didn't look as though keeping the ship clean was a huge priority.

Hawkins was grinning excitedly. 'This is great, man,' he said. 'You've got to see this.' Howarth followed him into the wheelhouse. At odds with the shoddy appearance of the rest of the ship, the wheelhouse was a shrine to state-of-the-art technology. There were banks of navigation instruments, ultra-modern radio gear, what looked like a fax, up-to-the-minute radar . . . Howarth looked through the radarscope and was impressed. Instead of the old-style radar with its sweeping line and circular motion, this was more like a computer screen. He could see the ship in the centre of the screen with the Iberian landmass behind it. The only problem was they appeared to be heading due west. Before he could think about this, the captain appeared at his shoulder. 'That's some radar you've got there,' Howarth said approvingly. The captain smiled proudly and patted the bulkhead. 'She's an old lady now, but she's still got life in her.' Howarth saw some steps leading to an alcove that functioned as a chart room. He went in and sat at the bench, on which was spread a map of the Atlantic. On the map a neat line had been drawn from Gibraltar to a spot north-west of Trinidad. Above him was an instrument giving their longitude and latitude.

Howarth began to plot their position the old-fashioned way, using dividers and parallel rules. As far as he could tell, they were following the line towards South America due west of Spain. There had to be a mistake. He did it again to make sure he had got it right. He had. The captain was watching his calculations over his shoulder with a bemused expression. 'We are here?' Howarth asked, pointing to the spot he had marked. 'Yes,' said the captain with a half-smile. 'But we should be going here,' said Howarth, tapping Portugal on the chart, assuming that the original plan to head for Vilamoura held good. The captain frowned and leaned over him to tap a spot near Trinidad. 'No – we go here,' he said. Howarth flushed red at his ignorance. 'What the fuck is going on?' he asked himself.

The captain turned and walked away, bored of this game. Howarth sat there, trying to take in what he now knew. It didn't take a genius to work out the reason why they might be heading to South America, particularly if Chadwick had anything to do with it. He got up and went back into the wheelhouse. Hawkins was still smiling, enjoying his adventure. That smile won't last long when he finds out our true destination, Howarth told himself grimly.

CHAPTER TWENTY-NINE

Just then, another crew member entered the room. The captain introduced him as his second-in-command, the ship's mate, calling him Sesu. Sesu barely looked at Howarth or Hawkins. He looked to be in his late thirties, with a fresh complexion and dirty blond hair down to his shoulders. He seemed to have more of a northern European appearance than a Spanish one, Howarth thought. Something about the man made Howarth feel very uneasy. At that moment, the fat cook's head appeared at the top of the steps, shouting something in Spanish before disappearing again. It was time for dinner.

Howarth realised he was starving and put aside the revulsion he felt for the cook. In the galley, six of the crew were sitting around the table – there would have to be a second sitting – and Jorge gestured for Howarth to sit next to him. The cook brought over two bowls for each man and returned carrying a huge pot, from which he ladled out some sort of bisque into one of the bowls in front of Howarth. In the soup were dozens of what Howarth thought were baby octopuses but soon realised were, in fact, cuttlefish. He watched as the others started to wolf it down and soon learnt what the second bowl was for as his fellow diners spat out the backbones of the tiny creatures and tossed them into the spare bowl. Howarth ate as much of the foul sludge as he could stomach, out of politeness, but prayed that there would be another course.

He was not disappointed. The cook collected up the bowls and returned a moment later, banging down an enormous leg of lamb in a roasting tin on the table. Mountains of roast potatoes and vegetables followed shortly after, and then it was every man for himself. Howarth did not restrain himself out of any misguided social nicety. This was only the second proper meal he had eaten since leaving Ullapool five days earlier and he was determined to make the most of it. He saw with satisfaction that he managed to heap more onto his plate than anyone else. He made light work of it.

After the meal, Chito looked over at him with his heavy-lidded eyes and gestured for Howarth to join him on deck. As the captain, Hawkins and Sesu sat down for their meal, he followed Chito out. They walked the length of the ship and sat on the foredeck. It was blisteringly hot in the midday sun, but at least it was sheltered from the wind. Chito lit a long, slender joint and sucked greedily on it. He winced in pain as he sat down. As neither of them spoke much of the other's language, they sat in silence, passing the joint back and forth between them in a ritual universally recognised by smokers and tokers. Eventually, Chito looked at him and, putting a finger over one nostril, mimicked snorting. 'You like coca?' he asked, his eyes darting around him lest he be overheard. 'I don't know,' said Howarth slowly so that Chito would understand. 'I've never had any.' Chito nodded his comprehension, handed Howarth the rest of the joint and limped off. 'What a strange chap,' thought Howarth. In fact, the whole trip was beginning to feel very surreal. It would get a lot more so.

Pleasantly stoned, Howarth fell asleep. The strange dreams were back. He had been kidnapped by a bunch of pirates and was being forced to walk the plank. Just as he hit the water, he awoke with a start. His shorts and T-shirt were indeed wet; the sea had become choppy and, with the swell, the odd wave was pouring over the rail onto the deck. Straight ahead of them, the sun was beginning its gradual descent, Phoebus in his chariot making his journey home as the ancients had it. Still heading west then, thought Howarth automatically. He headed back to the bow and made his way down to his cabin to put on jeans and a fleece.

In the cabin, the porthole was completely submerged like a fish tank as the ship rolled to the starboard side. Howarth sat on the edge of his bunk with his head in his hands. He was beginning to get a very bad feeling about this whole enterprise. He got up and headed back in search of human company. As he came out of his cabin, the door to the engine room opposite opened and Jorge appeared, gold tooth gleaming as he grinned at Howarth. The noise was deafening. Jorge gestured to Howarth to come in. He was inviting him to visit his domain. Howarth nodded in acceptance and Jorge handed him a pair of earmuffs that hung inside the door.

He followed Jorge down the ladder into the well of the engine room. The rails were greasy with oil, but he climbed down the 15-foot drop without incident. Jorge poured oil into a duct at the side of the huge engine, then beckoned for Howarth to follow him. He led him past the engine to a door on the far wall leading to his cabin. Inside, it was a mess. Clothes, pornographic magazines and an old guitar lay strewn across the floor and bunk. Jorge swept a pile off the bed to join the mess on the floor, patting the vacated spot and inviting Howarth to sit, which he did. Jorge reached into a locker and pulled out a bottle and two glasses, which he cleaned with some toilet paper before filling the glasses with a fiery, amber liquid. He downed his in one and Howarth did the same, feeling a burning sensation that warmed him to the core.

Jorge began to roll a joint and the two men attempted to chat, although Jorge's English was limited. The door opened and Chito came in. Howarth nodded and to his surprise, Chito said, 'Hello. You OK?'

Howarth said that he thought Chito didn't speak English, but Chito laughed and explained that he didn't want the captain to catch him speaking to Howarth so he pretended not to speak English at all when the captain was around – and it was better to keep it that way. Howarth asked him if he knew what they were doing here, and where they were heading. Chito gave him an amused look and said, 'You do not know where we going?' Howarth told him he didn't have a clue. Chito laughed, and said, 'We go to Caribbean for shipment.'

'A shipment of what?' asked Howarth, although he had a sinking feeling that he knew what was coming.

Chito was becoming uneasy. He looked at the door as if to check no one was there before whispering, '500 kilos of cocaine.'

Howarth nearly choked. 'You fucking what?' he spluttered, but Chito put his hand over his mouth to warn him to keep his voice down.

Chito looked at him in amazement. 'You do not know this? Then why are you here?'

Howarth's knee was twitching uncontrollably now, adrenaline pumping through his system. 'My God,' he said in shock. 'Half a fucking tonne of cocaine. That's it, I'm fucked.'

Chito looked at him without sympathy. He did not seem to believe that Howarth did not know the purpose of their journey. Howarth got up as though in a daze, his mind befuddled by the dope, alcohol and the news that he had just heard. He picked his way back through the engine room, climbed the ladder and headed for his cabin.

When he opened the door, he could see Hawkins stretched out on the bunk. His eyes jerked open at the sudden noise. 'Will you keep that fucking noise down? I'm trying to get some kip here.'

Howarth was in no mood for this. 'Shut the fuck up. We've got to talk. Let me roll a joint first. I think you're going to need it.' After expertly putting a number together, he passed it to Hawkins, who was watching him intently, his head propped up on one arm. 'Right,' said Howarth. 'Do you know why we're here?'

'Not really,' Hawkins replied nonchalantly.

'Well, how does half a tonne of coke suit you, then?' said Howarth. If he'd been expecting a shocked reaction from Hawkins, he was disappointed. The younger man showed no reaction. 'Look,' said Howarth, 'we've got to get off this ship. We can take one of the life rafts, there'll be stows for nine men. That'll keep us going until we get picked up.'

'Don't be daft, man,' said Hawkins. 'We're south of the shipping lanes here; no one's going to pass us.'

Howarth felt annoyed at Hawkins's stoical attitude. 'Look,' he said, 'Work it out for yourself. We're not on the crew list. If a US patrol boat turns up, what do you think they'll do.'

'I don't know, why don't you tell me?' said Hawkins.

'I'll tell you what they'll do. They'll slit our throats and throw us overboard.'

'Don't talk shit,' said Hawkins.

'I'm not talking shit, that's exactly what they'll do,' said Howarth. 'And I know who's going to do it as well. That cunt Sesu.'

'Look,' said Hawkins, attempting to be reasonable. 'The captain's told me all about it. They're going to build a cage on a sloping rail to put the gear in. If there's any sign of trouble, they slash the rope holding the cage and the whole thing shoots overboard. We'll be fine.'

Howarth looked at him in amazement. He clearly knew all about it. The time he'd been spending up in the wheelhouse with the captain hadn't been wasted, then. He might be only 20, but he was a pretty cool customer. Howarth sat fuming. Eventually he said, 'I should have known that slippery cunt Jonathan would get us into shit.'

'Why don't you take it up with him, then?' suggested Hawkins helpfully. 'He's on the radio to the captain the whole time. I heard them when I was up in the wheelhouse.'

'Christ, what else had he found out?' thought Howarth. They spent the next hour talking about the situation, with Howarth urging him to help him escape on a lifeboat. Eventually, Hawkins said, 'OK, Chris, whatever you say. Let's just pick the right moment, OK?'

'OK.' Howarth agreed. At least they had a plan now.

The two men got off their bunks to head up to the galley. Their stomachs told them it must be nearly time for supper. As they got ready to leave the cabin, Hawkins said casually, without looking at Howarth, 'There's one other thing I should tell you.'

'What's that, then?' enquired Howarth.

'These guys are with the Basque separatists. Pretty hardcore, I get the impression.'

Howarth stared open-mouthed at his departing back. Basque separatists? That was all he fucking needed.

Hawkins confirms many aspects of Howarth's account of what occurred on the *DIMAR-B*, although he says that there was never any real plan to escape from the ship in a lifeboat, that they joked about it from time to time but it never went any further than that. He says that Howarth began to crack up on the ship, becoming paranoid, aggressive and given to bouts of binge drinking. As Hawkins says, 'By the time we made it back to Scotland, everyone was well and truly sick of Chris – me, the captain, the crew, everyone.' For the record, Hawkins does not have any bad words to say about the crew. 'Everyone on the ship was perfectly friendly to me. I was sorry when I heard what eventually happened to Francisco, the captain, he was an alright guy.'

One can speculate that it is Hawkins's refreshing willingness to take responsibility for his actions that has allowed him to put his mistake behind him and rebuild his life. Even though he was only 20 at the time of this trip, he would frequently display a maturity beyond his years.

CHAPTER THIRTY

Over the next ten days, little changed on board. Howarth felt truly alone and wished he had never got involved. He and Hawkins were barely on speaking terms, Hawkins choosing to spend more of his time in the company of the captain. Finally, on Wednesday, 28 November 1990, things came to a head.

For their evening meal, the cook had prepared another cuttlefish bisque. Howarth watched Hawkins shovelling the soup into his mouth, spitting out the bones, until he felt he would be sick. 'I can't eat that fucking shit again,' said Howarth. Hawkins didn't bother to reply, or even to raise his eyes from his meal. 'Oh, fuck this,' Howarth shouted, jumping up from the table. The cook scowled at him, then turned his back to stir something in a pot on the stove. As he did so, Howarth caught sight of a box of Mars bars. While the cook's back was turned he snaffled five or six, like a naughty schoolboy at the corner shop. Muttering to himself, he headed back to his cabin to be alone.

In the corridor downstairs, he bumped into the captain coming up from the engine room. 'Chris, I wanted to speak to you,' said the captain. 'You weren't on watch today. What happened?'

Howarth flushed angrily. Who the fuck did this little twat think he was? 'I fancied a day off. What about it?' he said defiantly.

'Well, you must ask me if you want time off. While you are on my ship, you will do as I say. You are working for me until you get back to Scotland.'

'Fuck that,' Howarth blazed, 'I've had it up to here with this shit. And until I've spoken to that cunt Jonathan, I work for me, not you. Got that?'

With that, he stormed into his cabin, slamming the door behind him. He wolfed down his stolen chocolate until he felt sick then paced up and down the tiny cabin. He felt like a caged animal. Finally, he cracked. He needed to get properly pissed tonight. He stormed up to the galley, marched up to the fridge and grabbed a bottle of wine. As he pulled it out, the ship lurched as it rolled violently and the bottle slipped out of his hand, smashing on the floor. At the sound of smashing glass, several of the crew ran in, including the captain.

It is taboo to fight at sea as men are forced to rely on each other to survive. Hearing the bottle smash, they assumed the worst and came at a sprint. 'There will be no fighting on this ship,' the captain shouted, his eyes blazing. The red mist descended and the veins on Howarth's neck began to bulge. He pointed at the captain, screaming, 'You'll fucking know about it when I'm going to fight 'cos you'll be the first to get a bottle over your head.' At that, he laughed manically and pushed past the astonished group on to the stern deck where he came face to face with Sesu. 'And you, you fucking cunt,' Howarth roared, 'one word out of you and I'll fucking drop you.' He lunged at Sesu, who darted out of his way and ran into the galley. Howarth went after him but the captain stood in his way. 'Do you want some, then?' Howarth shouted at him. 'None of you fucking scare me any more. I've had it with the lot of you. Now get me a fucking drink, a proper one. None of that piss you call wine.' The captain just stared at him as though he was demented, which, of course, he was. 'Right, fuck you, then,' swore Howarth, 'I'll get one myself.'

He ran past the captain through the TV room into the captain's lounge. He had seen a case of vodka here the first night he'd been on the ship. It had to be here somewhere. He kicked the door to the captain's cabin open and saw the case of vodka on the floor by his desk, grabbed a bottle and turned to leave. The captain was blocking his passage along with three of the crew. Howarth held the bottle by the neck and brandished it at them. The captain said something to the crew and reluctantly they moved back to allow Howarth through. Howarth opened the bottle and took a swig, grimacing at the taste. He would have to get some Coke to wash it down. He laughed at the thought. Soon he would have all the coke he wanted.

Hawkins appeared, appealing to Howarth to calm down. 'Calm down? We're trapped on this fucking ship and all you can say is, "Calm down".' Howarth pushed past him and went out on deck. The night air was cool and felt good. He made his way to his favourite spot in the bow and sat looking at the stars, drinking the vodka. 'What am I doing here?' he thought in despair. 'Please, God, just let me get back to Fiona and the kids and I swear I will lead a normal life.' God wasn't listening. Getting drunker and drunker, Howarth stood on the deck howling into the night like a grief-stricken wild beast, his face streaked with tears. He finished the bottle and, thankfully, fell into a deep sleep.

Back in Ullapool the following night, at 10 p.m. on Thursday, 29 November 1990, Customs officers Craig Paterson and Tony Jackson were keeping an eye on Robbie Burns and Tony McDonald. They were in The Caley within earshot of the two men. They pretended to be making small talk over their pints but were listening intently to Burns and McDonald's conversation. Someone came into the bar and said hello to Burns and McDonald and asked them where Crazy Chris was. 'Och,' said Burns, 'Crazy's away in Spain. I got a postcard off him the other day saying he was well skint and thinking about heading back home.' Then Burns asked McDonald whether he wanted to see the boat and the two headed out of the pub.

They left their drinks and cigarettes on the table so Paterson and Jackson rightly deduced that they wouldn't be gone for long. Sure enough, the two men returned one minute later. They noted that Burns and McDonald were having a conversation about Crazy being 'drunk on board' and shouting, 'Is there anybody there?' They seemed concerned about his antics. Clearly, information about the ship's progress was getting back to Ullapool, presumably from Chadwick, who was in constant radio contact with the ship. It should be noted that there is no suggestion that Tony MacDonald knew of, or was involved with, the imminent drugs run – no charges were ever brought against him.

Back at sea, that morning Howarth had awoken with a throbbing hangover when the morning sun hit the bow deck. He slowly got to his feet and stretched, feeling stiff all over. At the far end of the ship, he could see Hawkins wave at him from the wheelhouse. Howarth would have to face the embarrassment caused by his antics the previous night.

He climbed up to the wheelhouse and nodded at Hawkins, saying, 'All right, Noel? How's it going?' Hawkins shook his head with a weary smile. 'That was some show last night. True Crazy Chris style.' Just then, the captain came around the corner, carrying a bowl of porridge. 'All right, Franco?' asked Howarth, testing the water. The captain did not deign to reply, simply giving Howarth a filthy look as he walked past. Howarth's blood boiled. Turning to Hawkins, in a voice loud enough to be heard by the captain, he said, 'Right, you can tell that cunt to go and fuck himself. I don't work for him – I work for me. I don't give a fuck about his shitty boat or his crew.'

With that, he turned and went back to his cabin, where he fantasised about being back in Ullapool with Fiona and the kids. Outside, a bad storm had hit them from the east, waking Howarth from his reverie as the boat lurched violently onto its starboard side. It was pitch black and, through the porthole, he could see forked lightning illuminating the violent black swell of the ocean. He glanced at his watch and saw that it was not yet 4 p.m. The boat rolled violently back the other way, onto its port side. Howarth put his head under the pillow, whimpering like a child. 'My God, why me?' he asked. No one was listening.

Over the next few days, Howarth felt truly alone. Since his crazed outburst, no one was talking to him and everyone kept out of his way. The storm lasted for several days and Howarth spent most of the time in his cabin, driven out only by hunger. On one such expedition to the galley to make himself a sandwich, he came face to face with the captain. Franco looked at him with something approaching a friendly expression. 'Hi, Chris,' he said pleasantly. 'How's it going?' It was as though the events of the previous few days had not taken place. Then, looking intently at Howarth with his black eyes, he said, 'You like to drink, Chris? OK, we drink. Come.' Howarth followed him through the TV room, where an old Norman Wisdom film dubbed into Spanish was playing. He led the way to his cabin, which, although no larger than Howarth and Hawkins's one, was fitted out with a sound system of which any household would be proud.

The captain pulled out a CD and put it on. It was one of Howarth's favourites, 'The Whole of the Moon' by the Waterboys. As the mournful lyrics sang of wandering out in the world for years, while the singer's love sat at home in her room, Howarth's thoughts turned to Fiona. He pictured her making supper, giving the kids a bath, watching *EastEnders* . . . Christ, how he longed to be in her arms again!

The captain pulled open the door of his wardrobe where he had stashed his vodka after Howarth's earlier stunt. As he did so, Howarth caught sight of a rack of rifles and some handguns. Howarth's heart sank. What was he doing here? The captain pulled out a bottle and, removing the top, threw it in the bin. A man after Howarth's own heart. The captain filled two tumblers to the brim and, handing one to Howarth, said, 'I, Chris, like to drink as well but not when I work. I am off watch now so now we drink.'

As Howarth took a draft of the fiery liquid, the captain studied him intently. Turning down the music, he adopted a serious manner. 'Chris, I now know that you did not understand the true purpose of our voyage.' He spread his hands in a conciliatory gesture. 'That, I cannot help. I am captain of this ship, and have a job to do, which I do well and I expect you to do your part. You are too far in for it to be otherwise. Your argument is with Jonathan. In the meantime, you and I both have jobs to do. You must do as you are told.'

Howarth reflected on what he had said. 'And if I don't?' The captain tutted and shook his head. 'Then I will have to make you do it, one way or another. It is out of my hands.' Howarth felt trapped.

Changing the subject, the captain said, 'Let me show you something.' He opened a drawer of his desk and pulled out an ink stamp, the type used by passport officials. It was a Nazi stamp, he said proudly, given to him by a friend in South America. Howarth could see the word 'Belsen' engraved on it, along with the German imperial eagle.

He recoiled and saw that the captain was now taking out an accompanying inkpad with Nazi insignia. Howarth pushed them away. He was not unduly squeamish, but this sort of shit was just too sick.

The captain saw his distress and tactfully put them away. Now it was Howarth's turn to change the subject. He asked the captain what his usual cargo was. 'Cocaine, heroin, anything that pays a lot of money,' he replied. 'If you wish to join us, and stop behaving so badly, you could make a lot of money. After this run, we are heading to Pakistan to pick up several tonnes of the best black.' Howarth told him that he would prefer to keep away from anything to do with Class A drugs, but wouldn't mind doing hash runs. The captain laughed. 'Good, good. I like you, Chris, but you drink too much.' Howarth sheepishly mumbled that his wife felt the same way.

'What other runs have you done in the past?' he asked.

The captain looked into space thoughtfully. 'Well, we made a lot of money from blacks in west Africa,' he said. Howarth asked how. 'For $6,000 a head, blacks would pay us to get them out of the country and take them to Europe.' Howarth asked how they managed it without papers. The captain paused to refill their tumblers. Howarth was beginning to feel woozy from the drink. 'We docked, unloaded our cargo and then that night, we loaded up the blacks. We pay off the port guards. We load up oil drums with air holes in them. Inside are the black bastards.' Howarth hated the way he spoke of these people and told him so. The captain looked at him in amazement. 'But they are only animals,' he protested. Howarth did not want to get into an argument about race so told him to continue. 'OK, so we put the drums in the hold, up to 50 at a time. A lot of money,' he laughed, rubbing thumb and forefinger together. Howarth was fascinated, despite the revulsion he felt for this short, fat, bearded man. 'Which country did you take them to?' he asked. The captain looked straight ahead. 'We take them out to sea, 10 or 12 hours from shore we pull them from the hold.' He opened the cupboard and pulled out one of the rifles, a Kalashnikov. 'Then we throw the black bastards over the side and shoot them with these.'

Howarth felt he would be sick. He gripped the side of the bunk as he fought to stay upright. Was the story true or was the captain trying to frighten him, letting him know what would happen if he did not cooperate? He was not going to take any risks to find out, to call his bluff. As the captain put the rifle away, he told Howarth that he was a member of a Basque separatist group. He said to Howarth, 'Did you read in your newspapers a few years ago about a bomb in a disco, where many were killed?' Howarth said that it rang a bell. Grinning, by now drunk, he put his arm around Howarth's shoulder, and leaned close enough to Howarth's face for his to smell the garlic on his breath. 'That, my friend,' he leered, 'was our man Sesu.'

Howarth pushed his arm away and stood up. The room was spinning. He had to get out of there, away from this man of death. As he stumbled from the room, the captain cried out, 'Come back, we will drink more vodka.' Howarth staggered out on deck and made for his perch in the bow. The sky was black, still lit by occasional flashes of lightning. The captain's message was clear. Howarth would need to cooperate if he wanted to see his family again. He huddled in the bow, shivering and praying for relief from the violent storm around him. It did not come.

CHAPTER THIRTY-ONE

The following day, Howarth awoke in his own cabin. The sun was streaming through the porthole, the storm having given way to balmy Caribbean skies. Up on deck, Jorge, the engineer, was pulling a hose along the salt-crusted deck. He attached one end to a filler cap and explained to Howarth in broken English that they needed to take on more saltwater as ballast. Leaving the water to fill up, he walked along the deck, stopping every few yards to scoop up armfuls of silvery fish. They were now in that part of the ocean where flying fish jump onto any boat in their path with a lemming-like collective death wish.

He banged on the galley porthole until the fat cook opened it, giving a cry of joy at the sight of the fresh fish. Jorge came back along the deck and told Howarth to listen until he could hear water from the hose splashing into the tank, showing that it was filling up. When that happened, he explained, Howarth should take the hammer that lay to one side and bang on the deck so Jorge could hear it in the engine room below. Howarth rolled a joint and lay there daydreaming until he could hear the water sloshing around the tank. He gave three blows of the hammer to the deck and heard a faint bang in reply. A few minutes later, Jorge reappeared and told him to keep an eye on the hose, that the tank would be full in around an hour.

Now stoned, Howarth suddenly noticed another filler cap to the right marked 'Oil'. He took a furtive glance to check no one was looking then pulled the hose out and into the oil tank. 'That should fuck things up,' he smiled to himself, not really thinking it through. Perhaps by the time they fixed it, they would have been spotted by a US Navy patrol boat. He went into the galley and ate some of the freshly fried flying fish. It was good to eat fresh food, he thought. After an hour, he went back and surreptitiously put the hose back into the water tank. As he did so, he became aware of Jorge looking down at him, frowning. 'Why is it not full yet?' he demanded. Howarth shrugged. Jorge looked across at the oil filler cap, gave him a sideways look, then headed off again. Howarth felt sure he had been rumbled.

Sure enough, the ship came to a stop an hour later, the engine groaning and thick, dense smoke pouring from the funnel. All of the crew came out on deck to see what the problem was. After an age, Jorge appeared with a filter cap in his hand. He spoke to the captain in Spanish and Howarth recognised the words for 'water' and 'oil'. Jorge did not confront Howarth and he gave a sigh of relief. The engineer explained that it would take six hours to fix the problem, around midnight, and Howarth cursed. He had hoped it would be more serious than that.

When he awoke the next morning the ship was on the move again. Howarth headed up on deck and lay in his corner sunbathing. At around midday, the engines stopped and the ship came to a halt. They must have reached their destination. He looked over the rail but could see nothing in any direction, no land – just the sea which was as flat as a millpond. Nothing happened for the next few hours and eventually the sun set to the west in a blaze of red. Not tonight, then, thought Howarth. That evening, he sat in the TV room and watched Pink Floyd's *The Wall* for what must have been the 20th time – the ship's collection of videos was pitifully limited. By the time first light came, he had not been to bed, too pumped full of adrenalin to sleep, wondering what the day would bring.

The ship did not move and there was no sign of any boat on the horizon coming to meet them. Howarth asked the captain whom, or what, they were waiting for. He laughed and, tapping his nose, said, 'Wait and see.' By 3 p.m., the heat of the sun had sent Howarth off into another doze. After a few weeks at sea, his skin had been burnished a deep bronze and his hair bleached. A humming noise, becoming gradually louder, woke him. The crew were tying a huge white cross across the deck. Just then, the noise grew to an ear-splitting crescendo and Howarth instinctively ducked as a plane roared over them, not more than 50 yards above.

The pilot was close enough for Howarth to see his features clearly. A deep brown skin with pointed nose, Howarth didn't doubt that he was Colombian. He gave a thumbs-up when he saw the cross and, flying past the ship, he banked and turned. By now, Hawkins had joined Howarth. 'Is this for real?' he asked in wonderment. Howarth was too stunned to reply. As the plane flew by, this time no more than 20 feet above the water, Howarth saw that the side door was open and he caught sight of two dark-skinned boys inside. On the pass, they pushed three bales out that hit the water with a huge splash. The crew sprang into action, launching the inflatable to collect them. As they did so, the plane turned again and carried out the same manoeuvre. Three more bales. And again, this time there were four bales. By now, the crew in the inflatable were fishing the bales out of the water, each one the size of a suitcase. The plane flew by yet again – another three bales. 'Christ,' thought Howarth, 'how many of these are there?'

Turning once again, the plane swooped back. Two bales were pushed out, then, after a little pause, a final one, almost hesitant as though reluctant to join the others. As it came tumbling out, Howarth saw with horror that it was going to land on the inflatable, sure to kill or cause serious injury to one of the crew. He screamed, but as it came down a wave pulled the boat just clear. It missed by an inch. The pilot of the plane waved and screamed off back west towards South America, which lay beyond the horizon, out of sight. Hawkins rushed to the foremast and clambered up to keep an eye on these expensive packages – each bale was worth around £6 million, as Customs would later learn. All 16 were accounted for and brought up onto the deck.

The bales were wrapped in hessian and from them emanated a strong, musky smell like the jungle. The mood on the ship had changed. No one was joking any more. In some countries, their cargo would mean certain execution. Howarth had no idea what it would mean in the UK, but he was pretty sure that it wouldn't be a few hours of community service, helping to build an adventure playground for deprived inner-city kids. The deck was now a hive of activity. Each man clearly knew what he was expected to do and they sprang into action. On the poop deck, one started welding a rail track, while another was cutting a groove into the deck. A third was using cutting gear to fashion a gate that swung open out of the handrail.

One of the bales had burst on hitting the water and a white soggy mess was seeping out. Jorge saw Howarth looking at this, and with a sly expression, said, 'Cocaine and water do not mix, Chris – like oil and water, eh?' Howarth smiled sheepishly and Jorge winked at him, saying, 'Only the once Chris, only the once.' The captain studied the wound with a serious expression and said to Howarth that it would be better to examine all the bags. Howarth said nothing and the captain asked, 'So, may we open the bags to examine them?' With a shock, Howarth realised that he was asking his permission. The relationship had changed. Now the cargo was on board, Howarth, as Chadwick's representative, had become the client and was in charge. He nodded his assent.

The crew ripped open the hessian to reveal hundreds of smaller packages in clear plastic, wrapped around with tape, most bearing the Gucci logo but a few marked for the attention of Virgilio Barco, the then president of Colombia who had declared war on the Medellin and Cali cocaine cartels. Someone at the processing laboratory had a sense of humour. Most of the packages were intact, though a few had split. These were taped up as well as possible. One, however, had burst in the middle and looked beyond repair. Howarth compressed the wet, white mess together and hit on the brainwave of placing it inside the funnel to dry out.

As the crew worked away, repairing packages, a white cloud rose up from the deck as the sun dried the cocaine. To a man, the crew were sniffing at the cloud as they worked, not letting any of the precious cargo go to waste. Howarth followed their example and soon his entire face was numb, his eyes bulging, as he snorted the uncut cocaine. Finally, they repacked the packages into the hessian bales, suitcase style. They counted the packages but could only count 499. One was missing. Then Howarth remembered the one drying out in the funnel.

He went to see if it had dried out. It had, but on inspecting it he could see four deep rake marks where someone had dug their fingers in and helped themselves to a big chunk of coke. He looked around him and caught sight of Jorge returning from below deck. The engineer looked away, refusing to meet Howarth's gaze. Howarth remembered that Jorge had refused to land him in it over the oil-and-water incident. It was payback time. 'Only the once, Jorge,' he warned, 'only the once.'

Back on the poop deck, the miniature railway system was finished.

169

Two grooves had been cut into the deck in which the rails sat. The gear had been loaded onto a cage, which sat on the rails, tied by rope to the ship. A gate had been cut into the handrail, which swung open. An axe had been left by the rope. If there were any sign of trouble, the rope would be cut, sending the entire cargo over the side and to the bottom of the sea. Howarth was impressed.

The days went by and they soon left the balmy weather of the Caribbean behind, heading back into storm after storm as they began the long journey across the Atlantic back to Scotland. One night, as Howarth left the TV room, he could hear water sloshing around. He stepped forward and realised it was coming from the toilet and shower room. The lights in the passageway had gone out, with only a nightlight giving a dim red glow, and the ship was now rolling drunkenly. Howarth opened the bathroom door and was hit by a wall of water. He tried in vain to close the door but too much water was flooding through, spilling out onto the passageway and down the stairs to below deck.

He ran back, drenched from head to toe, into the TV room, shouting, 'Agua, agua' to the crew. One of them waved at him to sit down, not taking him seriously. Howarth tried to grab one by the arm but he flinched and recoiled, staring at Howarth like he was crazy – which, given Howarth's form, was not an unreasonable assumption. It was only when the captain got out of bed to see what the commotion was that he was taken seriously. The captain ran through the TV room, shouting in Spanish at the crew to follow him to the shower room.

The water was pouring out by the gallon by now, flooding the galley to a depth of four inches and pouring over the lip of the stairs down towards the cabins and engine room. Howarth pushed past the captain and ran down the corridor, which was several inches deep in water. He pulled the door to the engine room shut to stop any more water getting in. He pushed open the door to the cabin where Hawkins was sleeping. There were several inches of water lapping around the floor. Hawkins looked at him groggily and said, 'You close that fucking door, Chris, I'm on watch soon.' Howarth excitedly tried to tell him about the flood. Hawkins replied acidly, 'Well, when you clear up, don't make too much noise. Goodnight.'

As he headed back upstairs, food boxes were floating out from the dry store. The engineer was in the shower room, fixing things. It seemed that, when the ship had taken a bad roll to the port side, a toilet valve had jammed open, filling the system with water. When the ship rolled to starboard, the water had rushed out, filling the room. Howarth shuddered to think what could have happened if he had not discovered the problem. They spent the rest of the night clearing up. Disaster had been averted.

CHAPTER THIRTY-TWO

For Customs and Excise, however, cocaine was not even on the radar. As far as they were concerned, this was still a routine, though sizeable, importation of cannabis. Back in Scotland, Graham Dick was waiting for signs of the cannabis being landed and dispersed. It was a shame that Howarth and Hawkins had slipped through the net at Malaga Airport, but it wasn't a disaster. They still had Forrest and Rae under surveillance and knew from their informant that they would be the couriers. They were also keeping a close eye on Burns and McDonald and had the two vessels *Shearwake* and *The Eastray* under tabs. *Shearwake* had not moved from its berth at Vilamoura in Portugal, and *The Eastray* was still in Sotogrande, near Jonathan's place in Estepona.

He had alerted Spanish and French coastguards to be on the lookout for anything out of the ordinary, in case Chadwick switched to another boat, and he had the RAF and the Ministry of Agriculture, Fisheries and Farming (MAFF) using their spotter planes to watch out for any unusual yachts off the coast of Scotland. The Scottish coast was being regularly patrolled by Customs and Excise cutters as well, so he could afford to be a little relaxed. The main thing was to keep an eye on Forrest and Rae. They would surely lead Customs and Excise to the cannabis. It would only be a matter of time, a waiting game for which they had had plenty of practice.

On Saturday, 15 December 1990, Jonathan Chadwick flew into the UK and took the shuttle up to Edinburgh Airport, hiring a car at the Hertz desk, plate number H492 XST. George Cockburn noted that the car was parked outside the Glenisla Hotel late that night. The following morning, Joe McGuigan drove past Rae's flat, noting the presence of

Forrest and Rae's cars, as well as Chadwick's hire car. He saw the three men walking in a nearby field engrossed in conversation. At 2.20 p.m., Chadwick drove past where McGuigan was sitting in his car in the main square at Blairgowrie. Two men were in the car with him. McGuigan cursed and threw the coffee he had just bought out the window, pulling out to follow the car without being seen.

He followed them onto the A9 at Dunkeld, where Maggie McKeand was waiting. McGuigan and McKeand followed them in separate cars as they headed north. It soon became apparent that they were heading for Ullapool and Maggie McKeand raced on ahead so she'd be there to keep an eye on them when they arrived. McGuigan stayed with them, taking care to keep two or three cars between him and his targets. At 4.45 p.m., they stopped at a filling station at Contin, near Dingwall. McGuigan got a good look at them and was able to confirm that his two passengers were indeed Forrest and Rae. He waited until they pulled off again, heading north on the Ullapool Road. He radioed ahead to let his colleagues know to expect company and then called it a day.

Up ahead, Frankie Cooper spotted Chadwick and his merry men sweep past the Harbour Lights Hotel at 5.26 p.m. and head north through Ullapool. Later, Forrest would state that they picked up Burns, who took them to a lay-by a mile or two north of Ullapool where, the plan was, the landed drugs would be transferred to Forrest and Rae's van from a four-wheel drive. They didn't hang about for long. Maggie McKeand and Tony Jackson saw them heading south out of Ullapool a little over an hour later, at 6.50 p.m. They followed them at a discreet distance as far as the Kessock Bridge, where Chadwick turned off and headed towards the town centre at 8.15 p.m. He began to carry out anti-surveillance measures, slowing down to a crawl, going three times round a roundabout and doubling back the way he had come. Perhaps he had clocked McKeand and Jackson.

Graham Dick explains: 'He's doing things like stopping at the side of the road to see if the cars behind him go past, he goes around roundabouts two or three times, he turns off roads then immediately stops, he goes the wrong way up one-way streets or simply slows right down on a dual carriageway to see who slows down behind him. So sometimes we had to let him go so he didn't rumble us, but usually we picked him up again soon afterwards. So he knows what he's doing to an extent, but really, proper anti-surveillance is much more sophisticated. He's just playing silly buggers but he thinks he's being really smart. So that's why we didn't see everything, like when he's in

Ullapool. It's a small place and you have to be careful not to get spotted so we had to be very subtle.'

Fortunately, Craig Paterson was at hand to take over, and he followed Chadwick to Inverness train station, where Chadwick pulled up in the car park at 8.30 p.m. When Paterson next came by at 9 p.m., he had gone, on the move south. At 10.20 p.m., Joe McGuigan reported that he was heading back through Blairgowrie in the direction of Rae's flat. There would not be anything else happening that night.

The next day, Monday, 17 December 1990, all three men's cars were parked outside Rae's flat. Late morning, Chadwick took off in his hire car and was followed by two teams to Perth train station, where he arrived at 12.40 p.m. Three minutes later, he came out of the station accompanied by Robbie Burns. The two men climbed into Chadwick's car and headed off on the M90. Despite more rudimentary anti-surveillance tactics by Chadwick, the surveillance team were able to follow him to Edinburgh. He made his way to Waverley train station in the city centre, parked and went with Burns into the station, where they were seen in the Travellers' Bite, Burns no doubt being treated to a display of Chadwick's largesse.

At 2.18 p.m., Chadwick returned to his car and Burns got on the 14.30 to King's Cross. Fortunately, this was no surprise to Customs and Excise, who had been tipped off that Burns would be taking the train down to Newcastle to stay with Tony McDonald, Howarth's cousin with whom he had spent the summer in Mull. Consequently, John Buchanan was waiting for him at Newcastle train station. At 4.05 p.m., he saw Burns get off the train and make his way to a public telephone, then sit waiting outside the station. At 5 p.m., McDonald pulled up in his blue Renault 18 estate, plate number JWB 739W. Burns climbed in and they were followed to a pub, the Foss, where the two men spent a couple of hours.

They headed back to one of two known addresses for McDonald in Orpington Avenue in the Byker area of the city. A few minutes later, they were picked up by a car and headed to the Wincomblee Hotel on Mitchell Street in a suburb called Walker, where they spent the evening, finally heading home at 11.25 p.m., presumably well oiled. In the car that picked them up was a girl called Elaine Miley. She recalls picking Tony up, or Benny as she calls him for some reason, and that he had 'a friend called Bunny, he had a Scottish accent, was thin and wearing a dark, woolly hat. I also remember that he had a beard.'

On Tuesday, 18 December 1990, Graham Dick was doing a spot of surveillance on McDonald's house at Orpington Avenue. He recalls:

'The next morning, a car picks up Robbie and Tony at 10.44 a.m. and takes them to Lloyds British Boatyard. Billy Reader sees Tony and Robbie looking at a large vessel, red hull, white superstructure, they're up on deck having a good look around. Then they clear off, go to a ship's chandlers, Fox and Hounds Marine Ltd, then go to a café.

'They muck around in Newcastle for a bit and later go to West Holywell, where they go to this bungalow where there's a blue and white boat outside, presumably for sale. And then they head off for the city centre and Robbie and Tony are off down the shops. I take a look in the car and in the footwell, I can see a box for an ICOM IC M5 VHF receiver, a ship-to-shore radio basically. This is at 1.30 p.m. A couple of minutes later, the guys are back and we follow them to Westminster Way, which is Tony's other place.'

Dick could sense that things were coming to a head. The ship-to-shore radio had to be to communicate with Howarth and Hawkins when they were bringing the gear in. He was perplexed as to why they should be looking at boats at this late stage, but put it down to forward planning for a future run – not that there would be one for these chancers, he thought with grim satisfaction.

That afternoon, Burns and McDonald set off on a serious pub crawl, starting at the Foss at 2.30 p.m., finally arriving back to Orpington Avenue at 11.35 p.m. that night. Customs officer Tony Jackson noted sparsely: 'Both unsteady on feet.'

While Burns and McDonald were having fun in Newcastle on Tuesday, 18 December, Chadwick had more pressing matters to deal with. He arrived at Edinburgh Airport at 8.44 a.m. with David Forrest. The two men bought tickets to Heathrow in the names Frost and Holm and did not return until 8.30 p.m. that night, when they headed to Forrest's flat on a maze-like council estate in Dundee – a nightmare to watch in surveillance terms. Forrest later told Dick that they had flown down to London and travelled to Brent Cross shopping centre in north-west London, Here, Chadwick showed him where he was to park the hire van with the gear on board, leaving it there to be collected by the next link in the chain. He was also introduced to the London connection, who would watch the van's arrival from a safe distance and then collect the van after Forrest had left it.

On Wednesday, 19 December, Burns and McDonald had an early start, setting off at 8.40 a.m. They headed to a café, Lizzy's Kitchen, where a taxi picked them up 45 minutes later. Dick had four different pairs of officers watching them now. Something was going to happen soon with this level of sudden activity. He was sure of it.

At the same time, over in Dundee, Forrest also had an early start. He headed off at 7.30 a.m. in his 2CV and was followed by one Customs team. Nothing of any interest was reported, so it seems that this was intended as a diversion – Chadwick's use of anti-surveillance tactics was in full flow, something which added to Dick's conviction that the landing was imminent. At 10.50 a.m., Chadwick himself came out of Forrest's flat and got into his hire car. For the next half an hour, he led his pursuers a merry dance, driving around in circles, doubling back on himself, slowing to a crawl. Finally, when he mistakenly convinced himself that he wasn't being watched, he headed back to the flat, arriving at 11.25 a.m. Two minutes later, Rae pulled up in his battered old Peugeot with one of his children. The two men looked around them and, satisfied that no one was watching, got into Chadwick's car and headed off with their various watchers pursuing in relay teams.

Dick's team were still following Burns and McDonald in their taxi. It would be an expensive fare. They took it all the way to Perth, a three-and-a-half-hour journey of some 155 miles. They arrived at Perth train station at around 1.50 p.m., a few minutes after Chadwick and Rae, who had been followed there, Chadwick parking by the museum and art gallery on Bridge Lane, a few minutes' walk away.

The four men (and Rae's child, who must have been very proud seeing his daddy at work) met at the station and got into a taxi together. An hour or so later, Burns and McDonald returned to the station to head home in separate directions, Burns to Ullapool and McDonald to Newcastle. Chadwick and Rae returned to Chadwick's hire car and headed back to Forrest's place in Dundee. Rae headed home and Chadwick's car was still there on a routine drive-by after midnight.

Graham Dick was beginning to get a headache: 'Wednesday 19th was a busy day for us. We've got a surveillance team in Dundee following Jonathan and Rae, we've got a team in Newcastle following Robbie and Tony, who get a taxi up to Perth and meet Jonathan and Rae, and we've got a team in Ullapool watching out for Hawkins and Howarth. And we're getting nervous now, wondering what all this movement is about and where these boats are. We're convinced that all this running about is to do with the arrangements for an imminent run, no doubt about it, but we don't know where the boats are. It shouldn't take this long to sail up from Spain, or even Morocco. And we've had the purchase of the ship-to-shore radio, so it's all happening.'

On Thursday, 20 December, Chadwick set off early from Forrest's flat and headed over to Rae's place at Glenisla. Later that afternoon, Forrest came over and joined them, spending several hours there – his car was still there at 9.30 p.m. Things had quietened down after the frantic activity of the previous day.

On Friday, 21 December, Forrest's car was seen back at his flat at 6.45 a.m. Chadwick was spotted at Edinburgh Airport at 8 a.m., returning his hire car to Hertz and taking British Midlands flight BD051 down to Heathrow. He was seen taking the Tube into central London, presumably to finalise his arrangements with the London connection. That afternoon, he made his way down to Gatwick and flew back to Malaga.

The tension was building. Dick was seriously concerned. Neither of the yachts they knew about had moved, but here were the principal targets looking as though they were planning for an imminent arrival of drugs. Perhaps Chadwick had switched yachts, after all. What if it had slipped into the country undetected, despite the combined might of three countries? He shook his head. It was crucial that they keep track of Forrest and Rae. Wherever the drugs would be coming ashore, Forrest and Rae would have to go. This job was stressful, he reflected, aware of how much egg he'd have on his face if he let this slip through the net. Surely the drugs had to be coming ashore soon. His other headache was that it looked like he'd be working over Christmas. He'd been in the job long enough to know that drug smugglers didn't really observe public holidays in the way the general population did, but it still rankled.

He looked out of the window in the control room in Dingwall police station. Outside, great swirling snowflakes were falling all around. It was St Lucy's Day, the shortest day of the year, and, on the radio, the Met Office had issued a severe weather warning for the north-west coast of Scotland, predicting a storm force ten coming in from the Atlantic, hitting the seaboard like a demolition ball. At least nothing would be happening tonight. Not even Howarth – Crazy Chris – would attempt a landing in these conditions. The thought of Howarth and Hawkins made him frown, though. Where the fuck were they?

CHAPTER THIRTY-THREE

Back at sea, the captain sent word that he wanted to see Howarth in his office. Howarth made his way to the cabin, feeling like a naughty schoolboy who had been summoned to the headmaster's study. He knocked on the door and went in. The captain was sitting at his desk. 'Ah, come in, Chris. Sit down,' he said. Howarth did as he was told. The captain tapped on the desk with a pen. Finally, he looked at Howarth. 'Well, Chris, it is time to make a decision. I need to know whether you are going to see this through.'

Howarth said, 'Well, it doesn't look like I've got much fucking choice, does it?'

The captain smiled apologetically. 'As I have said, that is a matter for you and Jonathan. The fact of the matter is I can take the cargo to Spain or I can carry on and take it to Scotland. It makes little difference to me, but the money is better for me if I take it to Scotland. So I need to know which it is to be.'

Howarth thought for a moment. If he refused at this late stage, and the captain diverted to Spain, what would happen to him and Hawkins? He could not be sure whether the captain had simply been trying to frighten him with his talk of death, but he wasn't prepared to call his bluff. 'I will see it through when we get to Scotland,' he said finally, 'but I am doing it under protest.' The captain nodded and took out a bottle, suggesting that they drink to their success. Howarth refused and the two men glared at each other with a mixture of hatred and respect. Howarth walked out of the room and headed back down to his cabin.

On the way, he bumped into Jorge, who beckoned for him to follow. They headed down through the engine room and across to Jorge's cabin. Inside, the room was thick with a pungent smoke. Hawkins was there, holding a sheet of tin foil, while Chito held a match underneath. In the middle of the foil, a liquid bubbled and smoked, and Hawkins leaned down to inhale the vapours through the case of a plastic Biro.

'Any good?' asked Howarth with interest. Hawkins looked up at him with heavy red-rimmed eyes. A burst of laughter told Howarth that it was. Howarth came over and took his turn. Within a few minutes, he felt deliriously high, sufficiently so as to forget his troubles. He noticed Chito wince again with pain and thought of the limp he always seemed to have. 'What's wrong with Chito?' he asked Jorge who laughed and said something to Chito in Spanish. As Hawkins leant down to take his turn on the cocaine mixture, Chito smiled and pulled his pants down, turning around to reveal the biggest, ugliest yellow boil on the bridge of his backside. Unfortunately for Hawkins, he had not seen this happening and, as he sat back up suddenly, he found himself face to face with the offending article millimetres from his nose. He let out a shriek of disgust and jumped up from the bunk, causing everyone to laugh.

Howarth stayed in there for what felt like a couple of hours. As he got higher and higher, he began to realise that he was now enjoying his adventure. It was like being in a film, he reflected, and the adrenalin surge was almost as good as the cocaine itself. More crew joined them later and the little party went on. Finally, the door opened and Sesu entered. He took one look at the gathering, frowned and left. This was the signal that the party was over and everyone got up and left. Howarth stayed behind and told Jorge that he knew that it was him who had taken the coke from the funnel. If he gave Howarth half, nothing further would be said. Jorge scowled but there was little that the engineer could do.

He rummaged through his drawers until he found a bag with a large amount of white powder in it. He split it into two, handing Howarth the smaller one. Howarth shook his head and pointed to the larger one. Swearing in Spanish, Jorge handed it to him and Howarth left the room. He was aware that all his sensations were heightened thanks to the cocaine and he could notice smell and touch with a clarity he had not felt for a long time. He made his way to his cabin and stretched out on his bunk, even though there was no way he could sleep: he was buzzing so much from the coke.

But sleep did come. When he next awoke, it was afternoon. He headed up on deck, where it was bracing and cold, not surprising now that they were well into December in the north Atlantic. Climbing up to the wheelhouse, he heard the radio burst into life, giving the call sign, 'Dinaris, dinaris.' The captain rushed over and, opening a notebook filled with numbers, began to switch to other frequencies to thwart any would-be eavesdroppers. He seemed to be having a three-way conversation. Howarth recognised one of the voices as Jonathan Chadwick's, and grabbed the mike from the captain. He shouted, 'Dinaris, dinaris.' Chadwick's voice came back as clear as daylight. 'How are you?' he said.

'Look, Jonathan,' said Howarth angrily. 'I don't want to do this; it's not my scene. This is too big for me.'

The captain pulled the mike away from Howarth, shouting, 'No business over the radio.' Howarth nodded his comprehension and took the mike back. By then, Chadwick was replying. 'Look, Chris, you have to. It's gone too far now. I'm sure I don't need to spell it out.'

'Is there no way out?' asked Howarth, knowing the answer.

'No, not now,' replied Chadwick. Howarth looked to the captain. He shook his head, confirming what Chadwick had said. Howarth asked Chadwick why he hadn't told him what they were getting into. He answered that it had been for security reasons, that the fewer people that knew what was going on, the less chance there would be of it getting out. He had chosen Howarth because he had been told that he would do it without asking too many questions and had a good knowledge of the Highlands coast. Also, he had acquitted himself well on the Gruinard Island run.

Chadwick finished by saying, 'Don't worry about Fiona and the kids. We're keeping an eye on them in Ullapool and they're fine just now.' Howarth claims that he took this to be a threat as to what might happen if he refused to comply. For the record, Hawkins dismisses talk of fear for personal safety, saying that at no time did anyone threaten him or imply that there would be repercussions if he did not do as he was told. To be fair to Howarth, however, the two accounts are not mutually exclusive. As ringleader of the landing crew, the sharper side of business would be more likely to be discussed with Howarth than with Hawkins, who was only 20 at this time, after all. The third possibility is that Howarth was becoming paranoid, as Hawkins has said, seeing threats and conspiracies where none existed.

Howarth then asked what would happen to Fiona and the kids if anything should happen to him, if he were arrested or – worse – killed trying to land the gear. Chadwick assured him that they would be looked after and that if they were caught, he would ensure that they had the best legal representation.

By 19 December, when Chadwick, Rae, Burns and McDonald were meeting up in Perth, the ship was approaching Ireland from the south-west. Howarth advised the captain to head around Ireland, heading north towards the Faroe Islands, then east towards Rockall and finally down into the Minch. If they came up through the Irish Sea, the risk of detection would be far greater, with British and Irish navy patrol boats on the lookout for gun-running. The captain took his advice.

By now, the TV was picking up flickering broadcasts from Irish and British stations. Through a blizzard on the screen, Howarth could just make out the news. While they had been away, the two sides of the Channel Tunnel met for the first time, Thatcher had been ousted as leader of the Conservative Party to be replaced by John Major ('John who?' thought Howarth) and at the High Court in London, Sonia Sutcliffe, wife of the Yorkshire Ripper, was facing a gruelling cross-examination by the legendary courtroom bruiser George Carman, who was representing the *News of the World* in a libel case brought against it by Sutcliffe. Howarth was not to know that soon *he'd* be the leading item on the news bulletins.

On Friday, 21 December, the captain summoned him to the wheelhouse. He was in the chart room with Sesu at the helm. Incredibly, Sesu smiled at Howarth by way of greeting. He was clearly prepared to let bygones be bygones, now that they were nearing the end of their journey. Howarth joined the captain and, on the chart, pointed out the approach through the Minch and Clashnessie Bay near Drumbeg, where they had been tasked with landing the load. This left a fingerprint on the chart that much later would provide damning evidence against the captain.

The captain told him that there were problems. There had been heavy snowfall in Scotland, making the roads impassable, meaning the pick-up van would not be able to get up there for a few days at least. The other problem was that there was a pig of a storm brewing up to the west that would hit them later that night, making the sea treacherous. He was thinking of cutting back out to the Atlantic until things looked a little less hazardous. Howarth was adamant that he wanted to go ahead, desperate to get back to Ullapool, and that he and Hawkins knew the coastline well enough to cope. The captain stroked his beard dubiously, then finally said with reluctance, 'OK – but it will be at your risk, not mine.' Howarth agreed readily, even though it meant that he would be risking millions of pounds' worth of product that belonged to the notorious Colombian drugs organisation, the Cali cartel. They were the least of his worries just now.

Howarth found out later that Chadwick had been urging them via the radio to head back out to sea, 'to get the fuck away from Britain', as Howarth puts it, which was just too hot, despite the snow blizzards. Chadwick had sent messages to this effect, but all Torres said to Howarth was that 'people were getting nervous'. As far as he was concerned, they were still all systems go. It was clear that someone in the chain of command was adamant that the landing must go ahead. Howarth does not know to this day whether the pressure was coming from the Colombians or from the captain, who wanted the gear off his ship.

There was a third problem as well. When Howarth had originally headed down to Spain, still believing that it was a cannabis run, the plan had been that Burns would rendezvous with them at sea to transfer the cargo onto another boat. By this stage, in view of the extent of the surveillance operation against them, the extreme weather and the fact that he had apparently been unable to get hold of a boat suitable for the job, it had been decided that he would meet them at the shore, with a four-wheel drive or van. This new plan had been explained to the captain by Chadwick over the radio. This left Howarth and Hawkins with no option but to load the gear onto the inflatable and try to land it that way. For now, he had no option but to focus on the deadly task in hand. With a storm force ten hitting them, this was almost suicidal, but Howarth would have done anything to get off that ship.

That evening, the cook prepared a special meal for their last night and beer, wine and spirits were flowing, although alcohol seemed to have no effect on Howarth, who was too pumped up to relax. At around midnight, the ship started heading down the Minch. A blizzard hit them and visibility was reduced to zero. The tension in the air was electric. Howarth went to check the radar but the blizzard was so heavy it had blacked out the screen. Hawkins muttered to him, not for the first time, 'I hope to fuck you know what you are doing, Chris.'

The snowstorm thinned a little, affording a degree of visibility. The captain called Howarth over to stand by him, saying, 'Chris, you are my eyes in these waters.' Howarth was feeling severely stressed with the weight of responsibility. Sesu came into the wheelhouse and said something in Spanish. The captain turned to Howarth and said, 'He wants to know when you want the inflatable loaded up.' Now Howarth was in control and he had to keep himself together. He went out on deck and supervised things. The inflatable was attached to the boat with two ropes, which would be used to lower it into the sea. Water was now washing violently over the deck and the waves looked enormous.

The bales were loaded onto the boat and a sheet of tarpaulin pulled over the top and tied to the sides to prevent the worst of the water getting in. At the rear, beside the outboard motor, there was just enough room for him and Hawkins. It was time to get ready.

CHAPTER THIRTY-FOUR

The two men got into the wetsuits that Sesu had given them, putting all their belongings into bin liners and taping them up in an attempt to keep them dry. When they were ready, Hawkins gave Howarth an anxious look, seeking reassurance. Howarth told him not to worry, that he thought they could make it. The look Hawkins shot him said that they must. Up on deck, the radar told him that the lighthouse at Stoer Point was on their port side. Howarth squinted but could see nothing through the wall of snow ahead of him. Well, he would have to put his trust in God.

The crew men lifted the inflatable over the side and began to lower it inch by inch. Suddenly, disaster struck – one of the ropes snapped and the inflatable fell lengthways, dangling with its nose just above the angry black sea. Several bales slid out from under the tarpaulin and dropped into the water. Hawkins guided the inflatable into the water and, jumping in, started up the motor to begin searching for the bales. The captain came about to provide shelter in the lee of the ship from the storm that was hitting them with full force from the west.

Howarth shone his flashlight all around. In the arc of light, they could make out bales bobbing in the water. Hawkins gathered up five of them and, unable to find any more, concluded they had rounded up all the strays. Unbeknown to them, they had not. A sixth bale slipped away, to be washed up further along the coast a couple of weeks later, providing yet more evidence against them. It was time to risk their lives trying to get ashore. There was little room to spare behind the tarpaulin-covered cargo. Howarth squeezed in and the men pulled the tarpaulin back up to their necks, leaving just their heads exposed. They could pull it back over the outboard motor if any big waves hit them. If too much water got into the outboard motor, it would die – as they then surely would.

Howarth left Hawkins to steer the boat, shouting instructions to him above the howling wind as he struggled to get his bearings. He could see nothing through the snowstorm. Occasionally, he could have sworn he had seen the light from the Stoer Point lighthouse but then he realised that he could see traces of light everywhere that he looked. His eyes were deceiving him and he was being dazzled by the snowstorm. His problems were about to get a whole lot worse. As the *DIMAR-B* pulled away from them, they moved out of its lee, losing the protection it had afforded them. Howarth looked out behind and saw to his horror a huge wall of water heading straight for them, threatening to engulf their craft. It hit and washed over the tiny boat, drenching them from head to toe.

The engine cut out and they were spinning in the water, as helpless as a cork on the sea. Howarth shouted to Hawkins to help him try to lift the outboard out of the water to try to get it started again but in his heart he felt it was a lost cause. By now, he was terrified, thinking that there was surely no way out of this, that the cruel sea would claim them. Above the wind, he could make out the sound of breakers dashing on 300-feet-high cliffs. They would smash like matchwood in the same way if they drifted much closer.

Hawkins grappled with the motor, but, petrified, shouted to Howarth that it was stuck fast. Howarth stuck his arm into the freezing water and felt around the motor. Thick rope had trailed around the propeller, causing it to cut out. If he could remove it, then they would have a chance. He pulled but it was too entangled and would not budge. He shouted to Hawkins, asking where the knife was. Hawkins gave him a helpless look and pointed to the cargo. The knife was trapped somewhere underneath half a tonne of cocaine.

Howarth groaned and the two fell to their knees, sliding their arms up to the shoulder under the bales in a desperate search for the knife. If it was towards the front of the 15-foot boat, they were lost. Suddenly, with a triumphant cry, Hawkins pulled his arm out, holding the knife aloft. He leaned over the stern side of the craft and put his arm into the water, hacking away at the rope. After what seemed like an eternity, during which Howarth felt sure they would be dashed against the rocks, which sounded nearer and nearer, Hawkins managed to cut the propeller free of the rope. He managed to get the motor going once again, and Howarth tried to work out where the passage between treacherous reefs and the murderous cliffs of Oldany Island lay.

At that moment, another huge wave hit them. They began to slide down the follow-through and Howarth looked to the starboard side. An enormous wall of water was building up and closing in on them. It would fold in on top of them, surely capsizing them and sending them to the bottom. Howarth pushed with all his strength on the outboard motor. The inflatable gave a kick and shot forwards just as the wave was coming down on them. They made it by the skin of their teeth.

Again, Howarth thought he could just make out a flash of light from Stoer Point ahead of them. If he was right, it was time to turn in to the port side and find a way through to Clashnessie Bay. If he was wrong . . . well, it didn't bear thinking about. He began to turn in where his best guess told him the passage would be. Behind them, another huge breaker was coming in that lifted the boat up high. Ahead of them lay a trough of at least 20 feet. Howarth and Hawkins leaned back as far as they could, praying that the nose would not pitch forward into this valley of water, pulling them to their deaths. They were hurtling on the crest of the huge wave, completely out of control and, for all Howarth knew, sending them to be dashed against the cliffs of Oldany Island.

The two men began to scream, terrified, knowing that their destiny was now out of their hands. Suddenly, they were pushed into the flat, calm water of Clashnessie Bay. They had made it. They were alive.

It was by now 7 a.m. and the light was breaking from the east. All around was pristine snow. The journey from the ship to shore had taken the best part of five hours, though it felt like a matter of minutes. The bay was deserted but it might not stay that way. They would have to move fast. There was no sign of Burns with the van. Howarth was furious but this was not the time for recrimination; he would deal with Burns when he saw him.

They worked methodically for the next two hours, taking the bales off the boat and hiding them under rocks near the beach. This was below some cliffs at the point of a peninsula that jutted out on the northern side of Clashnessie Bay, separated from Oldany Island by the narrowest of inlets, a channel leading through to the next bay, Eddrachillis Bay. The stash could only be reached by boat. It would be safe enough until Chadwick could organise collection. They marked the point with a white pole and got back in the inflatable to head for shore.

The inflatable was in a pretty sorry state. Howarth wanted to destroy it to dispose of evidence. 'We had been planning to turn the fucker around and point it out to sea with the engine still going,' says Howarth, 'and let it end up at the bottom of the Minch. But when the four-wheel drive didn't show, we had no choice but to stash the stuff in the trickiest place we could find and we left the inflatable there so we could get back out to it when we needed to.' It was a decision they would come to regret.

By 9 a.m. their work was done and the two men took the inflatable to the shore where they hauled it up against some rocks to beach it. Still in their wetsuits, they pulled open their bin liners to find that all their clothes were, unsurprisingly, completely sodden. Keeping their wetsuits on for warmth, they pulled on trousers and a pullover each to try to look a little less conspicuous. Some chance – two heavily sun-tanned men with wetsuits poking though at their pullover sleeves was not a common sight on a snowy Saturday morning just before Christmas in this quiet part of the world.

They started the three-mile trudge uphill to Drumbeg and got there an hour later, gasping for a smoke. Their duty-free cigarettes were soaked so they rummaged through their pockets looking for British currency. Pooling their resources, they found they had enough for a packet of ten cigarettes and a couple of ten-pence pieces to phone Ullapool to be collected. There is little in Drumbeg – a newsagent's, a payphone and a pub – but it served their immediate needs. Hawkins went into the newsagent's. If the husband and wife behind the counter were startled by his appearance, they contrived not to show it. They politely commented on the weather and handed over the packet of ten Embassy.

Outside, the two men lit a cigarette each and inhaled deeply, still harrowed by their near-death experience. Howarth went to the phone box and phoned home to persuade Fiona to undertake the 40-mile trip in a blizzard to come and collect the conquering heroes. There was no reply. He thought for a moment, then, realising it was a Saturday, concluded she must be up at her mum's. He dialled the number and, hearing the pips, pushed in the coin. It was her dad. 'Hello, Chris, you back then?' Fiona's dad enquired.

'Aye, just back. Listen, I've only got the one ten pence. Is Fiona about?'

'No, she's away down to Inverness shopping with her mum and the kids. Stocking up for Christmas, you know.'

Howarth groaned. 'Have they taken the car?'

'Aye. Is there a problem?'

'Not yet, but I think there will be soon. Look, I've got to go, I'll see you over Christmas.'

Howarth thought hard. He had one coin left and he couldn't afford to waste it, stuck out here in the middle of nowhere. He had a mate, ex-army guy named Paul, who had a van and who'd helped him out with errands before for a few quid. He'd better be in, he thought grimly as he dialled the number. Thankfully, Paul picked up.

'Paul, it's Crazy. Can you do me a favour?'

A little over an hour later, Paul's van came lumbering up the hill at Drumbeg. By now numb with the cold, Howarth and Hawkins gratefully climbed into the van and began to thaw out in the heat of the cab. They made small talk as they headed back down to Ullapool. Before they reached the town, they stopped at the brow of a hill from where they could see the village below, a snow-draped toy town like a scene in a department-store window at Christmas, now only three days off. Paul pulled over to the side of the road and got out on the pretext of having a piss. He motioned with a sideways jerk of the head for Howarth to do the same. Outside the van, he said in a low voice, 'Listen, Chris, it's no business of mine what you're up to, but Ullapool is crawling with Customs – and they're all looking for you. Whatever you're doing, Customs are everywhere, and they'll be watching. That's the word, anyway, just be careful.'

Howarth thanked the man and they got back into the van. As they drove down hill towards the village, Howarth got him to pull into the estate and reverse as close to his door as he could. They checked there were no suspicious-looking cars about and climbed through the back of the van, out through the rear doors and ran up to Howarth's front door as though a wildcat was after them. Once inside, the two men whooped with joy that they had made it back without being killed or caught. They took it in turns to have a hot bath and let all the stress and dirt of recent weeks seep away.

In the kitchen, Howarth checked the fridge and found that Fiona – bless her – had stashed several four-packs of strong lager. They cracked a couple of tins open and spent the next few hours getting drunk and laughing hysterically as they relived the last few weeks at sea and the suicidal landing they had carried out the previous night. At last, Howarth went upstairs to climb into a proper bed and sink into a delicious, deep sleep while Hawkins set off on his short journey home. He had kept his promise to his mum. He was home in time for Christmas, after all. But it would be the last he would spend with her for some years . . .

CRIME AND PUNISHMENT

CHAPTER THIRTY-FIVE

Graham Dick was having a bad day. His scouts had reported that there was still no movement on *Shearwake* and *The Eastray*, he had spotter planes all around the Minch and the Irish Sea, but nothing untoward had been spotted and the weather was filthy. There were three Customs cutters, Sea Riders, patrolling the Irish Sea and the Minch, MAFF was helping out with spotter planes, the RAF with helicopters, but all the time they were looking out for a yacht big enough to have taken four tonnes of cannabis up from Spain or Morocco. They would certainly not have attached any significance to a battered old inflatable beached at Clashnessie Bay – even if they had spotted it.

His day was about to get even worse. In the late afternoon, he got a phone call from Sergeant Mike MacLennan of the Northern Constabulary. Although based at Inverness, MacLennan lived in Ullapool. He was not directly involved in Operation Klondyke, but local police had been briefed on it and told to keep an eye out for anything unusual. MacLennan called Dick with some monumentally bad news. He had just seen Hawkins, he reported, on Quay Street in Ullapool, sporting a healthy suntan and a big grin.

Dick was perplexed. How the fuck had Hawkins got back into the country? He quickly called the team together for a meeting. The atmosphere was grim. If Howarth and Hawkins were back in town, there was every chance that they had landed the gear and that it had been distributed and could be anywhere by now. He detailed a couple of the team to get onto the airlines, airports and ports to see whether there was any sign of the two men having entered the country legally, although in his heart he felt that he was clutching at straws. He also gave instructions for the three Customs and Excise cutters to patrol the coast on the lookout for any unusual vessels and contacted the RAF and the MAFF yet again to beg some spotter planes to tour the coastline, hoping against hope that it was all not too late.

After a couple of hours he got the news that he'd been dreading.

There was no record of Howarth and Hawkins entering the country through normal channels, which made it all the more likely that they had come ashore with the drugs and got them out from under their very noses. That slippery bastard Chadwick had pulled it off. He'd been playing cat-and-mouse with them, or, to borrow further metaphors from the animal kingdom, leading them on a wild goose chase, making asses of Customs and Excise. *Shearwake* and *The Eastray* had been red herrings. He felt thoroughly depressed, and the atmosphere in the control room did little to lift his spirits. Everyone went about their work woodenly, mechanically, feeling that it was Good Guys 0, Bad Guys 1. What a Christmas present. He passed his hand over his eyes and shook his head, feeling a headache coming on.

Several members of the team refused to give up, and felt that it was not all over. 'Look, just because Howarth and Hawkins are back, that doesn't change fuck all,' one of the team argued passionately. 'The drugs must still be somewhere. We've been watching Forrest and Rae and they haven't stirred. We know they're the transport crew so it stands to reason the drugs have been stashed somewhere. We've just got to wait for them to make their move.'

Dick smiled wearily. He wanted to believe, to share the enthusiasm. Perhaps the spotter planes or the cutters would turn something up, he told himself without really believing it. What if Forrest and Rae were also decoys? And what if they'd been promoted from transport crew to principals after acquitting themselves on the Gruinard Island run? It would have been a simple enough matter to recruit a couple of neds to pick up the gear and take it off. He couldn't help but feel that he was witnessing 18 months' hard graft disappearing down the Swanee. Christ, he needed a drink. He was going to have to put up with some serious piss taking from elsewhere in the department over this.

As Dick says: 'There was general gloom as we're thinking that they must have got away with it, although several are saying, 'Bollocks, it's not gone anywhere, Forrest and Rae haven't moved, and we know they're the transport team,' so there's still a faint glimmer of hope. Personally, I'm thinking that they've done it and, although it wouldn't be a black mark in career terms, there would be a few sniggers. It would be a big blow to my professional pride. It completely, utterly, totally ruined my Christmas, and that of everyone else on the team.'

Back at 13 Morefield Place, Howarth was awoken later that evening by the sound of the front door closing with a bang and voices in the hall. He came to the top of the stairs to find Fiona and the kids back from their shopping trip to Inverness. The kids went wild when they saw him, shrieking with excitement as he picked them up in turn and threw them up in the air. At last, the kids were enticed into having their baths and going to bed. They could play with their father the next day, Fiona said sternly as she put out the light.

Downstairs, she shut the lounge door and stood, hand on hip, facing Howarth. 'Well,' she said eyebrow raised, 'where have you been all this time, then?' Howarth sat down and began to tell her everything that he had been through, finding it hard to know where to begin and what to include. As he recounted his adventure, there was a knock at the door. Fiona got up to answer it. She was back a moment later, rolling her eyes. 'It's Robbie,' she said. 'He wants to see you.' She headed off to the kitchen, leaving the two men to talk. Burns shuffled into the room almost apologetically, as though awaiting the outburst from Crazy Chris that would surely ensue. He was not disappointed.

'So what the fuck happened to you?' roared Howarth. Burns put out a placating arm. 'Hang on, Chris, it's not my fault.'

'Not your fault? Where the fuck were you? We could have been killed on that fucking inflatable.' Howarth was in no mood to make peace.

'I couldn't sort out a boat,' pleaded Burns. 'I looked at some down in Newcastle but I couldn't find one that was suitable, and I wasn't able to borrow one. And then the storm hit, I thought it would be suicide to go out in it anyway, even if I did have one.'

'What the fuck do you think it was like for us in the inflatable, you twat? And what happened to the four-wheel drive? Why didn't you meet us at Clashnessie Bay as planned?'

'Well, Jonathan said he was going to sort out some money to cover a four-wheel drive, but I never got it, what was I meant to do?' Burns looked at the backs of his hands nervously before clearing his throat. 'The thing is, Chris, the reason I wanted to see you this evening is I've got a bad feeling about the whole thing. I want out.'

'What did you say?' asked Howarth incredulously.

'I don't want anything to do with it any more, it's all been a terrib . . .'

Burns didn't get to finish his sentence. Howarth's fist came crashing into the side of his face, hurling him back against the wall and knocking over a table and lamp in the process. Howarth stood over him, apoplectic with rage. 'You want out? You fucking cunt, I should fucking kill you. Because of you, you spineless prick, me and Noel could be at the bottom of the Minch by now. And then all you had to do was get up to Clashnessie with a vehicle and you even managed to fuck that up.

Well, thanks to you, the gear's still sitting up there, and you're going to fucking help sort this fucking mess out.'

Burns didn't argue, all the fight having been knocked out of him. He was still part of the team, like it or not. In a twist of irony, Chadwick would shout the same speech practically verbatim down the phone at Howarth when he called the following day, only to find Howarth saying that he would have nothing further to do with it, that he had discharged his duties and it was now down to Forrest and Rae to take over and earn their money. If Howarth was going to see his £150,000, Chadwick made clear, he would ensure that the gear was loaded onto Forrest and Rae's van and sent south. Howarth tried to explain that Ullapool was crawling with Customs and that it would make far more sense for him 'to fuck off down to Oban or somewhere' to try to draw his pursuers with him, but Chadwick was having none of it.

Dick was still feeling sick. On Sunday, 23 December 1990, he learnt for sure that Howarth was back along with Hawkins. Joe McGuigan and Craig Paterson had spotted Howarth at 3.50 p.m. in The Caley with Burns. There was still no sign of movement by Forrest and Rae over to the east of Scotland. By Christmas Eve optimism was fading. In the surveillance log, Billy Reader makes the following bitter note at 6 p.m. on Christmas Eve: 'Saw Howarth and Burns in Caledonian Bar, drinking with others. Howarth exceptionally happy.'

The whole team had become despondent, convinced that they had let the drugs slip through their fingers. On the evening of Christmas Eve, Dick decided that it was time to cut their losses. He stood the team down, giving them some much-needed time for rest, save for a couple of volunteers to stay on with him in Ullapool on the now remote possibility that something might happen. Billy Reader volunteered, as did Joe McGuigan. That evening, Reader kept tabs on Burns and Howarth, who spent the evening in The Caley. At one stage, in an episode reminiscent of Dick's encounter with Chadwick at the Glenisla Hotel, Howarth recalls that Reader slipped off to the loo for a piss. As he did so, Howarth, who had been keeping an eye on Reader, got up and followed him into the urinals, taking up position right next to the Customs officer. He looked over at Reader, nodded affably, and said: 'So what brings you up to Ullapool at this time of year? I've not seen your face around here before . . .' Reader said the first thing that came into his head. 'Och, I'm looking for work. You don't know of any work going around these parts, do you?' Howarth fixed him with a long, steely gaze, before throwing his head back and guffawing. 'You expect me to believe you're looking for work? Come off it, pal – it's Christmas Eve, for fuck's sake.' He walked out, still laughing to himself and shaking his head, leaving Reader feeling lonely and small. He'd been rumbled, his cover blown. It was the perfect, shitty end to a perfect, shitty Christmas.

Things improved immeasurably for Dick and the team, however, on Boxing Day. They received word from an informant that the drugs had not been moved and were stashed somewhere along the coast. Dick was jubilant, punching the air as he began to ring around to tell the team they were back on and required back at work. No one minded their Boxing Day being interrupted in this way; they were just relieved to learn that all their hard work had not been for nothing, after all.

Back at Morefield Place, Howarth was getting the jitters. As well as Reader on Christmas Eve, he'd spotted one or two strange faces looking at him as he went about the village. He was being watched day and night, and it was doing his head in. By Wednesday, 27 December, he had had enough. He told Fiona and the kids to go and stay with her mum for a few days. He had decided to head down to Muir of Ord to be with Val for a few days and try to draw some of the heat of the surveillance with him. He slipped out of the house that morning and, looking around to make sure he wasn't being followed, headed out to the right, towards the beach. He broke into a sprint and ran along the river that flows from the village down to the sea. As he reached the front, he sprinted the last few hundred yards to the back of a block of flats a few streets back from the sea. He climbed over the wall of the last one, then made his way through the back gardens until he came to the one owned by a friend, Davey Hilton. He crouched by the back door and, reaching up, rapped on the kitchen window. A moment later, the door opened and his mate appeared. 'Fuck's sake, Crazy, you gave me a heart attack. What the fuck are you up to?'

'Let me in, man, I've got to use the phone.' As his pal made him a cup of tea, he dialled Val's number.

'Val? It's Chris. You've got to help me out . . .'

An hour or so later, Val pulled up outside and, as instructed by Howarth, reversed as close as she could to the front door. Davey came out, looked about and, seeing nobody, told Howarth the coast was clear. Howarth scuttled out, climbed into the back of the car and, lying on the floor, pulled some rugs over him. They were soon back at Val's and for the first time in weeks, he felt relaxed. They had managed to get there without picking up any surveillance. Maybe he could have a few days' peace and quiet.

It was not to be. That evening, he got a call from Chadwick. Fuck, he'd forgotten that he'd given him Val's number. Chadwick was not happy that he'd left Ullapool without telling him first. The pick-up was scheduled for the following night. Forrest and Rae would be heading north in a hired blue Transit van. They would call Howarth to report on their progress; he was to meet them en route and take them to the landing point. Things were moving towards their conclusion. Howarth felt sick. Surely they couldn't get away with it?

CHAPTER THIRTY-SIX

The following day, Dick was back into his stride. Klondyke was back in full swing, the control room at Dingwall police station was buzzing. The team were working the phones, the surveillance crew were radioing in reports and all was right with the world. He grabbed a cup of the foul brew that passed for coffee and headed for his desk. It was 3 p.m. Suddenly one of the team who was working the radio called him over excitedly, with a thumbs-up. 'It's Forrest – he's on the move.'

Dick permitted himself a smile of satisfaction. He should have had more faith. Their instincts had been right all along. Three-quarters of an hour later, the radio crackled again. Forrest had hired a blue Transit, plate number H739 MOH, from Eurodollar in Gellatly Street, near Marketgate in Dundee city centre. Dick felt a surge of adrenaline. This was surely it. Followed by his Customs tails, Forrest drove north, up through Dunkeld and onto the A9 for a short stretch, before heading for Pitlochry, an attractive Victorian resort in the Perthshire Highlands, popular with holidaymakers in general and hill walkers in particular. He pulled up in the car park at the bus station and his tails, two police officers named Matthieson and Alexander, pulled into a vacant space a few down from the van. It was 5.16 p.m.

Three minutes later, they got a shock. A blue Ford Sierra, plate number A950 YSC, pulled into the space next to them and a man dressed in full hill-walking kit got out. With a flash of recognition, Alexander realised who it was – and he was staring straight at them. 'Fuck, it's Ian Rae,' muttered Alexander under his breath. Quick as a flash, he wound down the window and called over to Rae, 'Excuse me, mate – can you tell us where the chip shop is?' It may not have been the best line in the world, but it seemed to work. Satisfied, Rae relaxed and explained that he wasn't a local, that he was here to go on a climbing holiday in the Grampians near Dalwhinnie, some 30 miles or so north. The two men thanked him, and he climbed into the van with Forrest. 'Shit, that was close,' said Matthieson as they watched the Transit pull off. They radioed ahead to the next leg of the relay team, who took over and kept tabs on the van as it travelled up the A9, finally stopping at Aviemore at around 7 p.m.

Forrest and Rae had stopped for a much-needed pint at the Winking Owl, a pub popular with the hardy – and hopeful – skiers prepared to risk a week of their annual leave for the capricious conditions of the Cairngorms. After 40 minutes, they headed back to the van and got on their way again. Every so often, they were seen to stop at telephone kiosks, phoning ahead to Howarth, as it later transpired, to check that they were still on. The news from Howarth was not good – the roads north of Inverness were impassable due to the appalling conditions. Only the main roads south of Inverness were being snow-ploughed. Ullapool was effectively snowed in, and there was no chance of the situation changing imminently.

An hour later, they pulled off the slushy main road and onto the virginal snow covering the car park at the Milburn Hotel in Inverness. The hotel was kept under surveillance overnight until 9 a.m. when they left. Throughout the evening, Forrest emerged every so often to use the telephone kiosk, eschewing the one in the hotel. The following morning, they climbed back into the van and headed south on the A9. The run had clearly been aborted until the conditions improved. Two Customs cars followed the van as it headed south. They soon found themselves in a slow convoy of cars stuck behind a snow-plough that was doing its utmost to clear the overnight fall on the A9.

It was a long, slow journey back to Pitlochry, where the two units saw Rae return to his Sierra and then drive in convoy with Forrest's hire van south on the A9. At 2.45 p.m., when they radioed in that Forrest was approaching Perth, Dick took the decision to stand the team down. Nothing was going to happen in the next couple of days with the roads up north in this state. The guys had worked hard and selflessly over the

Christmas period. It was time to give them a break. He asked for one volunteer to stay on in Ullapool with him – Frankie Cooper put himself forward – and a couple of guys to watch Forrest's place to discover when he was on the move again. Once Forrest set off, Dick reasoned, he'd have time to call everyone back to be in place by the time the van reached Ullapool.

And it was a welcome break for Howarth. Now assured that nothing would happen until sometime in the New Year, he could kick back and relax a little. A few days later, sick of being cooped up in the house, he proposed to Val that they take a run into Inverness. Val, feeling a little on edge from Howarth's persistent pacing up and down and peering out of the front window for, as she believed, non-existent watchers, readily agreed. She dropped Howarth at his favourite watering hole, the Eagle on Baron Taylors Street, the one he had visited before his first trip down to Malaga more than a year previously. She told him she'd be off shopping and would be parked behind the station if he got bored, otherwise she'd pick him up from the Eagle when she was done.

Howarth bought himself a pint and sat at a table in the window, watching the great whorls of snow swirl and swoop outside, settling gently in a carpet on the streets outside. The warmth of the bar, and the beer in his belly, made him feel cosy and for a few minutes, he forgot his woes and his feeling of being hunted and trapped. Then on the other side of the street, he saw a parked car with two occupants who seemed to be looking at him. Fuck, it's got to be Customs, he thought angrily. Damn them, could they not give him a moment's peace? On a whim, he finished off his pint and marched out into the snow.

He turned left and headed towards the station, casting an eye over his shoulder as he did so. Sure enough, one of the men got out of the car and began to follow him as he picked his way through the shoppers and office workers. He ducked into the station and threaded his way through the crowds to the station pub, Bertie's Bar, pausing only to check his pursuer was still in his wake, before going in.

Like most station pubs, Bertie's was doing brisk business, mainly from men who sat on their own nursing a pint and reading the back pages of the tabloids. Howarth ducked into a corner and watched the door. A moment later, the door opened and in rushed his pursuer. He looked young – 'too young for this job,' thought Howarth – and looked around anxiously until he came face-to-face with Howarth who was grinning at him, the tables having been turned.

'All right?' asked Howarth, not maliciously.

'Er, not bad,' stammered the man, clearly caught off guard. Recovering, he nodded outside at the black sky and the heavy snow. 'It's getting cold just now,' he offered by way of conversation.

'Oh, I don't know,' flashed back Howarth with a wide grin. 'I'd say things were beginning to hot up.' He chuckled at the man's retreating back, delighted to have caused discomfort.

It should be pointed out here, however, that Dick disputes whether it was one of the team. Dick says, 'When Chris and Noel came back from the run, they thought that there were Customs everywhere. They saw things that made them suspicious and sometimes, yeah, it was us, and other times, they were just being paranoid. There was the time that Craig Paterson was down outside Val's in Muir of Ord, and the car got stuck in a snowdrift and one of the neighbours had to dig them out.

'The people that Chris says he confronted weren't us. We had some guys keeping an eye on him in Muir of Ord and Inverness, but no one would be following him closely enough to be picked up by him. The people he tackled were probably just passers-by.'

Whatever the truth of it, just after the incident at Bertie's Bar, an acquaintance of Howarth's from Drumbeg, a fisherman named Donnie Mathieson, came in. He spotted Howarth and came over. The two men bought a pint and Mathieson explained that he was visiting his father in hospital, and that he'd been given a lift down by a neighbour, Donnie McLeod, who joined them a few minutes later. The conversation turned to fishing, and one of the men mentioned that an inflatable had appeared on the beach opposite Oldany Island. Howarth told them that it was his boat, that he had just left it there for a few days. It was to prove another piece of damning evidence, tying him to the boat.

A couple of days later, the call Howarth had been dreading came. Val answered and, giving him a look, passed him the receiver. 'Some guy called Jonathan,' she said.

Chadwick was brisk and to the point. 'Right, it's on for tomorrow night. Tam and Raz [Rae] are picking up a hire van and heading up your way. There's a lay-by with a bus stop at Braemore Junction, a few miles south of Ullapool.'

'Aye, I know it,' said Howarth, reflecting that everything would be finished – one way or another – shortly.

'Right,' said Chadwick. 'You're to meet them there at 8 p.m. and go with them. I've arranged for the gear to be left by the track near the road at Clashnessie Bay. Take the boys there, help load up the van and then your work is done.'

'What about my money?' Howarth wanted to know. He had received one package from Spain since getting back, containing £3,000. By his reckoning, there was a lot more to come. That package, suspiciously, had been opened and labelled 'Damaged in transit' by the Royal Mail.

'Don't worry, you'll get it in the next few days,' Chadwick assured him.

The next day, 6 January 1991, Howarth peeped out of Val's front window. In the street outside, he could see a stranger looking at his car, perplexed. He'd been snowed in overnight. Must be Customs, he thought. As it happens, he was right. He grinned as he saw the man knock on a neighbour's door to ask for help digging his car out. Serves you right, you bastard, thought Howarth. He called Val in and told her that he needed her to do something, to get in her car and drive off towards Inverness. If she was sure she wasn't being followed, she should double back and head up the Ullapool road. He'd slip out the back door, across the fields and wait for her there. With a sigh, Val agreed. From her statement to the police, she was beginning to tire of Howarth's cat-and-mouse games and would be glad to see the back of him, even if he was the father of her child. She went out and Howarth crawled to the back door, keeping down in case anyone was looking in.

He slipped out and quietly shut the door behind him. Outside, the sun shone brightly over snow-mantled fields. He set off in a loping run and eventually intersected with the Ullapool road a mile or so north of Muir of Ord. He waited by a frosty hedgerow and a few minutes later Val pulled up. There was no sign of anyone following. An hour later, she was pulling up outside Howarth's house in Morefield Place. Howarth thanked her for everything. She just nodded, and swung the car around to head back south. Inside, Howarth dialled Paul's number. 'Hi, Paul, it's Crazy again. Listen, mate, I need another favour . . .'

That evening, Paul drew up outside Howarth's house at 7.30 p.m. Howarth jumped in and the two men headed south out of Ullapool, down through wooded glens until they reached the lay-by at Braemore Junction. Howarth thanked Paul for his help and slipped him a few quid. He jumped out and, as he watched the van's tail-lights disappear back up the road, he suddenly felt very alone – and very afraid. Just before 8 p.m., he saw headlights coming down the road towards him from the direction of Ullapool. Howarth shrank back into the bus stop and, to his horror, the car swung into the lay-by. It was a police patrol car. It drew up next to the bus stop, close enough for him to hear the men's conversation. 'Fuck, is this it?' he asked himself. Apparently not – not yet, anyway, The patrol car swung back out onto the road five minutes later and headed off.

Howarth walked out onto the road and watched it go. Then, turning the other way, he could see headlights appear over the brow of a hill in the opposite direction. The pinpoints grew bigger and more dazzling as they grew closer, until they were on top of him. It was Forrest and Rae in a bright orange Transit van, bearing the legend 'Baxter's self-drive, Forfar' in huge letters, and a telephone number for good measure. 'Great,' said Howarth. 'That's fucking subtle, lads.' Forrest began to protest that it was the only van they'd had, but Howarth cut him off. Some international drugs smugglers they made – more like the Keystone Kops, he thought with a hollow laugh.

They headed back down to Inverness, keeping well clear of Ullapool, by now crawling with Customs, as they – rightly – imagined. Instead, they headed up the east-coast road and made their way to Bonar Bridge, a pretty little town famous for its bridge across the Kyle of Sutherland, first built in 1812 by our old friend, the prolific Thomas Telford. It had once been an important staging post on the Edinburgh–Caithness road. Although it had declined in importance throughout the 1980s, following the building of the Dornoch Firth Road Bridge, which, being much closer to the sea, cut out a good 20 miles' driving, it remained popular with tourists and hill walkers.

They pulled up at their destination for the night, the Dunroamin Hotel. Forrest and Rae entered to book a room (Howarth was going to stay in the van to check no one tried to fit a tagging device). Margaret Riddoch, the hotel proprietor remembered them. She said that they booked a twin room for one night. They said that they would be leaving at 4 a.m. to go to work and asked if they could borrow an alarm clock. She offered to get up to cook them breakfast, but they said that they wouldn't put her to the bother, and that she should just leave out some sandwiches for them. They paid cash in advance for their room, and she asked them to sign the register. In what is not the finest example of the workings of a master criminal mind, David Forrest signed in as 'D. Forrest.' But he was not stupid enough to use his own address. Oh no. The crafty old fox used his parents' address. That should fool them. At least Rae had the wits to use a false name and address – 'B. Robertson of Westmuir' – though on reflection, he tried to score out the 'B' and replace it with a 'D'. They then went up to their room.

199

Marilyn Dunoon, a 36-year-old bar assistant was on duty that night. She recalled that, shortly after Forrest and Rae went up to their room, a fair-haired man 'of Scandinavian appearance' – Howarth – came into the bar and ordered a pint of Special. A few minutes later, he was joined by Forrest and Rae, and the three sat at a table studying a map of northwest Scotland. A couple of interesting points arise from her testimony. The first is that she says: 'The fellow who was not resident only came to the bar when he first came in. After that, it was the two residents who bought the drinks.' This is fitting with a far more central role than Forrest and Rae would ever admit to, more like Chadwick's lieutenants, with Howarth the hired help who would expect his drinks to be paid for. And the second relates to Ian Rae's appearance, which had led Howarth to wonder what Rae's beautiful wife Lucinda, or Lucy, was doing with him. Describing Rae as 'late thirties, slim build, light brown short, straight hair, wearing blue denim jeans and jersey,' Marilyn Dunoon added, unnecessarily, that he 'struck her as quite good looking', stating that she would know him again.

Margaret Riddoch heard her two guests get up at 3 a.m. They went downstairs at 3.20 a.m., collected the sandwiches she had left for them in the dining room and then left. Looking out the window, she saw them climb into the van and drive away in the direction of Lairg.

It's a tough drive through bleak Highlands terrain from Bonar Bridge to Clashnessie Bay, beautiful in summer but forbidding in the depths of winter and the middle of the night. Howarth recalls that they arrived at the track leading to the beach at around 5.30 a.m. Burns had been told to make sure the gear was moved up to the roadside gate by the track the previous night. As instructed, Burns was there with several other local figures he had drafted in. The van reversed into the gateway, chipping a post as it did so. The rear doors were pulled open and a shadowy army of helpers moved swiftly, loading up the priceless cargo in a matter of minutes.

Forrest and Rae offered Howarth a lift, but he declined with a shake of his head. He told them that, if he were them, he would go the long way around the north and then down the east coast, avoiding Ullapool at all costs. Howarth bade farewell to the two men and they set off – heading south towards Ullapool. They had chosen to ignore his advice. Howarth jumped in a vehicle with a few locals and they headed back down to Ullapool. He felt drained and relieved. His deadly work for Chadwick appeared – finally – to be over.

CHAPTER THIRTY-SEVEN

It had been a relatively stress-free New Year for Graham Dick. The gear was still waiting to be moved, the key suspects were under constant surveillance and Operation Klondyke was in full swing. He had stood most of the team down for the New Year, except for Frankie Cooper, who volunteered to stay on in Ullapool – 'much to our families' disgust,' says Dick. They had gatecrashed a Hogmanay party at the Harbour Lights Hotel on New Year's Eve. They started off on beers and later moved on to gin and tonics. Dick recalls: 'Around three in the morning, Frankie said, "What the hell are all those wee bottles on the table?", squinting at them, trying to focus. So we looked at them, and they were all bottles of tonic, all full. And then we twigged. We were so drunk, we'd been drinking neat gin with ice all night!'

They'd earned it. From looking as though they would snatch defeat from the jaws of victory, a few basic slip-ups and displays of amateurism by Chadwick and his crew meant that Customs were very much back on. Nothing would be happening for a few days – the foul winter weather that was hitting them just now would ensure that the roads would remain impassable for at least a few more days. Dick could afford to relax. A few days later, they received intelligence that the boys were ready to go, that the pick-up was imminent, so Dick recalled everyone to get back into position. What happened next was designed to ensure that his stress levels would go shooting through the roof.

Because of the locale as previously described, Rae's flat was unsuitable for surveillance without it 'showing out' (that is, without being detected by the party under surveillance), especially in the blizzards that were hitting the Highlands – cars would stand out like a sore thumb, and car tracks on freshly fallen snow would give the game away. The Glenisla Hotel was a regular haunt of Chadwick and Rae, and so would be too risky to use as a surveillance base. So the decision was taken to concentrate all resources on Forrest over in Dundee.

A team of four cars was despatched to watch Forrest. The way the system worked is that three cars would be spaced at intervals along the road from the estate where Forrest lived, and they would act as a relay team once the move was on. The fourth car would be 'the eyeball', watching the entrance to Forrest's estate closely. As soon as Forrest made a move, the eyeball would notify the other cars, which would then move into position, ready to take up the pursuit. The advantage of the system was that no one car would have to follow for long stretches, being able to drop back and let colleagues take over to avoid the risk of 'showing out', of being detected by the quarry.

Unfortunately, the system failed that night. Forrest's home was at Aberlady Crescent in the Whitfield area of Dundee, a tough and deprived neighbourhood. Aberlady Crescent is part of a council estate with a maze of dead-ends, cul-de-sacs and covered walkways between blocks – a nightmare for surveillance. Add to that the fact that the night of 6 January 1991 was a black one, with blizzards obscuring the view, and it was a recipe for disaster.

The eyeball unit had seen no sign of Forrest leaving the previous afternoon. By 2 a.m., the lack of movement from Forrest's flat was seriously concerning Dick. He gave the order to one unit to head for the previous parking spot at Pitlochry – he knew from the aborted run on 28 December that Forrest would head for Pitlochry to pick up Rae – sweeping by Rae's place, just in case Forrest had managed to give them the slip, after all. Driving conditions were atrocious as they headed up through Blairgowrie to join the tortuous A93 that leads up into the Cairngorm mountains. The snow was coming down furiously and, even at full speed, it was all the wipers could do to clear the fall from the windscreen. From Blairgowrie, they should have turned left towards Pitlochry some ten miles along the road; in these conditions, they missed their turn and carried on up to Braemar, a further 20 miles up into the mountains. The team was made up almost exclusively of Glaswegians who were not familiar with the area, and trying to map-read while driving through twisting mountain roads, in pitch black during a blizzard, had proved too much. Up ahead they saw through the swirling snowflakes a sign proclaiming that they had reached Braemar; a deer stood in the middle of the deserted, eerily snow-lit road, looking at them with mild curiosity. Cursing heavily, they did a U-turn and started heading back over the hills the way they had come. They finally arrived at the bus station car park in Pitlochry at 5.45 a.m. to find Rae's car there; there was no sign of Forrest's hire van.

Back in Dingwall at the control room, Dick was growing frantic. Forrest had managed to slip through the net. They now had no surveillance and no vehicle description or plate number to go on. He acted quickly, consulting a roadmap. Any vehicle heading south from Ullapool would inevitably have to pass through the Maryburgh junction between Dingwall and Inverness. Similar lookouts had been set up on the east coast road. He sent someone down there immediately to watch for passing vehicles. He also put out an all-points broadcast to police units of the Northern Constabulary to be on the alert for any vans on the move, with instructions that the registration numbers be radioed in to be checked against the police national computer, or 'PNC'd'. Says Dick, 'If the van showed as coming from Dundee, Angus, Tayside, anywhere on the east coast, we were going to have it.'

He was pacing up and down now, praying for some news. Just after 7 a.m., the radio crackled. It was Jim Conroy, radioing from Ullapool to say that he had seen a van coming down the hill towards the village from the north. Could this be it? A few minutes later, at 7.10 a.m., Maggie McKeand, who was watching Howarth and Burns's houses, reported that lights had just come on at both. That must be them back from the run, thought Dick with grim satisfaction and a feeling of relief. Now all they needed was the van.

At 7 a.m., Sergeant Mike MacLennan of the Northern Constabulary had left his home in Ullapool. He was due at police headquarters in Inverness at 8 a.m. for a training course. A few miles south of Ullapool, as he passed through Corrieshalloch Gorge, he spotted a stationary bright-orange Transit van with 'Baxter's self-drive, Forfar' blazoned across its side. One man was sitting at the wheel; another man was walking back to the van from the public toilet. Aware of the hunt for the landing crew, he radioed in the registration – B79 VSL – to the control room at Dingwall. It was 7.15 a.m.

A couple of minutes later, they had a match for the van from the PNC. It was registered as a hire van, owned – unsurprisingly – by a company named Baxter's in Forfar. Dick whooped and punched the air in triumph. It had to be them. He got on to Tayside Police and asked them to send some uniforms around to wake up Mr Baxter to find out to whom he had hired the vehicle.

Lewis Baxter was awoken by a knock on his door at 8 a.m. on Monday, 7 January 1991. The 57-year-old had been running his hire business for some 30 years without trouble and he was surprised to have an early morning visit from the police. They explained that they needed to know to whom he had hired this particular van. Baxter pulled on some clothes and headed over to the office to check his paperwork. Running his finger down the entries, he found what he was looking for. 'Ah, yes, here we are,' he said. 'I hired that Transit on Saturday to a David Michael Forrest . . .'

At 8.15 a.m., the Transit passed through the Maryburgh junction, picking up a police tail as it did so. At the control room, Dick says, the feeling of relief was indescribable after all the highs and lows. There was a debate about whether they should allow the van to continue to its destination and try to pick up the next link in the chain as well. Says Dick, 'Were we tempted to let the van go on to London? Well, we had a lot of conversation about that, and a couple of the guys wanted to do it. We just didn't have the resources to do that. We'd been up for 48 hours, don't forget, the troops were scattered all over the place and we were just dead on our feet. You're talking a 15-hour drive down south, so I don't think we could have done it physically, and I don't think we could have done it without it showing out.'

Dick decided that they would take the van as soon as they had enough men and vehicles to do the arrest. They had enough to take out the transport crew, the landing people and the organisers, Jonathan Chadwick and his associates in Spain. The troops were being called in from the various parts of Scotland where they were scattered. By 9.20 a.m., when the Transit van had reached Newtonmore on the A9, they had enough manpower to pull them. When Forrest and Rae were pulled over at Corrieshalloch Gorge, they had put the bales of drugs into green garden waste liners and had labelled them 'Inert samples – Dounreay', a nuclear-processing plant near Thurso, on the north-eastern tip of Scotland, and created a fake delivery note that purported to show that they were to be delivered to a Professor Davidson, Department of Geophysics, Campbell House, Taviton Street, London WC12. There was no department of geophysics at University College, no Professor Davidson, Campbell House was a student hall of residence and there is no area of London with the postcode WC12. Other than that, it was a pretty good cover. The van was being tailed by two marked police cars and two unmarked Customs vehicles. When the order was given at 9.20, the police cars put on their sirens and pulled out to stop the van. Forrest pulled over on the hard shoulder and he and Rae jumped out, all idea of a cover story gone, with their hands in the air, saying, 'We were told it was cannabis.' As Dick says, 'That struck us as odd, although we didn't attach the proper significance to it at the time. I mean, no one was saying it wasn't cannabis.'

One detail concerned Dick. A Transit van would not be capable of transporting four tonnes of cannabis, more like half a tonne (which it, in fact, turned out to be). All their intelligence was that four tonnes of hash would be arriving in Scotland from Spain or Morocco. Where the fuck was the rest of it?

Forrest and Rae were taken back to police headquarters in Inverness and interviewed, later being charged with being knowingly concerned in the importation of cannabis, and possession with intent to supply cannabis. During his interview, Forrest told the interrogating officers that he had been instructed to pick the cannabis up from Clashnessie Bay, drive it to London and leave it in a parking space at Brent Cross Shopping Centre on the North Circular road, the A406. He was then to make a phone call to a number he had written down. An officer was despatched to trace the number. It was a payphone on Fann Street, part of the Golden Lane council estate, near the Barbican in the City of London, where social housing sits cheek-by-jowl with the affluent buildings of one of the world's richest financial districts. No one was seen waiting for the phone call that never came.

Forrest did a double-take when he first saw Graham Dick. 'I know you,' he said. 'I've seen you on the telly!' He had recognised Dick from the video of *The Duty Men* that Jonathan had made them watch repeatedly. He claimed that he had been promised £15,000 for his part in the job. Interviewed by Frankie Cooper and George Cockburn of Customs, he sang like a canary, as they say in some of the more poorly scripted films. He admitted that he had tried to do a run on 28 December but had had to turn back due to the appalling weather. He confirmed that Jonathan Chadwick was the head of the organisation, and said that he and Rae held equal rank further down the chain. He claimed that he understood that the cannabis was brought to the UK on a boat crewed by Chris Howarth, who was to be their main contact for collecting the stash. He went on to confirm details of his various meetings with Chadwick and Howarth.

In another room, Rae was saying much the same thing to Joe McGuigan and John Buchanan, although he claimed that he was less of a player than Forrest, having been offered only £5,000 for his role. He also landed Burns (or 'Greasy' as he called him) in it, saying that he had met him on a number of occasions, including one time in Newcastle, and again on 16 December. Then he had travelled up to Ullapool with

Chadwick and met Burns to agree a pick-up point where the four-wheel drive would take the gear. He also said that he was 'fairly certain' that Burns was one of the men who had helped load the gear onto the van earlier that morning. So much for honour among thieves.

The van had by now been driven to the pound at police headquarters at Inverness and arrangements were being made for the gear to be transferred to the forensic laboratory at Pitt Street, Glasgow, for analysis. It was time to pull in the three musketeers – Howarth, Hawkins and Burns.

CHAPTER THIRTY-EIGHT

When Howarth got home at 7.10 a.m. on Monday, 7 January 1990, he was physically and emotionally drained. He sank into his favourite armchair, then, remembering that he had filched a bottle of Spanish brandy from the galley on the *DIMAR-B*, he got up to fetch it. Throwing away the cork, he began to swig liberally. As he says, 'It didn't even touch the sides.' After a while, Fiona got up and he told her what had happened, talking 19 to the dozen, high on adrenalin and brandy. After a couple of hours, he took himself off to bed, saying to Fiona, 'Call me at midday, love.' As it happens, Customs and Excise were to beat her to it.

Howarth awoke to find his bedroom crowded with people. His initial reaction was one of fear, that it could be the vengeful owners of the drugs that had gone missing overboard, anyone. One spoke up. 'Christopher Eric Howarth? We are arresting you on suspicion of being knowingly concerned in the importation and supply of a controlled drug, namely cannabis.'

'Thank fuck for that,' was all Howarth could reply, bizarrely relieved that his nightmare was heading to its natural conclusion. He got dressed and went downstairs with his newfound friends. Among them was one local policewoman whom he recognised. She shrugged apologetically, as if to say, 'It's out of our hands.' Leading events was a Detective Sergeant Angus Chisholm, a moustachioed 38-year-old whom Howarth remembers as 'a hard bastard'. He gave the order to search the house.

Howarth could only stand by as they did so. He decided to make himself useful. There was little he could do, after all, under the circumstances.

'Anyone fancy a coffee?' he asked pleasantly. Chisholm glared at him, and carried on searching. On a bookshelf in the front room, he found a matchbox. Opening it, he exclaimed, 'Aha!' Howarth couldn't help but laugh.

'What, you're accusing me of being behind a huge amount of drugs coming into the country, and you think £5 of hash is going to be evidence?' Chisholm said nothing, dropping the matchbox into a polythene bag with exaggerated care.

A few minutes later, he had cause to look satisfied. Holding a piece of paper aloft with a triumphant smile, he said to Howarth, 'Did you write this?'

Howarth said, 'No, the Poet Laureate sent it to me as a present.'

Behind the cockiness, he was shaking with fear. Christ, why had he been so stupid as to leave that poem lying around? It read: 'I'm carrying a cargo/A cargo in a ship/Carrying a cargo/A cargo full of shit/ Doing time, doing plenty/ Doing all of my twenty . . .' And at the bottom, after several similarly incriminating verses, he had scrawled in huge letters: 'OH FUCK I WILL DO MY TIME.'

Other officers were taking away samples of Howarth's clothing in polythene evidence bags. Things were looking bad, concluded Howarth. Just then, the front door opened, and Fiona came in with the kids. 'What the hell is going on?' she demanded. Howarth tried to explain, but one of the officers gently took his elbow. 'Come on, Chris,' he said, not unkindly, 'It's time to go.' The enormity of what was happening, together with the sight of the baffled expressions on his little girls' faces, overcame Howarth. Great salty tears began to roll freely down his cheeks. 'Come here and give your old man a hug,' he said, knowing it would be the last time they would do so for a long while.

Over at Burns's and Hawkins's places, it was a similar story. All three were being taken separately for questioning, Howarth and Hawkins to Inverness, and Burns to Dingwall. Burns got into a van with Customs officer Malcolm Sharp and Detective Constable Walker of Inverness CID. During the journey, Burns appeared depressed. He asked what colour the van was that had been pulled. When he was told that it was red or orange, he gave a resigned look, and began to talk. He only did it, he said, because he'd been told that he'd receive £75,000 for his part, enough money to get a new boat and start again. He asked them why they hadn't taken them out when they'd been loading the van, but received no reply. The comments were duly recorded in Sharp's notebook and corroborated by Walker, but after seeing a solicitor at Dingwall, Burns denied ever having made them and refused to answer any questions put to him.

Over at Inverness, Billy Reader and Tony Jackson interviewed Howarth. He denied pretty well everything. He admitted to having been out of the country for seven or eight weeks, but when pressed for details, he developed a severe case of amnesia. He could recall only that he had been in Spain hitchhiking, but could not remember the names of any places he had stayed. He denied ever having met Jonathan Chadwick. Shown a photo of him with Chadwick in Benalmádena, he changed his story, saying that he had met him once but knew him as Dave. Confronted with details of the surveillance operation against him, and his repeated meetings with Chadwick, he changed his story again and accepted that he had met him a few times socially and by chance around Ullapool. He denied ever having met Forrest and Rae; they were brought into the room separately and he continued to deny ever having met them, even when he was told that they had confessed and named him. He denied knowing Tony McDonald in Newcastle – until it was pointed out to him that McDonald was his cousin and that he was known to have spent the summer with him diving on Mull.

Down the corridor, Maggie McKeand and Jim Conroy were not making much better progress with Hawkins. They asked him when he had last been out of the country and he told them that he could not remember. He was asked if he might have been to Spain, and he told them that he had never been to Spain in his life. When asked where he had been during the six weeks prior to Christmas, he said that he had been staying in Newcastle, but could not remember where, or with whom. He was told that they had evidence that a Noel Hawkins had travelled from Ullapool to Malaga on 11 November 1990 – was there another Noel Hawkins in Ullapool that he knew of? Hawkins now clammed up, replying 'no comment' to everything that was put to him.

That afternoon, Howarth, Hawkins and Burns were each charged with one count of being knowingly concerned with importation of a controlled drug, namely cannabis, into the UK, two charges of supply, to Forrest and Rae, and one charge of possession. Things were not looking good for the boys. They optimistically sought bail, which was, of course, refused, and were placed on remand in Porterfield Prison in Inverness to await trial.

208

It was time for Dick to get cracking. Under Scottish law, the Crown has 110 days from the time of charging a suspect to bringing the case to court. There was a lot to be done. His first, and most pressing, concern was where the rest of the cannabis was. As Dick says: 'It was extremely disappointing just to have half a tonne of cannabis. It's OK, but it's not that big a deal, something that drugs squad could just as easily handle without bringing in Customs. We'd been expecting the full four tonnes and we were baffled as to where the rest of it was.' He called out the spotter planes again and, having been told by Forrest and Rae exactly where they had picked up the gear, he sent several poor sods up there in the slush and snow to stumble around in their Wellington boots, searching for non-existent cannabis. By the evening, it was clear that it was nowhere around, and he called it off. They did, however, find the beached inflatable, which was tagged and removed as evidence.

That evening, the team went for celebratory drinks in Dingwall, although, given the eventual size of the haul, the affair was slightly muted. The following day, they learnt they had real cause to celebrate. Across the corridor from the control room, John Buchanan was with the forensic team as they did a preliminary analysis. As they told him their initial findings, he listened intently, growing increasingly wide-eyed, before returning to the control room. Buchanan looked at Dick, with a shocked expression. 'Graham, I don't know how to put this. That hash – well, it's not hash. It's half a tonne of Colombian cocaine.' There was a stunned silence, during which everyone else stopped what they were doing, trying to take in what they had just learnt. Finally, Dick let out a long, low whistle. 'Fuck me,' was all he could say. Later, during the trial of the three men, he was asked in the dock what his reaction was when he learnt the true nature of the haul. He replied: 'I don't remember exactly what I said, but it would certainly have been stronger than, "Oh, gosh".'

The team had, almost inadvertently, managed to pull off the UK's largest ever drugs bust. Had colleagues down in London suspected for one minute what they were dealing with, they would have applied immense pressure for the case to be taken off Dick and his team and passed to a unit down south. Noses had been put out of joint, but there was a grudging admiration for what the team had pulled off. A spate of stories appeared around the time, no doubt the result of meetings between envious colleagues in the Department and friendly reporters on national and local press over a pint or two, claiming that it was only thanks to an alert local copper, Sergeant Mike MacLennan, or 'Eagle-eyed Mike' as he is now known around Ullapool, that the van was taken out. Dick has nothing but respect for MacLennan, but feels that this version of events belittles his team's achievement: 'It was bloody good police work by Mike, there's no question about that, but to be fair to ourselves, it was us who had put out the call to watch out for the van. We had guys stationed at the Maryburgh junction and various other key points in the north of Scotland, meaning that whatever route the guys had come, we would have had them.'

This was not the time to be bickering over who should get the credit, however. They had a lot of work to do, gathering evidence. They took paint samples from the inflatable, which matched samples found on some of Howarth's clothing, tying him to the boat. They also had statements from the two Drumbeg fishermen, Mathieson and MacLeod, in which they stated that Howarth had freely admitted the boat was his when they met him in Bertie's Bar at Inverness station. They had found hair samples in the back of the hire van that belonged to Howarth, tying him to the run. And most importantly, they had Forrest's and Rae's statements incriminating Howarth, Hawkins and Burns.

The Procurator Fiscal, David Hingston, was also keen to prove importation beyond any reasonable doubt, so they had traces of sisal in the inflatable and, of course, the bales themselves, that expert witnesses said could only have come from South America. The outboard motor on the inflatable contained petrol with a green dye; Dick and his team made enquiries all over the world but were unable to discover where the petrol had come from. No matter; the case against the three men was pretty watertight.

On 15 March 1991, at the High Court in Edinburgh, Forrest and Rae pleaded guilty to possession with intent to supply a controlled drug, namely cocaine. Although Customs felt that they had enough through their surveillance of the two men to make an importation or conspiracy charge stick, their lawyers made it clear that they would fight it all the way. As Customs needed their testimony in the imminent case against Howarth, Hawkins and Burns, it was decided to accept the plea bargain. Forrest's and Rae's claims that they were simply couriers on the periphery of the operation, who would be paid respectively £15,000 and £5,000, seem to have been accepted by the trial judge, Lord Marnoch, who imposed relatively light sentences. Lord Marnoch said that Forrest was prepared to act as a courier in the supply of a substantial amount of illegal drugs and jailed him for ten years. He told Rae that he was satisfied that his role was subordinate and jailed him for seven years. As this was in the days when prisoners could get up to two-thirds remission for good behaviour, the boys could have expected to be out after just two or three years. Which was nice. Howarth, Hawkins and Burns could not hope for such leniency.

CHAPTER THIRTY-NINE

Towards the end of April, Howarth was told to pack up his belongings at Porterfield Prison in Inverness, and be ready in an hour. 'Why, where am I going?' he asked. The screw remained impassive. 'You'll find out soon enough, laddie,' he said. An hour later, Howarth was in the back of a meat wagon heading for Saughton Prison, in Edinburgh. Their trial was scheduled to begin at the High Court in Edinburgh on 29 April 1991, in Court Nine, before Lord Penrose. Howarth was represented by Kevin Drummond, QC.

The sheer weight of the evidence against the three men meant that the outcome of the trial was always going to be a foregone conclusion. None of them chose to take the stand in their own defence. Early on, Kevin Drummond approached the Crown to indicate that his client, Christopher Howarth, was now prepared to plead guilty in return for a reduced sentence. This plea bargain was rejected by the Crown. As the Americans might put it, it was a day late and a dollar short.

Witness after witness took the stand to add to the mountain of evidence against the three men. At one point, Roy Stoddart, head of the cocaine intelligence unit, was called. He was asked whether it was conceivable that the cocaine could have been synthetically produced in this country. He explained that cocaine hydrochloride was a derivative of the coca plant only grown in South America and that the sisal, or hessian, found in the bales had been analysed and shown to come from there as well. Hingston was determined to leave nothing to chance on the main charge of importation. He was then asked to value the haul. He paused for a moment, then said, 'It is worth in excess of £100 million.' There was a gasp from the jury. The following day, all papers carried screaming headlines, such as '£100 million coke haul was biggest ever!'

The methodology for valuing the coke was as follows. Previous seizures of coke on the street revealed a purity of 39 per cent, and Customs stated that, at this time, the street price for coke was £87 per gram, as against a price today of £50.

The equation, then, is a simple one:

$$87/_{39} \times 91 = £203 \text{ (price per gram)} \quad 203 \times 500,000$$
$$= £101,500,000 \text{ (value of haul)}$$

We will look more closely at this methodology in the final chapter.

At one point in the proceedings, the Procurator Fiscal, David Hingston, deduced that the line of questioning by Howarth's barrister, Kevin Drummond, appeared to be leading to a defence that the inflatable would not be capable of transporting 500 kg of cocaine without capsizing or sinking. Hingston slipped out of court and gave some instructions to Graham Dick. The following day, members of the team purchased an identical inflatable which was then loaded up with 500 one-kilogram bags of salt and two Customs officers had a lot of fun sailing the craft around Troon harbour. Needless to say, the boat coped admirably with its cargo. This evidence was adduced in court, much to Kevin Drummond's fury, who claimed that he had been ambushed and that the Crown must have been approaching witnesses unlawfully for them to have known what was coming. Hingston countered that he had surmised that this would be a possible line of defence and so had sensibly taken precautions to counter it. The trial judge, Lord Penrose, ruled in the Crown's favour and the evidence stood.

On 28 May Drummond summed up, stating that 'there is not a shred of evidence that anything about drugs was ever mentioned', that his client had believed he was being taken on to do a yacht delivery. He ended his elegant summing up by saying to the jury: 'I invite you to acquit on what you have heard – and on what you have not heard.' That courteous invitation was declined. That night, back in Saughton, Howarth made the following entry in his journal.

> I continue to read my newfound book, *Insights from the Prophet Isaiah*. I turn to this book when I need strength. Are my prayers being answered? I ask myself as I take a shower. I rub my skin to cleanse myself, and say over and over again in my head, "I stand

before you, God, naked. Please help to cleanse me, God, please help to cleanse me, God, please" . . .'

His prayers fell on deaf ears. On 30 May the jury returned. Howarth recalls that he was not expecting anything less than he got. Howarth now says: 'I knew I was fucked. I'd known I was fucked since we'd landed the sodding stuff. Ullapool was crawling with Customs; it was madness to try to move the gear, but Jonathan wouldn't listen. The only questions in my mind were: "How long will I get? Will it be more than a 20-stretch or less? And will Robbie and Noel get off?"'

He didn't have to wait long to find out. The foreman of the jury stared straight ahead impassively as he announced that all three were guilty as charged, although they returned a verdict of not proven on a couple of charges for Hawkins and Burns. It made little difference.

Lord Penrose moved swiftly to sentencing. Howarth recalls that he tossed aside pre-sentencing reports prepared for the court by social workers, scornfully insisting that he had no interest in reading them. He accepted that they were pawns in a bigger game, but said that he had no choice but to impose hefty sentences *pour encourager les autres*. Addressing Howarth first, he said that he was the undoubted ringleader of the landing party. He sentenced Howarth to 25 years on the importation charge, and 15 years each on the charges of possession and supply. Howarth's mind was reeling. All he could think was that 55 years would mean that he would die in prison, that he would never know freedom again. It wasn't for another hour or so that his lawyer explained that the sentences would run concurrently.

Howarth's entry in his prison journal for that night makes for grim reading. It reads:

> As I write this, I find myself in a single cell, classed as a Category A prisoner, which means that I am locked up 24 hours a day. What more do they want? I have given everything. I have been given 25 years, and still they want more. I just do not have anything left to give – except my life, which is getting closer now than ever. If I dwell on it any longer, it will happen. I will end it. The only thing that keeps me going now is a photograph of my Fiona, and the kids, who have lost their dad. The pain hurts me, hurts me hard, more than ever before. I feel numb to the bone.
>
> I will try to put it into words. Life is lost, has lost all true

sense of place. I cry openly in front of grown people. I cannot help it. My face feels hot, my head thumps. I am a man without hope, a man with nothing left. They have taken it all. Twenty-five years. That figure will not leave me. Twenty-five years. My God, why me? Why do I deserve this? My skin tingles and moves without thought from me. In 25 years, my oldest daughter will be 33, my age now, and the youngest will be 28. Oh my God, no, no. I hate God and all he stands for. I prayed to be saved. I believed, not just for me, but for Fiona and the kids. Now I am destroyed in one afternoon.

There will be those who will say that Howarth should have thought about the consequences before getting involved with Chadwick. But it is hard not to feel some compassion for the man. Winston Churchill, no woolly liberal, once said: 'The mood and the temper of the public with regard to the treatment of crime and criminals is one of the most unfailing tests of the civilisation of any country.' Anyone that can take delight in such bleak and unrelenting punishment for weakness and venality must surely have failed this civilisation test.

Hawkins and Burns each received 15 years for their part in the case, although Burns was cleared on the charge of importation – not that it did him any good. Hawkins recalls that when he heard his sentence, his legs began to buckle. A screw gripped his arm tightly and whispered, 'Stand up and be proud for your mother, laddie.' Howarth was moved straight to Shotts, a notoriously severe Category A prison 15 miles south-east of Glasgow. During his time there, he was chosen to be one of ten high-profile prisoners to be moved to the 'Special Unit', an experimental segregated wing of the prison. As a result, he would be listed in a feature in the tabloid *Daily Record* as one of 'Scotland's ten most dangerous men'.

Hawkins and Burns both successfully applied to be transferred to prisons in England, Hawkins on the grounds that he had relatives in Falmouth, Cornwall, Burns on the grounds that his son lived with his partner Karen Doffman's mother in London. Howarth explains that there might have been another reason for their transfer request. 'Up here, this was a massive case, with wall-to-wall coverage, so they're more likely to make an example of you. Down there, they've got loads more nasty bastards inside to worry about, so they're more likely just to want to get you through the system and back out as quickly as possible, with minimum hassle.' If this is true, it seems to have worked. Hawkins was released at his earliest possible parole date, five years into his sentence. He used his time inside wisely, getting training and qualifications that, arguably, he would not have had on the outside. He is now married and lives quietly and respectably in the south of England, seldom returning to his former life in Ullapool. Burns was released after his second parole hearing, six years into his sentence. He returned to Ullapool and lives much as he did before. Howarth sees him around the village, but the two are not on speaking terms.

As for Jonathan Chadwick, a warrant for his arrest went out via Interpol in January 1991, shortly after the seizure. Dick had intelligence that *Shearwake* was due to do another run. During the trial of the three men, one spectator watched the proceedings with a great deal of interest from the public gallery. Legal reasons prevent him being named, but he was known to Customs as an associate of Chadwick's, a man from Fife on the east coast of Scotland. On 26 October 1991, he flew out to Spain with two other men. One was another Fifer, who was under surveillance and was seen to board *Shearwake* along with our old friend Ditus Neumann. Spanish Customs were one step ahead of them, however; on 13 January 1992, *Shearwake* was taken out near Almeria. On board were Neumann, a fellow German national, an Italian national and the Scotsman from Fife. Also on board was 500 kg of cannabis resin.

Shortly prior to Chadwick's associates from Fife flying down to Spain, there was another interesting development. Operación Galicia was a major Spanish operation against drugs smuggling, Galicia being notorious for providing smugglers. It was the home region of Francisco José Boo Torres, the captain of the *DIMAR-B* that had taken Howarth and Hawkins for their not-so-pleasant cruise to the Caribbean and back home for Christmas. Operación Galicia was headed by an ambitious young judge named Baltasar Garzón, who would later achieve notoriety by having the Chilean fascist dictator (and close personal friend of former British Prime Minister Margaret Thatcher) Augosto Pinochet arrested for suspected crimes against humanity when he came to visit England. On 16 October Garzón's men took out a boat named the *MV RAND* on the high seas 50 miles off the Portuguese coast. On board were two crew members who were listed as being on board the *DIMAR-B* during the run for Chadwick, José Francisco Trigo Freijoo and Francisco José Rodriguez Rajoy. They had on board 50 packages, each containing 20 kilos of uncut Colombian cocaine – neatly wrapped in

Gucci tape, from the same Cali cartel laboratory that had supplied the cocaine seized in Operation Klondyke. Clearly, Torres's men had decided to go freelance.

Dick was now chiefly concerned with Chadwick and Torres, the two main villains as he saw it: 'The sentences that Chris, Noel and Robbie got were tough, very tough. I think there was a degree of politics behind it. It's not breaking any state secrets to say that it would be nigh on impossible to police every inlet, every estuary, every inch of coastline in Scotland. The coast of Argyll alone is longer than that of the whole of France, and that's just one area.

'So the thinking was probably to send out a very strong message as a deterrent, to say that if you do smuggle drugs, and you get caught, you're going to get the book thrown at you. I think there's a strong case for arguing that Forrest and Rae were more central to the operation than the others. As for Chadwick and Torres, they were professionals, far more ruthless, who knew exactly what they were doing and were quite happy for the others to carry the can when the whole thing went belly up.'

We'll come to Torres shortly. With regard to Chadwick, he gave his followers the slip for some time. As the song has it, though, he could run – but he could not hide. Not forever.

CHAPTER FORTY

As has been previously pointed out, Jonathan was very close to his mum. An analysis of her accounts shows she was heavily involved with Jonathan's financial matters. After selling Mackay's Hotel in Strathpeffer, £211,000 went into her business account. The overdraft was almost £80,000, leaving her around £130,000 to take into retirement in Spain. She put £20,000 into a current account, the rest being transferred to a high-interest account. A sum of £29,000 was transferred from an account Jonathan held in Luxembourg to his mother's high-interest account, which then went back out to another account held by Jonathan in Gibraltar, so it seems that she was effectively laundering her son's money.

Added to these various transactions, her diary entries suggested an intimate knowledge of Jonathan's affairs. 13 June 1990: 'Jonathan got boat today.' 23 June: 'Jonathan to UK.' 8 August 1990: 'Ian [Rae] and Lucy back home.' 4 January 1991: 'David [Forrest] paid for ticket to Spain.' This was presumably a sign that Forrest was preparing to bolt to Spain after doing the run three days later. Then on 9 January 1991, after the bust: 'Jonathan and Moina rang, saw piece in paper. May be Rae. Worried.' By now living back in Scotland, in Stanley, near Perth, Dorothy Chadwick was still popping over to Spain to see Jonathan and Moina from time to time. On 27 January, she writes: 'Went to Spain. Moina met me, picked up Jonathan. Went to Gibraltar, went to both banks. Got my money matters cleared. Took out £2,000.' One has to question why her son, a drugs smuggler, had to fly her over to Spain to take her to a bank in Gibraltar to draw out large sums of cash if she believed everything to be above board.

On 15 March 1991, she writes: 'Tam [David Forrest] and Ian [Rae] sentenced at Edinburgh today. Tam 10 years, Ian 7 years. Dreadful.' There is no record of her showing the same compassion later on to Howarth, Hawkins and Burns. On 16 March, she writes, 'All in papers about the boys. Wonder if Jonathan knows.' A picture begins to emerge of a Violet Kray-like figure who could see no wrong in her son, and referred to his criminal associates as 'the boys'.

Jonathan managed to avoid arrest for a long time, despite an Interpol warrant. He was eventually picked up 18 months after the cocaine bust, on 26 May 1992 at Fuengirola, on the Costa del Sol. He was with his mother. He was travelling under the passport of one Alan Archibald Lumsden, a Fifer – the identity had clearly been organised by some of his Scottish associates, although there is no suggestion that Lumsden knew that his passport was being used in this way. The car he was driving was also registered in this name. He attempted to run away, but was soon caught. A photograph of him taken in custody clearly shows a black eye; he must have put up a fight. Both he and his mother refused to comment, and he was placed in Alicante Prison.

Chadwick fought the extradition order tooth and nail, but his options finally ran out after 18 months of judicial wrangling on Wednesday, 24 November 1993 when it was approved by the Spanish Supreme Court. Then a miracle appeared to happen. Despite the fact that he was due to fly back to the UK imminently to stand trial, the authorities decided to move him to Valencia Prison on 4 December

1993. As he was about to be transferred from Alicante Prison, and was being taken outside to be put in a meat wagon, Chadwick ran away, together with another prisoner, an Algerian. How he managed to get out of the prison, away from the guards and avoid being picked up is a mystery. Some, naturally, suspect corruption within the Spanish prison service, and on 6 December 1993, the Lord Advocate – Scotland's equivalent to the Attorney General – wrote to his opposite number in Spain, protesting in the strongest possible terms about this lapse in security. Chadwick has not been heard of since, and the best guess is that he now divides his time between Spain and Morocco.

That just leaves Francisco José Boo Torres, the captain of the *DIMAR-B*. Dick had learnt his identity, and the name of the boat, through intelligence not long after Howarth, Hawkins and Burns had been arrested. Following their conviction, Dick arranged to come and see Howarth at Shotts, on 4 July 1991. Howarth claims that he was told that if he cooperated, Customs would use their influence to have him taken off Category A, transferred to a more amenable English prison and that they would ensure that his parole was unopposed, indeed rubber-stamped, at the first opportunity, meaning that he could get out after eight years. Howarth agreed to meet Dick. His statement at best could be described as grudging, containing as it did a farrago of fabrications and half-truths.

The only thing that mattered to Dick, though, was that he told Howarth that he knew the ship was called the *DIMAR-B*. Howarth naively confirmed this to be the case. Dick had what he needed. Using Howarth's statement as a deposition, he had enough to bring Torres to trial – if he could find him. He began to do some research. He found that Torres came from Pontevedra, a Galician fishing village north of the Portuguese border, 'where they've got smuggling in the blood', says Dick, 'and they're brilliant at it. They've got traditional colonial links with Colombia. A hell of a lot of the ships on the high seas smuggling cocaine into Europe are going to be Basque or, more likely, Galician, and that's where Francisco is from.'

The Rough Guide to Spain says the following:

> Smuggling is a long-established tradition in Galicia. Not all the boats you see sailing into the picturesque fishing harbours are carrying fish; not all the lobster pots sunk offshore are used for holding crustaceans; not all those huts on the mussel-rafts are

occupied by shellfish-growers. All along the coast, you'll find beaches known locally as the 'Praia de Winston' [Winston Beach], notorious for the late-night arrival of shipments of foreign cigarettes.

Recently, however, it has become more difficult to laugh off the smugglers as latter-day Robin Hoods. Taking advantage of the infrastructure developed over the years by small-time tobacco smugglers, and of the endlessly corrugated coastline frequented by innumerable small boats, the big boys have moved in. At first, there were stories of large consignments of hashish brought in at night; now heroin abuse has become a major concern. At some point, the Medellín cartel of Colombia began to use Galicia as the European entrance point for large consignments of cocaine. Several major police crack-downs, particularly on the Isla de Arousa where certain segments of the population seemed all of a sudden to have become inexplicably rich, have yet to reverse the trend that has locals worrying that Galicia is heading towards becoming 'another Sicily'.*

Torres was very much a product of his region. Dick has a grudging respect for him. 'When we finally nicked Torres, he was only 25, but he had a full captain's ticket, which is incredible – very smart guy, very ruthless. He comes from a small fishing village, Cambados, near Pontevedra, brother Marco, sister Diane, mum and dad still alive. Marco and Diane are students, and he's paying for them. He got his captain's ticket in '87 when he was 22.'

Dick learnt that Torres had bought the *MV CITO* – as it was then called – in June 1990 from a Danish company for $300,000. It was bought using a Panamanian front company at least part-owned by Torres, named Ocean Ship International. From June to November 1990, Torres made two legitimate voyages to provide a front for the vessel, taking sand from Morocco to Portugal. He also spent some £20,000 having the renamed *DIMAR-B* fitted out with ultra-sophisticated radar, radio and fax equipment. On 14 November 1990, as we know, Torres sailed from Gibraltar to the South American coast with Howarth and Hawkins on board, collected the cocaine and returned to Scotland, where he offloaded his passengers. The weather was so terrible that Torres was obliged to put in at Galway Bay until the

---

* This extract is taken, with permission, from *The Rough Guide to Spain*, 9th edition, published by Rough Guides Ltd.

weather improved, before setting sail for Gibraltar, where he arrived in late January 1991.

From then until July 1991, Dick learnt through intelligence and informants, Torres had been planning to import vast quantities of cocaine from Colombia into Europe but, following the arrests in Scotland, his suspicion of interest in his activities meant these plans were put on hold. In May 1991, the *DIMAR-B* left Gibraltar for Djibouti and then Dubai. In July 1991, it managed to disappear. Dick had lookouts all over the world keeping an eye out for it, but no sightings were reported over the next few months. Where was that slippery seaman and his boat?

On Friday, 1 November 1991, Dick was out on the beers with his boss, Mike Stannard, in London. Stannard had taken over from Andy Barr as senior investigations officer in Glasgow during the closing stages of Operation Klondyke. The two men had had business at Custom House, Customs and Excise's traditional head office by the River Thames on Lower Thames Street in the City of London, close to the Tower of London. Above the noisy conversations and laughter in the pub, Dick heard his mobile go. It was long distance, one of their drugs liaison officers in Miami. 'Dick,' came the drawl, 'you know that ship you're looking for, the *DIMAR-B*? It's in fucking Halifax . . .' Dick was trying to think. Halifax? Halifax doesn't have a port. 'Halifax?' he repeated, unsurely. 'Yeah, Halifax . . . Halifax, Nova Scotia.'

On Sunday, 27 October, Royal Canadian Mounted Police, or RCMP (no, they're not really Mounties any more, but the name has stuck) had pulled over a dump truck near Chester, Nova Scotia. Inside were 3.5 tonnes of cannabis. The following day, the *DIMAR-B* had limped into harbour in Halifax. It didn't take a genius to put two and two together. Gerry Pretty of RCMP's drugs section boarded the ship to speak to Torres. He found colleagues from Customs, including Peter McTiernan, were already taking an interest. Pretty questioned Torres at length about what had brought him and his crew to Halifax, but Torres had his cover story off pat. He also pretended not to be able to speak much English. He claimed they had been berthed in the Bahamas for some weeks and, on heading up the eastern seaboard, they had developed trouble with a turbine, forcing them to come into port for repairs, and to take shelter from an impending storm.

The following day, Tuesday, 29 October, Pretty returned to find Torres in the Customs Office making a phone call to the Spanish

Consul in Halifax. When he had finished, Pretty explained that he was not buying Torres's story and that he was, in fact, arresting him on suspicion of importation of a narcotic, namely cannabis, into Canada. Torres seemed unperturbed, requesting only that he be put in touch with the Spanish Consul in Halifax, a Luis Holmes, whose card he inexplicably had. Pretty, displaying the courtesy for which Canadians are renowned, agreed to do so, and phoned Holmes himself. Holmes redirected Pretty to a Mrs Barrio, the chancellor of the Spanish Consul in Montreal. Pretty explained the situation to her, and asked that she arrange counsel for Torres. Torres, however, insisted that he did not require counsel, and agreed to a discussion of his activities.

Due to a lack of evidence, Torres was effectively offered immunity in return for telling RCMP what he knew. They had no evidence against Torres, but if they could use his testimony against the six Nova Scotians caught with the 3.5 tonnes, it would have been a deal worth making. Pretty writes: 'It became very evident, after I had spent only a short period of time interviewing Torres, that he clearly understood English perfectly. He began to speak very fluently, and was easily understandable. In fact, he often used very precise nuances of the English language. For example, he described various suggestions I made concerning his activities in terms of some being "logical" and others "illogical". He appeared at times to be quite nervous, but was polite and attentive throughout.'

Pretty continued to interview Torres over the next two days and seems to have bonded with him, discussing his family, girlfriend and impoverished background (which was why he was paying for his siblings' education). Trust appears to have been established between the two men, and Torres finally told him the truth. Between 7 July and 15 July, the *DIMAR-B* had been moored at Dubai. After this, the ship headed for the high seas near Pakistan, where it rendezvoused with a vessel that transferred 17 tonnes of hash on board – as Torres had told Howarth would be happening.

The *DIMAR-B* then sailed to Nova Scotia, and used two radio frequencies in an attempt to contact a vessel, which was to receive the offload of hash. The crew arranged a shift to watch for the vessel. Torres would be on the bridge daily 'from 2000 hours to 2400 hours, and 0800 hours to 1200 hours. At 00zulu (midnight) he would use frequency 8341, and at 1200zulu (noon) frequency 26518 in an effort to contact the vessel,' reports Pretty.

The vessel finally answered his call on Tuesday, 22 October, and approached the *DIMAR-B* in very rough seas. Torres, an experienced seaman despite his age, saw immediately that it was unsuitable for the offload. It was only eight metres in length, and did not have a steel hull. Torres indicated via the radio, in less than pleased terms, that it should turn back and send a man to do a man's job. He continued to make the calls on the designated frequencies until Friday, 25 October, when a vessel called the *MV NOVA SEA* arrived at the specified coordinates 150 miles out on the turbulent Atlantic waters to the east of Halifax. His crew was obliged to carry out the offload by hand as, along with the rest of the once-gleaming ship he had managed to trash, the hydraulic boom was no longer working.

On Monday, 28 October, as previously reported, the *DIMAR-B* made its way gingerly into the port of Halifax, and by Thursday, 31 October, Gerry Pretty had the evidence he needed against the Nova Scotians. Torres would be free to go when he desired. Torres arranged for money to be wired through to the account of the Seaman's Mission in Halifax, where he and the crew were staying, to cover their board and to pay for flights from Montreal to Madrid via Amsterdam. The flights were booked for 8.30 p.m. on Sunday, 3 November.

Pretty had logged all the phone numbers in Spain called by Torres while he was at the Seaman's Mission. They were all Pontevedra numbers. Pretty writes in his report: 'Torres spoke openly with the writer in relation to his fear of the individuals in Spain who were behind this hashish importation. He expressed concern that he could, or would, receive "a bullet in the head" if the people in Spain heard, not only that he had been arrested by the Canadian authorities, but that he had talked about his involvement in the importation and the organisation behind it.' Never mind 'a bullet in the head' from assailants in Spain, real or imagined, Torres was about to get an almighty kick up the arse from Scottish Customs and Excise. *That* is what he should have been concerning himself with.

CHAPTER FORTY-ONE

Back in London, Dick and Stannard had to move quickly. The drugs liaison officer had told them that Torres had been given immunity and would be flying back to Madrid from Montreal 48 hours later, on Sunday, 3 November. They legged it back to the office, Custom House, and called the Procurator Fiscal, David Hingston, at home for advice. Hingston told them that, in order to get an extradition warrant over to Canada pronto, he would need what is called an 'information and summons' in order to have the warrant signed by the Sheriff at Dingwall in the morning and faxed through to Halifax. This essentially meant putting together, in record time, an outline of the material facts in the case and the grounds upon which Torres could be shown to have a case to answer in a Spanish court. It would be a long night for the boys.

Dick called his counterpart at Customs in Canada, Peter McTiernan, and explained the situation, assuring him that the paperwork would be following in due course. Finally, they finished and whacked the documentation up to Scotland by fax, following shortly after by plane. The extradition warrant was faxed over to Halifax the following morning, Saturday, 2 November 1991, and Torres was once again taken into custody without being told why. The case was taken up by Marian Fortune-Stone, senior counsel within the Federal Prosecution Service of the Department of Justice, acting on behalf of UK Customs and Excise. Torres had been within a slice of chorizo of tasting freedom.

On Monday, 4 November, Gerry Pretty attended court in Halifax along with Peter McTiernan from Customs. During a pre-court discussion with a baffled Torres in the waiting room, Pretty told Torres that the hold-up was due to the fact that Scottish authorities were about to travel to Nova Scotia to secure his extradition to stand trial for 'a 500 kg offload of cocaine which had occurred along the north-west coast of Scotland in December 1990'.

Pretty told him that the Scottish authorities had determined that the

DIMAR-B had been the mothership in the offload, and that he was responsible. Torres was not mucho alegre at this news. Pretty writes: 'He looked shocked, and immediately became very flushed in the face.' Pretty went on to explain that the cocaine had been seized, and various of the players involved. He asked Torres whether he knew Chris Howarth or Noel Hawkins. Torres insisted that he had never heard of them, and that they had never been on his ship.

Pretty went on to explain that Howarth had confirmed that the *DIMAR-B* had been the ship involved. He had talked of conversations with Torres in which he had learnt that crew had fired automatic weapons on board the *DIMAR-B* (presumably Howarth was referring to Torres's talk of his humane way of ensuring that African refugees reached another life – just not the one that they had expected when they handed over their life savings). Pretty pointed out that this was consistent with the expended shell casings that they had found on the deck of the *DIMAR-B*, along with a belt designed to hold banana-shaped clips for an automatic rifle, although there was no longer any sign of the firearms themselves, presumably having been 'offloaded' before putting into port. Pretty says: 'Torres made no comment to these disclosures, but looked increasingly uncomfortable as we talked . . . McTiernan and I showed several photographs from the Scottish report to Torres, and he commented, "These are only words, and the opinion of someone else." He further stated, "I would have to see the person who said this with my own eyes – it is all a fantasy in someone's mind."' At that morning's court appearance, he was remanded in custody, pending further hearings. Bail was not granted. He was – not to put too fine a point on it – well and truly shafted.

On 15 November 1991, Graham Dick and Malcolm Sharp flew over to Canada to start building their case against Torres in anticipation of his eventual extradition to Scotland. They arrived in Halifax armed with warrants to search both the *DIMAR-B* and the RCMP vaults, the RCMP having lifted a lot of evidence from the ship. Dick got his first look at Torres on 20 November in court for a bail hearing. Bail, not surprisingly, was denied. On 22 December, he and Sharp served the warrant on the RCMP to allow them to look through the vaults. And that's when they struck gold. Among a lot of inconsequential material taken from the ship, Dick found a note, later proven to be in Torres's handwriting. At the top was Howarth's ex-directory phone number in Ullapool. Beneath it, Torres had scrawled 'Crazy Chris + Super Noel = Tom & Jerry.' No, I don't get it, either. But his little joke would ultimately wipe the smile off Torres's face. It would form a key part of evidence tying him to the Clashnessie Bay offload.

While Dick and Sharp were there, they also took samples of paint from the side of the ship. These looked as though they would match the samples found on the inflatable at Clashnessie Bay, presumably where the inflatable had smashed and scraped along the side while being lowered into the Minch the previous December. On 27 November, Dick and Sharp were back in court for a Supreme Court hearing regarding the validity of their search warrants, which they won. Two days later, Torres wrote a beautiful and elegantly handwritten five-page suicide note to the judge, and slit his throat, using the blade from a safety razor issued in prison. The note began (translated from Spanish):

> Señor Judge,
> This letter is addressed to you as the representative of that utopic and platonic term that humans call justice. First of all, I beg of you not to make an autopsy of my dead body, for I consider that such an action would be a waste of public money that, most probably, could be used for much better public purposes.

He goes on to say that:

> You have built up an image of me that is nothing else than that of a pariah of society, someone lacking dignity and value, ideally to become the easy prey for exaggerating journalists whose only aim is to achieve popularity using sensationalist and non-objective data in order to make up a selling product to be consumed by this boring and sick society of which you, and I, up until recent times, are part of. That is why it is better to die with honour than to live in dishonour.

This last line is taken from the Book of Kings by the eleventh-century Persian poet Firdawsi, and is clearly the expression of a cultured and refined mind.

Unfortunately for Torres, as the blood spurted from his slit throat, soon causing unconsciousness, his head fell forward. As he was sitting upright, this effectively stemmed the flow, which kept him alive until he was discovered. The great thing from Dick's point of view, though, was that the suicide note provided an uncoerced handwriting sample that tied Torres to the 'Crazy Chris + Super Noel' note. So in one sense, it did prove to be a suicide note.

On 20 December, his barrister, a man named Craig Garson, handed the brief back, saying, 'I am for hire – not for sale.' He added, 'I don't want to spend the rest of my life looking over my shoulder.' In a conversation with Marian Fortune-Stone, a clearly shaken and nervous Garson said, 'You lot [the authorities] don't know what you have got yourselves into.' Torres's case was then taken up by two high-profile Canadian defence lawyers, Warren Zimmer and Kevin Burke. On 9 January 1992 – four days before Ditus *et al.* were taken at sea with 500 kg of hash – they appealed against Torres's extradition to Scotland. Their appeal was rejected on 23 February.

That spring, there were two interesting developments. The first was that Torres again tried to commit suicide. As he was no longer allowed razors, he had to be a little more imaginative. Says Dick, 'That spring, he made himself a concoction of ink, melted plastic and various other foul ingredients which he drank. The upshot was that he gave himself a very sore throat.'

More interesting was the second development. RCMP began to receive intelligence from as many as five separate sources that an audacious attempt was to be made either to break Torres out of prison, or to assassinate him in the process, silencing him. The order had come from Colombia, it was believed.

RCMP treated the information seriously. The previous year, US Customs had tracked a suspicious aircraft heading up the eastern seaboard from Colombia. The Americans notified Canadian Customs that the suspect plane was heading for their airspace. Canadian Air Force planes were scrambled and forced the craft down at New Brunswick, Nova Scotia. On board were a number of Colombians. One source close to the case says: 'If I remember rightly, one was a woman with strong family connections to Pablo Escobar, the notorious late head of the Medellin cartel' – and one tonne of cocaine.

The source continues: 'Around this time, a guy at a filling station has a van pull in for petrol. A Hispanic guy gets out and fills up but the garage guy doesn't like it so he phones up the local police. And further down the road someone else doesn't like it – they'd pulled in for some Coke or whatever, no pun intended – and he phones up the locals. And by the time the locals have three or four calls, they decide to pull the van and there's ten Colombians in the back with a huge arsenal of machine guns, assault rifles, you name it. They're going to take out the whole courthouse, you know, this little dinky, maple syrup-type place in eastern Canada, that's how serious they were.

'The people behind the cannabis importation that they first got Francisco for were probably the same people behind the earlier coke importation, and they were more than capable of taking out Torres because they didn't want him to speak. You'll probably find that the cannabis guys in Canada were also buying cocaine from the Cali cartel so the wheel comes full circle, there's enough people wanting Torres kept quiet to give RCMP a headache.

'All Scottish Customs and Excise did, with Klondyke, was disrupt the supply temporarily. In parochial terms, it was a great haul but in global terms, what's half a tonne of coke to the Cali cartel? It's a drop in the ocean, it's a setback for them, but that's all it is. The only thing that would scare them would be if Torres started talking.'

RCMP didn't need persuading. Their informants told them that two well-known hitmen in Quebec and Montreal had been offered CAN$600,000 (slightly less than £300,000) to break Torres out – or take him out. They were armed with Uzis and aerial photographs of the detention centre in Halifax where he was being held. Security was stepped up massively, there were outriders and armoured vehicles used each time Torres had to attend court, there were armed units on the roof of the courthouse . . .

His lawyers fought the extradition process every inch of the way. Finally, in July 1993, Graham Dick and Frankie Cooper travelled over to Halifax for the final Supreme Court hearing, which took place on Monday, 12 July. Everything went their way – they were given authority to bring Torres back and, just as importantly, to bring back the evidence from the *DIMAR-B*. It was crucial that they get Torres back to Scotland safely. His defence was not notified of the departure until two hours after the plane had left Halifax, an Air Canada flight bound for Glasgow. Dick had had the passenger lists vetted for security and was leaving nothing to chance.

Dick says: 'We rolled into the prison in Halifax and went into the governor's office. And he picked up the phone and said, "Tell Torres to come up, I want to see him." And Torres came up and saw us and looked gutted, didn't say a word. The governor sent someone down to his cell to get his belongings and he was handcuffed to us and we got into a van. We had outriders and escorts front and back and we swept straight into Halifax airport, where we got a direct flight to Glasgow on Air Canada. We swept straight through security and Customs, straight up to the plane and onto the plane first and up to the back where we'd booked seats. So it was me, Frankie and Torres and a box of evidence on another seat. He was so pissed off, he didn't say one word all the way to Glasgow. When we did the passenger lists, we found there were five suspected Lebanese Mafia on board, which didn't go down too well, and there were two Spaniards.

'Anyway, we got back and we'd arranged a police escort from the airport, again it was outriders and escorts front and back and it was straight up to Dingwall so he could be taken in front of a sheriff and charged. And then I got the train back down to Glasgow from Inverness after an overnight flight handcuffed to Frankie Torres and I think I probably slept for a week. Torres was taken to Inverness initially and then transferred to Barlinnie.'

Torres appointed high-profile defence barrister Donald Findlay QC as his brief. Many readers will remember Findlay for the furore caused when he was forced to resign as vice-chairman of Glasgow's Rangers Football Club after being caught on camera singing anti-Catholic sectarian songs. The case was finally heard at the High Court in Glasgow in February 1994. During the trial, Howarth was brought to court to testify against Torres, which he refused to do. The trial judge, Lord Weir, warned Howarth that he would be found in contempt if he continued to refuse to answer questions put to him by the advocate depute, but Howarth stood his ground. Consequently, Lord Weir sentenced him to two years' imprisonment for contempt, the maximum sentence Parliament allowed him. The time would run consecutively with his prison sentence, so adding another two years to Howarth's time inside.

On 25 February 1994, Torres was found guilty and convicted for his part in the landing of the cocaine near Oldany Island. Lord Weir handed down 30 years for Torres, the heaviest sentence ever given for a drugs offence in Scotland, though this was later reduced to 25 years on appeal, on 28 May 1997. Three days after the conviction, Torres again slit his throat in Barlinnie Prison, again unsuccessfully. Findlay expressed astonishment that his client, with a history of repeated suicide attempts, should have been allowed access to a razor. He was then moved to Shotts Prison, where, in October 1994, came suicide attempt number four – this time, he fashioned a homemade crossbow in the workshop and pointed it at his chest. Needless to say, he missed his heart and survived. Up on the special unit, Howarth heard the news about his old chum, but decided not to send flowers.

On 25 June 1997, proving that the law really can be an ass, Torres was ordered to pay a confiscation order to the court of £1 – the smallest confiscation order ever made in Scotland – or face having seven days added to his 25-year jail sentence. Confiscation orders are routinely made in the case of convicted drugs smugglers to seize their assets in order to show that crime really does not pay. In Torres's case, no assets had been found. Says Dick: 'We traced a few accounts belonging to Torres in Pontevedra, but we were advised that it wouldn't be wise to turn up in his home town asking questions.'

In October 1999, Torres was escorted to Glasgow Airport from Shotts to be flown back to Madrid to serve the rest of his sentence in Spain.

In the autumn of 1999, Howarth had his first hearing before the parole board but was knocked back, as he was the following year. Then in 2001, the board agreed that he was suitable for parole. Howarth was overjoyed – until it was pointed out to him that he now had to do the two years for contempt relating to the Torres trial. His lawyers decided to fight it on the grounds that his human rights had been breached as he had not had legal representation in this matter, and was therefore denied natural justice. The case was scheduled to be heard at the High Court in Edinburgh on Friday, 21 December 2001, at 10.30 a.m.

That morning, he was told sarcastically by one of the screws at the open prison to which he had by now been moved not to bother packing his bag as he'd be back later. A natural optimist, Howarth did so anyway. In court, there followed a five-minute round of arcane legal debate, in which his lawyers argued that he should be given a fair trial on the charge of contempt, and be given parole until that trial took place. To his amazement, the court agreed. He was free to go. He was escorted to the front of the courthouse by the scowling screw who had travelled to court with him that morning. Outside, it was a grey December morning, but Howarth felt blessed to be alive. The screw handed over the bag containing Howarth's personal effects and money for transport costs, around £40 cash. The screw looked at Howarth with disdain, then said, 'Well, Howarth, what are you going to do now?'

Howarth looked one way down the Royal Mile towards Holyrood Palace, then the other way up towards the castle. Opposite the courthouse on the next corner was a pub, the Deacon Brodie. Brodie was reputedly the inspiration for Robert Louis Stephenson's *Dr Jekyll and Mr Hyde*. He grinned and pointed. 'See that pub there? I'm going to go in there, and get well and truly rat-arsed.'

Three hours later, and six pints to the good, he was on a train to Inverness, where he would catch a bus back home to Ullapool, where Fiona, as she had done for many years, would be waiting for him.

The contempt case is still hanging over him. His lawyers expect that it will be heard at some point in the next two or three years, though they don't expect him to go back inside for it. Howarth now lives quietly, eschewing the pubs around the village, such as The Caley, in which he seems to have spent most of his formative years. He makes a modest living restoring furniture, a skill he picked up doing woodwork inside. Not so much Crazy Chris these days; more like Cosy Chris now.

CHAPTER FORTY-TWO

So just how important was Operation Klondyke? As has been pointed out, half a tonne of pure cocaine is a tremendous haul, but is a 'drop in the ocean' for the Colombian cartels. The distinctive Gucci tape on the packages made it easier to trace the original owners and source of the drugs, the Cali cartel in Colombia. Dick found there had been five other seizures of drugs with similar markings over the previous 18 months. Six kilos taken in Florida in 1989, 450 in Puerto Rico, 635 in Guatemala, then in 1990, 253, also in Guatemala and 798 in New York.

Customs and Excise currently work on the following approximate figures. Total global production of processed cocaine hydrochloride over the last few years has been put at between 850 and 900 tonnes per annum. Peru, Colombia and Bolivia are the biggest producers of coca leaf, in that order. It's worth pointing out, however, that virtually all reports put Colombia as the number-one producer of cocaine hydrochloride – according to the now defunct Observatoire Géopolitique des Drogues, a French drugs research body, in 2000, Colombia alone accounted for between 500 and 700 tonnes of cocaine, which makes Customs and Excise's suppositions look decidedly conservative. Around 300 tonnes makes its way to Europe, according to Customs and Excise, with around 50 tonnes destined for the UK. By the early 1990s, the Cali cartel was emerging as the main competition to the Medellin cartel and was responsible for up to 30 per cent of the country's cocaine supply, meaning as much as 200 tonnes. The hauls cited above come to around 2 tonnes, 1 per cent of output. Even a legal business that involved global shipping of product to market could live with that sort of percentage of goods lost or damaged in transit.

The Updated National Drugs Strategy of 2002, a UK Home Office mission statement, concludes that: 'There will be a renewed focus on middle markets to address a critical point of supply to UK streets, and on local policing and tackling crack.' Typical of the 'middle market' is Colin, a north London cocaine dealer. Through contacts, I arranged to meet him to get background for this book. Although reluctant to begin with, after I gave assurances that I would change his name and not include any information that could identify him, he finally agreed to meet me. He took my address and came to visit me one afternoon – 'I generally play football in the evenings,' he explained at my home in London.

Colin is as far from the stereotype of a drugs dealer as is possible to imagine. He was casually dressed in a pair of Chinos and a regulation Gap T-shirt. The only outward sign of wealth was that he drove a brand-new BMW, though in London, that is nothing remarkable. He seemed interested in what I did for a living – 'My girlfriend's training to be a journalist,' he explained with evident pride – and came across as affable and intelligent.

He had been dealing cocaine since the late 1980s, he told me, and in that time had seen no great fluctuation in the wholesale price. He was a middle-ranking wholesaler, turning over around two kilos per week. In his time, the most he had ever paid for a kilo was £30,000, and the least £26,000, which equates to between £26 and £30 per gram, as against a street price of £50 per gram, so it's not difficult to see where the profits are to be made. He currently pays around £27,000 per kilo. By way of comparison, the price for the purest form of a kilo of gold (the official category is London good delivery – the Bank of England classification for pure gold) as quoted by the Bank of England, is £6,900. You do the math, as they say across the Pond.

'My target profit margin is £2,000 per kilo,' he explained. This would put him on an annual take-home salary of £208,000 – to earn the equivalent legitimately, taking into account tax and National Insurance, he would need to be on a salary of some £338,569, according to chartered accountants Cox, Costello and Horne of Rickmansworth, Hertfordshire. This is the same amount as Paul

Reynolds, the head of business sales at UK telecoms giant BT, took home for 2002, according to their annual report. Not bad, when you're your own boss, work from home and get to meet new and interesting people in your line of work – Colin, that is, not Paul Reynolds.

Colin explained that he didn't touch the stuff himself as he found that when he used to, he ended up bingeing on it. 'I generally just deal to the same handful of people, usually nothing smaller than half an ounce at a time. I don't deal from home, and because I'm meeting so few people, the risks are minimal.'

How does he know how pure the stuff he's buying is? 'Well, I generally buy from the same source, and it's always the same, 90 per cent. It's very easy to work out. You weigh out one gram, wash it with ammonia and heat it over a flame in a spoon. The impure stuff will flake off. You take what's left – the pure stuff – and weigh it on digital scales. If it shows as 0.9, which it always does with my source, you know it's 90 per cent.'

He corrected a common fallacy. 'It's a myth that if it comes in a rock, it's pure. You can get pressing machines; I've seen it done, which allow you to re-press the coke with a cheaper substitute. Novocaine – the stuff they inject you with at the dentist's – is the best because the user feels their mouth and gums go numb, as they do with the real stuff. The machine basically consists of two horizontal plates with metal sides. You place the compound in the lower tray, then you use a vacuum hand pump to lower the top plate until it's all nicely compressed.

'Generally, the guys who are going to cut it with powder are small time, and they'll mix it in with glucose, or if they're really cheap, they'll use baby laxative.'

He expressed incredulity at the Customs claim that street price in 1991 was £87 per gram, that street coke was typically 39 per cent purity then and that only 50 tonnes per annum are consumed in the UK. He thought for a few minutes, then said: 'Look, I've been doing this since the late '80s, and the price per gram has always stayed fairly static around the £50 mark. If you were paying £60, it was because the person you got it from only sold a few grams here and there and had to make his money up somehow. As for 39 per cent – either they get really shit coke up there, or someone's got it wrong. The stuff I knock out is 90 per cent, and I'm sure my customers will only cut it a little bit. You'd have to go a hell of a long way down the chain, with people cutting it more and more, before you got to 39 per cent.

'As for 50 tonnes used in the UK per annum, I don't know about that. I know three guys just in my postcode who turn over ten kilos a week each. That's one and a half tonnes a year, just off three guys in one little bit of London – and I'm sure there are plenty of others round my way that I don't know about. So 50 tonnes throughout the whole country . . . When you consider the whole of London, Leeds, Manchester, Glasgow, whatever . . . I don't think so.'

It's easy to see why people are prepared to take the enormous risks involved with smuggling cocaine. But has the government got it right regarding prohibition and tackling the middle market – in other words, the sort of person like Colin who acts as a distributor to those who supply the end user? *The Updated National Drugs Strategy* states that the aim is to continue to target the supply side by focusing on international trafficking, particularly heroin from Afghanistan and, of course, cocaine from South America, but to place more emphasis on the middle market at the same time. The document goes on to say:

> Substantial quantities of heroin and cocaine destined for the UK market are successfully being taken out, but the impact of the international drug trade on the UK market needs to be explored further. There are gaps in our knowledge of how the drug trafficking business works and the routes and methods used to supply the market, especially within UK borders, and these must be addressed.

Not all drugs enforcement professionals agree with the new emphasis. One senior drugs enforcement officer, who asked not to be named, told me: 'The thing about the middle market for cocaine is that it generally doesn't cause attendant problems of criminality – armed violence, that sort of thing – as, say, the crack market does, which is a policing nightmare. In the past, we've been content to leave the middle market be to an extent, as it often caters for recreational users who want to have fun at the weekend, then go back to work and lead normal lives during the week. That left us free to worry about tracking the drugs at source before they even came into the country, and to worry about the nasty end of the market. But the new strategy is that the middle market is to be targeted, and that's what the powers-that-be have decreed.'

In September 2001, the former British ambassador to Colombia, Sir Keith Morris, who served in Bogota from 1990 to 1994, gave evidence to the House of Commons Select Committee on Home Affairs regarding his views on the war on drugs. Morris opened by saying:

My conviction that legalisation of drugs is the only way to limit the harm that drugs can do stems from my experience as a participant in the drugs war in Colombia from 1990 to 1994 and my observation of developments since. I have been witness to the costly failure of prohibition and have finally been driven to the conclusion that policies, which I implemented and in which I believed, were doomed to failure because they came from an era which has passed.

Morris went on to say that the policies he helped implement were designed to focus on the supply side in, especially, Colombia, and would ultimately lead to all-out war with the drugs cartels. As the war intensified, the drug cartels became more and more determined to protect their revenues. Finally, they succeeded in killing Pablo Escobar, head of the Medellin cartel in 1993.

But as Morris pointed out, 'the cost had been thousands of lives, three presidential candidates, two justice ministers, many judges, soldiers, policemen and countless civilian victims of his indiscriminate bombing attacks'. Yet the supply of cocaine had not been affected, for 'The Cali cartel had simply replaced Medellin as number one [supplier] and heroin production had started.'

As well as the numerous medium-sized organisations that sprang up to fill the vacuum by the disbanded Medellin and Cali cartels, there was also the problem that cocaine production was a big source of revenue for the paramilitary Marxist revolutionary groups, such as the Revolutionary Armed Forces of Colombia (FARC). Over the years that he had been observing the drugs wars at close quarters, Morris noted, the number of lives lost ran into many thousands, but cocaine production and supply to the rest of the world barely fluctuated. The drugs war was imposing a terrible price in terms of human loss, but made no difference to the market.

Morris concluded:

> Demand is clearly the key. I simply do not see any hope of reducing it significantly. Many now regard recreational drug use as normal. Prohibition worked in the 1950s when I was young because hardly anyone even thought of using drugs other than alcohol and tobacco, which were taken enthusiastically. But there has been immense social change since with either the law or social attitudes liberalised on homosexuality, abortion, extra-

marital sex, drinking, gambling, broadcasting, Sunday trading, you name it. Personal choice is the credo on everything except drugs, where the law has been made even tighter. In this climate, prohibition not only does not work but it does great damage. Users are at risk from impure drugs, millions of law-abiding people break the law just because they use drugs occasionally, addicts are pushed into crime to feed their habit and the rest of society suffers intolerable levels of crime as a result.

He pointed out that if appropriate regimes were established pragmatically for each drug, with product testing and taxation used for increased research, education and treatment, the harm drugs now do could be greatly reduced. He finished his evidence by saying:

> Of course it would not be easy. There would be a black market and the defenders of prohibition are probably right in saying that it would encourage greater use and hence addiction. But I do wonder whether those psychologically likely to become addicts are often put off by current laws. And they would be looked after as normal members of society with a health problem.
>
> The benefits would be immense both to consumer – less drug deaths, less crime – and producer countries – less conflict and corruption. We would have to convince our American friends, who were the architects of the present system. But as prohibition is a major source of terrorist funds, they may now look at it differently. And no consumer country would benefit more. More young black Americans are in jail than in higher education.

In a piece that Morris wrote for *The Guardian* in July 2001, he said:

> It has been difficult for me to advocate legalisation because it means saying to those with whom I worked, and to the relatives of those who died, that this was an unnecessary war. But the imperative must be to try to stop the damage.

The Home Office's British Crime Survey report – *Drug Misuse Declared, 2000* – suggests that around four per cent of the population – around two million people – have used ecstasy at some point, and widespread acceptance of recreational drug use is likely to increase. At time of going to press, a new Department of Health survey showed that the number of teenagers admitting to using cocaine has risen from 1 per cent in 1994 to 5 per cent today, and for ecstasy, from 4 to 7 per cent. Over a third of all 15-year-olds now admit to using drugs of some sort in the past year. This would suggest a total figure of Class A users in the UK in excess of 2 million, and rising, which compares to a figure of around 940,000 people who usually attend a Church of England service on a Sunday in the UK.* To criminalise such a swathe of the population, many of whom break no laws except the one of prohibition in their recreational drug use, seems draconian and ultimately self-defeating. The glamour and pull of cocaine is one that evidently draws too many people to be swayed by the knowledge that what they are doing is illegal. In a modern democracy, policing is done by the consent of the majority – witness the popular revolt against the poll tax, which led to its withdrawal and, arguably, the downfall of its architect Margaret Thatcher. Recreational use of cocaine is becoming so widespread that many younger people view it as being on a par with exceeding the speed limit – a little naughty but a fact of life.

The glamour associated with cocaine is not simply limited to those who use it. Hit songs about it have reached the top of the charts, films about it have enjoyed huge box-office success and it has spawned dozens of books and thousands of magazine articles. Even those employed to enforce its prohibition benefit from a little of its glamour, with cocaine investigation one of the most sought-after positions within Customs and Excise. One senior drugs enforcement officer told me: 'I remember the first time I saw cocaine. We were down in London on a job and we had a warrant to search this guy's house and we took a load of stuff down to the station. And there was this big block wrapped in tinfoil . . . So we opened it up and my mouth just dropped. It was this incredible, sparkling crystalline block, just beautiful it was. It just had this incredible aura, this lure . . .' And this from an agent of the prohibitionists rather than a user.

Testifying to the House Select Committee on Crime on 17 September 1969, US educator and congresswoman Shirley Chisholm said: 'It is not heroin or cocaine that makes one an addict, it is the need to escape from a harsh reality. There are more television addicts, more baseball and football addicts, more movie addicts, and certainly more

---

* Source: *Church of England Gazette*, Volume 3, Edition 3, 2003.

alcohol addicts in this country than there are narcotics addicts.'

Meanwhile, the great rush of white gold continues to beat a path to the market. Seizures and busts cause but the tiniest of disruptions, like trying to thwart a mighty river. The foaming torrent simply gathers more pace, more persistence, and forces its way through, ever onwards towards the sea, the market, where young professionals and socialites in the clubs, bars and living rooms of London, Leeds and Livingston do not care what death and destruction has been caused to bring them their illicit thrill, their little bit of intoxication, of glamour, of a buzz on a Saturday night.

POSTSCRIPT

Operation Klondyke resulted in the most valuable seizure of drugs in the UK (although readers should note the comments about the methodology for valuation in Chapter 39). This was due to its intense purity, and the reason that other big hauls were less valuable is because they were significantly less pure, according to Customs and Excise.

Other significant seizures include:

Operation Eyeful, which resulted in a seizure of 400 kg of almost pure cocaine, with a street value of £90 million, taken by yacht to the Isle of Wight from southern Caribbean Island Bequia in October 2000.

Operation Ypres, which resulted in a seizure of 800 kg of cocaine found in a consignment of groundnuts in Winchester, Hampshire, May 2003. Although the haul was 800 kg, it was only valued at £50 million.

Operation Elysian, which resulted in a seizure of 650 kg with a street value of £40 million hidden among heavy plant machinery, which arrived by ship from Ecuador at Felixstowe in November 2002.

Operation Extend, a six-year operation that resulted in the seizure of 500 kg of cocaine with a street price of £61 million in 2001. This led to a 14-month trial and a record total of 215.5 years in jail for 16 defendants. The ringleader, Brian Brendan Wright, is still on the run and is believed to be in northern Cyprus.

The largest seizures involving UK Customs and Excise tend to take place at sea. In May 2003, a joint UK and Spanish Customs operation led to the seizure of a motor torpedo boat in the mid-Atlantic. On board they found a record 3.6 tonnes of cocaine, worth over £250 million.

And the following month, June 2003, a joint operation between UK Customs and Excise and the Royal Navy resulted in the interception of a Panamanian-registered merchant ship *Yalta* some 400 miles west of St Lucia. On board was 3.3 tonnes of cocaine, again worth over £250 million.

These seizures are what is being caught – but how much is getting through?